# ADVENTIST CLASSIC LIBRARY

Reprints of Important Publications
in the Adventist Tradition

Edited by
George R. Knight

A SERIES BY ANDREWS UNIVERSITY PRESS

Current Volumes in the Adventist Classic Library

> *Life Incidents*, by James White
> *Seventh-day Adventists Answer Questions on Doctrine, Annotated Edition*
> *Autobiography of Joseph Bates*

Projected Volumes (Partial List)

> *Memoirs of William Miller*, by Sylvester Bliss
> *History of the Sabbath*, by J. N. Andrews
> *Feed My Sheep*, by H. M. S. Richards
> *Earliest Sabbatarian Adventist Periodicals*
> *Answers to Objections*, by F. D. Nichol
> *Life Sketches of James and Ellen White* (1888 edition)
> *History of the Second Advent Message and Mission, Doctrine and People*, by Isaac Wellcome
> *Early Sabbath Tracts*, by Joseph Bates
> *Bible Adventism* and other early works by James White
> *Our Firm Foundation* (the report of the 1952 Bible Conference, 2 volumes)
> *A History of the Origin and Progress of Seventh-day Adventists*, by M. E. Olsen
> *The Sanctuary Service*, by M. L. Andreasen
> *Evidence from Scripture and History of the Second Coming of Christ about the Year 1843* and other works by William Miller
> *The Cross and Its Shadow*, by S. N. Haskell

The term "Adventist" in this series is used broadly. While most of the selections in the Adventist Classic Library will be directly related to Seventh-day Adventist heritage, some will come from Millerism and other branches of the Millerite tradition.

# AUTOBIOGRAPHY OF
# JOSEPH BATES

with Additional Material
from Two Later Editions
of the Same Work

Introduction by Gary Land

ANDREWS UNIVERSITY PRESS
BERRIEN SPRINGS, MICHIGAN

Andrews University Press
213 Information Services Building
Berrien Springs, MI 49104-1700
Telephone: 269-471-6134
Fax: 269-471-6224
Email: aupo@andrews.edu
Website: www.andrews.edu/universitypress

Original Edition (1868): The Autobiography of Elder Joseph Bates; Embracing
a Long Life on Shipboard, with Sketches of Voyages on the Atlantic and Pacific
Oceans, the Baltic and Mediterranean Seas; also Impressment and Service on
Board British War Ships, Long Confinement in Dartmoor Prison, Early Experience
in Reformatory Movements; Travels in Various Parts of the World; and a Brief
Account of the Great Advent Movement of 1840-1844, by Joseph Bates. Steam Press
of the Seventh-day Adventist Publishing Association, Battle Creek, Mich. 1868.

Reprint Edition (2004): Autobiography of Joseph Bates. Introduction by Gary Land.
Copyright © 2004 by Andrews University Press
All rights reserved
Printed in the United States of America
07   06   05   04        5   4   3   2   1

ISBN 1-883925-44-4
Library of Congress Card Number 2004105699

|  |  |
|---|---|
| Project Director | Ronald Alan Knott |
| Project Consultant | Deborah L. Everhart |
| Typesetting | Thomas Toews |
| Cover Design | Robert N. Mason |

Adventist Classic Library

|  |  |
|---|---|
| General Editor | George R. Knight |
| Series Director | Ronald Alan Knott |

For reading convenience and balanced layout on the page, the facsimile reprint of
the type from the original edition is enlarged by about 30 percent.

Typeset: 10.5/12.6 Sabon MT

# HISTORICAL INTRODUCTION

Prisoner of war, sea captain, moral reformer, and itinerant preacher, Joseph Bates led a varied and fascinating life and, as recognized by several scholars, achieved historical significance by co-founding the Seventh-day Adventist Church. C. Mervyn Maxwell, for instance, stated in his survey of Adventist history that Bates might "rightly be considered the father of the Sabbath truth among Seventh-day Adventists" while Bates's biographer, Godfrey T. Anderson, observed that Bates and James and Ellen White formed a "staunch triumvirate whose faith, foresight, and influence would become a major force in the formative years of the Sabbatarian Adventists."[1] Yet despite this acknowledgment of Bates's importance, relatively few writers have focused their attention on the man.

## The Biographers of Joseph Bates

The first extended treatment of Joseph Bates's life appeared in Everett N. Dick's *Founders of the Message*.[2] Although Dick was a trained historian who had earlier written his doctoral dissertation on the Millerite movement and an acclaimed work on the Great Plains,[3] he stated that in this book he was not writing "critical, scientific history" but rather "a popular work which will inspire to nobler living and greater sacrifice the young people of this denomination."[4] Instead of analyzing Bates's contribution to Adventism, therefore, Dick presented a narrative of his life, which appears to have been largely based on Bates's *Autobiography* and the recollections of John Loughborough, a pioneer Adventist minister.[5] Nonetheless, at various points in his story Dick characterized the man. Calling Bates a "Pioneer of the Pioneers among Seventh-day Adventists," he stated that the former sea captain was "probably the most interesting character" among the denomination's founders. Dick further described him as "an enterprising businessman," a "prodigious worker, never sparing himself," and "a great pathbreaker."[6] He also noted Bates's constant itinerating, commenting that "perhaps the spirit of the sea rover was too strong in his veins. At any rate he seemed ever intent upon traveling here and there, stopping only a day or two at a place."[7] Emerging from Dick's narrative is the portrait of a man of nearly endless energy and devotion without whom the Seventh-day Adventist Church would probably have never taken the form that it did.

Somewhat more analytical, a master's thesis by Clarence Edwin Stenberg[8] similarly narrated Bates's life, largely following the *Autobiography*, letters and articles in the *Review and Herald*, Bates's pamphlets, and some surviving unpublished correspondence. Attempting to identify Bates's contributions to Adventism, Stenberg noted his development of the theology of the Sabbath and the heavenly sanctuary, although his writings were little read after the 1840s, and his role as "a standard bearer for health reform." But, he concluded, the most important contribution was "the *life* of the man himself. Joseph Bates, the stout-hearted, dominant sea captain, the leader of men, became Elder Bates, the kindhearted, persevering pastor, the shepherd who sought out people and led them to Christ."[9]

The first book-length treatment of Bates's life after the *Autobiography* was Virgil Robinson's *Cabin Boy to Advent Crusader*,[10] a biography written for young people in which the author invented dialogue but otherwise stayed close to known facts. Robinson largely followed Bates's own *Autobiography*, devoting about half of his 190 pages to Bates's life at sea and another twenty pages to his experience in the Millerite movement. The final seventy pages of the biography addressed Bates's activities in the developing Sabbatarian Adventist movement, emphasizing his selfless devotion to this cause. Because Bates spent only a few pages of his *Autobiography* on his sabbatarian period, Robinson drew on the published recollections of John Loughborough and J. O. Corliss,[11] two early Seventh-day Adventists who had known Bates. In addition, Robinson used some of the letters that Bates wrote to the *Review and Herald* between 1851 and 1853. The author closed his sympathetic portrayal of Bates by saying, "to the very end his life was consistent with the principle he had adopted when he first became a Christian: All that I am, all that I have, belongs to God."[12]

In 1972 Godfrey T. Anderson, a trained historian and previously president of Loma Linda University, produced the first scholarly biography of Joseph Bates, *Outrider of the Apocalypse*.[13] Anderson considerably expanded knowledge of Bates's early life through his study of legal records, Dartmoor Prison materials, and Bates's surviving logbook and correspondence. While Anderson placed Bates within the context of American economic and social history, he presented a primarily factual account of Bates's life and avoided overt interpretation. Rather than analyzing Bates's continuing fascination with dating the Second Coming of

Jesus, for instance, Anderson simply stated, "By some logic he interpreted the wave sheaf which was waved seven times by the priest as meaning seven years, which he proceeded to add to 1844, thus coming up with 1851 as a new date for Christ to come."[14] Anderson gave little attention to Bates's thought, emphasizing instead his "constant itinerating"[15] in behalf of the Sabbatarian Adventist cause. As a result, Anderson said little about Bates's tendency toward legalism, noting at one point only that Bates's "concept of the high privilege of church membership caused him and the body of members [in Monterey, Michigan] to feel that they would be delinquent in their responsibility if they did not deal drastically with offenders against the law of God and the principles of the church."[16]

Although he offered little analysis and interpretation, Anderson carefully reconstructed much of the chronology of Bates's life and provided information about such things as his personal finances, relationship with his wife, and role in the conferences that led to the organization of the Seventh-day Adventist Church. Through contacts with descendents of Bates, Anderson was also able to publish a painting of Bates as a young man and the only known photograph of his wife Prudence. Through his research, Anderson provided a foundation on which other scholars could build.

Jerry E. Daly followed Anderson by devoting his master's thesis to the transcription and analysis of Joseph Bates's logbook.[17] When George R. Knight, who had previously written widely on nineteenth-century Adventist history, wrote *Joseph Bates: The Real Founder of Seventh-day Adventism*,[18] he extensively used Daly's transcription to supplement information provided in the *Autobiography*. Knight, however, spent relatively little space on Bates's seafaring days, focusing instead on the captain's contributions to the development of Adventism. In contrast to Anderson, Knight examined Bates's thought, analyzing the pamphlets that he wrote between 1846 and 1850 to argue that Bates's understanding of history and theology

> would make the Sabbatarians an aggressive, mission-oriented people from 1848 onward. Thus he was not only Sabbatarian Adventism's first theologian and first historian, but also its first mission theorist. The combined understanding of those three fields...would become a driving force as he becomes the movement's first missionary.[19]

Knight also discussed Bates's legalistic tendencies and recounted disagreements between Bates and the Whites over such issues as the pre-Advent judgment, date-setting for Christ's coming, the time for beginning the Sabbath, and the publication of the papers *Present Truth* and *Advent Review*. Looking beyond the specific issues in these conflicts, Knight placed them within the larger context of a "generational transference of leadership from Bates to [James] White. Bates as a leader had provided essential functions in the 1840s, but new challenges called for new talents and a new leader....From 1850 onward White would be the undisputed head of the Sabbatarian movement."[20] As the issues in conflict were settled, Bates traveled constantly, spreading Sabbatarian Adventism northward into Canada and westward into Michigan, which in 1855 became the center of the movement. Knight concluded that "we can honestly say that without Joseph Bates there would be no Seventh-day Adventism. He was the source of a great deal that was true and helpful."[21] Knight's work thereby complemented Anderson's factual emphasis by providing an interpretive biography that demonstrated Bates's essential contribution to the development of Seventh-day Adventism.

## Joseph Bates's Life

Joseph Bates[22] was born on July 8, 1792, in Rochester, Massachusetts, but within a year his parents moved to the seaport of New Bedford. Growing up in an important whaling center, Bates felt strongly the call of the sea and at age fifteen sailed to London as a cabin boy on the *Fanny*, thereby initiating the first major period of his life. Although his father had hoped that this voyage would cure his wanderlust, two years later Bates sailed again, this time to Archangel, Russia. This trip brought Bates into unanticipated trials and adventures. Through the captain's apparent incompetence, the ship was caught in an ice-pack off Newfoundland; Danish privateers later captured it. After the Danes confiscated the ship, Bates made his way to Liverpool where, while staying in a boarding house in April 1810, he was "seized and dragged" by a "press gang"[23] and subsequently forced into the British navy.

Bates had begun his maritime career during a very dangerous time. In 1803 war had broken out once again between Great Britain and Napoleon's France; the young United States sought to remain neutral as it supplied food to Europe. Great Britain, however, experienced a shortage of sailors, many of whom had deserted the Royal Navy for American ships. In an effort to get its sailors back, Britain began forcibly removing or "impressing" suspected deserters from American ships and British port towns. As the British did not carefully distinguish between actual and alleged deserters, they caught up many American citizens in their net, perhaps as many as 6,000 between 1803 and 1812.²⁴ Bates, unfortunately, was among these illegally impressed sailors.

For the next two and a half years Bates served on first the *Rodney* and then the *Swiftshore* in the Mediterranean. When impressments among other causes led to the outbreak of war between the United States and Great Britain in 1812, Bates and other Americans demanded to be treated as prisoners-of-war. After spending eight months as a prisoner-of-war on the *Swiftshore*, Bates was moved first to Gibralter and then to England where with 700 others he was kept on a prison ship. After at least two attempted escapes, in September 1814 the prisoners were transferred to Dartmoor Prison, about fifteen miles north of Plymouth, where Bates stayed until released on April 27, 1815.

Bates's adventures were not over, for he was involved in two mutinies on his way back to the United States before finally being reunited with his family in June 1815. Within a few weeks, however, Bates obtained a position as second mate on a ship sailing for Europe. For the next thirteen years he spent more than three-quarters of his time at sea, rising ultimately to the position of ship captain in 1820 at the age of twenty-nine and eventually becoming part owner of his ship. During these years he made at least ten voyages to such destinations as Europe, the West Indies, and South America.

Meanwhile, Bates married a childhood friend, Prudence Nye, in 1818. They had five children: Anson (who died before his second birthday), Helen, Eliza, Joseph, and Mary. Like his father, Joseph followed the sea but died of dysentery while on shipboard in 1865. Although her husband was gone much of the time, Prudence appears to have had the help of her widowed mother, who lived with the family for forty years.

The second major period of Bates's life, that of Christian reformer, began while he was still a seaman. Joseph's parents were staunch Congregationalists, but as a young man he made no religious profession. In the 1820s, however, he adopted certain personal moral reforms that appear to have ultimately led to his Christian conversion. Bates's experiences on shipboard and in prison, where he saw the effects of drunkenness, awakened him to the dangers of alcohol. Between 1821 and 1824, therefore, he made a series of decisions—to stop drinking first "ardent spirits," then wine, and finally such things as beer and ale—that led to his adoption of teetotalism, except for medicinal purposes. In 1823 he also gave up tobacco, first discarding cigars and then chewing tobacco. About the same time, he also sought to break himself of the habit of swearing and began reading the Bible. As Bates recognized later, all of these actions depended on his own effort. "By so doing I concluded that I was *making myself* a good Christian."[25]

In 1824 Bates's religious awakening began. His wife had inserted into a New Testament she had placed in his trunk a poem that dealt with the theme of death.[26] Deeply moved, after reading the poem several times Bates began to experience a dark night of the soul, longing to be a Christian but realizing his desperate state as a sinner. When one of his sailors died and Bates had to read the prayer book at the burial service, he "felt indeed that I was a sinner before God" and from that point "felt a sinking into the will of God."[27] Bates still had trouble believing that his sins were forgiven until he attended a revival near his home about two years later. In 1827 he joined the Fairhaven congregation of the Christian Connection—also spelled Connexion—in part because he agreed with its belief in adult baptism and its anti-Trinitarianism.

Bates's frequent references to revivals in the late 1820s remind us that his conversion was not an isolated incident. Instead, it was part of a great religious revival, known as the Second Great Awakening, which had started around 1800 and swept through the northeastern and western United States and dipped into the South, lasting at least until the mid-1840s. Its effects were significant. Between 1800 and 1830, for instance, church membership in the United States doubled. Emphasizing personal conversion, a generally Arminian theology that rejected predestination in favor of free will, perfectionism, and an optimistic postmillennialism, the revival contributed greatly to the many reform efforts of the era. Historian Steven Mintz writes that these religious revivals

> were at once a force for social discipline and for social reform. Many social conservatives viewed evangelical religion as an indispensable tool for taming the frontier and subduing the urban working class by combating violence, profanity, intemperance, and vice. But evangelicalism not only targeted the sins of the poor: it also sought to reform the manners of the rich and high-born, to make them moral as well as genteel. In the words of revivalist Charles Grandison Finney, revival sought to remove "the starch and flattery of high life": luxury, idleness, fashionable display, and gluttony.[28]

Bates appears to be a classic example of the evangelical reformer. Embracing personal reform even before his conversion, immediately after becoming a church member he helped form a local temperance society. The modern temperance movement had begun only one year earlier when Lyman Beecher and others had formed the American Temperance Society. On his next voyage, Bates applied his personal convictions to the behavior of the crew, banning the use of alcohol and profanity and requiring observance of the Sabbath each Sunday. After this voyage Bates retired from his seafaring life in 1828, having accumulated a "competency" of about $11,000, to take up farming and real estate ventures, but his interest in reform continued to grow. After observing the conflict between colonizationists, who wanted to solve the problem of slavery by sending the slaves back to Africa, and the abolitionists, who proposed immediately ending the institution by freeing the slaves, Bates joined the latter group. He also helped organize the Fairhaven Seaman's Friends Society and participated in the American Tract Society until he decided that it did not take a clear enough stand on slavery. On his farm he experimented with growing mulberry trees and envisioned establishing a manual labor school centered on the production of silk. Unfortunately, this project did not prove viable and the school never materialized. Meanwhile, about 1831 Bates embarked on additional personal reforms when he gave up the drinking of tea and coffee; in 1843 he became a vegetarian.

But Bates's interest in reform was not finished. In 1839 a Christian Connection pastor invited Bates to hear him present the views of William Miller regarding the second coming of Jesus. As a result of studying Bible prophecies, particularly those of Daniel 8 and 9, Miller, an upstate New York farmer, had concluded that Jesus would return about the year 1843. His premillennial understanding of Christ's coming conflicted with the Second Great Awakening's postmillennialism, but nonetheless he slowly attracted interest after beginning his public speaking in 1831; by the late 1830s, other ministers, such as Bates's friend, were beginning to advocate his ideas.[29] The lecture prompted Bates to obtain and study Miller's lectures, and he soon became a believer.

Bates quickly became active in promoting Miller's ideas. Having already become acquainted with Joshua V. Himes, pastor of the Christian Connection Chardon Street Chapel in Boston, through his reform activities, Bates joined with Himes and others in calling for a general conference of Millerites to be held in October 1840. Bates first heard Miller preach in 1841 and that same year helped organize a regional conference. The following year he chaired a second general conference, which took place in Boston. Bates's involvement with the Millerite movement led to tension with his Christian Connection church, resulting in his withdrawal in about 1842. His participation in moral reform societies also ended, for "so much more could be accomplished in working at the fountain-head, and make us every way right as we should be for the coming of the Lord."[30] In short, for Millerites the second coming was, as David L. Rowe calls it, "the ultimate reform, the sudden and total obliteration of all evil."[31]

In 1844 Bates sold his home and most of his real estate and paid off his debts. With H. S. Gurney, a blacksmith, he traveled to Maryland to preach the prophecies in slave territory. Despite threats from some who did not like abolitionist Yankees with strange religious doctrines, the two missionaries returned safely to New England. In April Bates suffered what he called the "first disappointment in the advent movement"[32] when Christ did not return as expected. Puzzled regarding where he had been wrong, Bates continued to study the Scriptures. At a camp meeting held in Exeter, Massachusetts, in August, he learned "new light" from Samuel S. Snow, a Millerite preacher. Snow believed that Jesus would come on October 22, which he had determined to be the Day of Atonement. Alas, there was "another sad disappointment."[33] Believing that the Millerite system of prophetic interpretation held truth, however, Bates persevered.

In the early spring of 1845 Bates began the third major period of his life after reading Thomas M. Preble's article advocating observance of the seventh-day Sabbath, which appeared in *The Hope of Israel*, a Millerite paper. Bates quickly accepted this new doctrine and soon thereafter traveled to Washington, New Hampshire, where he met with Frederick Wheeler and other Adventists who were observing the Sabbath. Consistent with his long-standing interest in reform, Bates began working to return Christian practice to its biblical roots. "In the course of his lifetime," Godfrey T. Anderson wrote, "Joseph Bates was a sturdy pioneer in many worthy projects. Now he was the first of his erstwhile advent companions to proclaim, in season and out, the Sabbath reform message."[34] In August 1846 he published a tract, *The Seventh-day Sabbath a Perpetual Sign*, in which he presented biblical arguments for observance of Saturday. That same month he met James White and Ellen Harmon (a visionary who was speaking to Adventist groups in northern New England) but was unable to convince them of the Sabbath. Later that autumn, however, Ellen and James White, recently married, studied Bates's tract and accepted the Sabbath doctrine. The following January he published an expanded version of his pamphlet, drawing connections with the prophecies of Revelation 14 and the idea that the change of the Sabbath from Saturday to Sunday constituted the "mark of the beast."

Other of Bates's books included *The Opening Heavens* (1846) in which he reaffirmed the literal second coming of Jesus. He followed this with *Second Advent Waymarks and High Heaps* (1847), *A Vindication of the Seventh-day Sabbath* (1848), *A Seal of the Living God* (1849), and *An Explanation of the Typical and Antitypical Sanctuary, by the Scriptures*

(1850). Meanwhile, he participated in most of the "Sabbath Conferences" that took place in 1848 and 1849 in which the Sabbatarian Adventist movement coalesced around its key doctrines. In his writings and at the conferences Bates played a key role in linking the Sabbath doctrine with what became known as the Sanctuary doctrine. The interpretation of the sanctuary, first proposed by O. R. L. Crosier and his associates in 1845, argued that Daniel's reference to the cleansing of the sanctuary, which Miller had understood as referring to Christ's return to the earth, instead meant that on October 22, 1844, Christ had entered the Most Holy Place of the heavenly sanctuary described in the book of Hebrews.

In 1849 Bates traveled to Michigan where he contacted former Millerites and presented to them the new Sabbatarian Adventist understandings. For the next twenty years Bates itinerated nearly constantly, repeatedly visiting the New England and Midwestern states, as well as New York and Canada. Increasing numbers of believers in Michigan led James White to move the office of the *Review and Herald*, the Sabbatarian Adventist paper, to the town of Battle Creek in 1855. Three years later, Bates himself moved to Michigan, establishing his home in the village of Monterey.

As the Sabbatarian Adventist following grew, it became apparent to the leading figures in the movement that what they called "gospel order" was needed. Like many other former Millerites, Bates originally opposed denominational organization, but he gradually changed his mind. In 1853 Bates and James White introduced the first step toward the practice of ordination when they signed a ministerial card for John Loughborough; other ministers subsequently received similar credentials. That same year Bates's home church selected a deacon and the following year Bates helped other local congregations choose leaders.

As the Sabbatarians began holding general meetings, Bates played a leading role. In 1855 he chaired a conference that addressed the issue of the hours that the Sabbath should be observed. Bates had long promoted the idea that observance should begin at 6:00 P.M. Friday and continue to 6:00 P.M. Saturday. The conference, however, adopted the view of J. N. Andrews—whom the Sabbatarian leaders had asked to study the problem—that sundown marked the beginning and closing of the Sabbath. In 1857 Bates chaired a conference that voted to purchase a power press for the Review and Herald Office and resolved to build a meeting house in Battle Creek. Two years later he chaired another conference that created a "systematic benevolence" plan for economic support of the Adventist ministry. Bates then chaired a series of conferences that chose the name

Seventh-day Adventist (1860), established the Seventh-day Adventist Publishing Association (1861), and formed the Michigan Conference (1861). He served as chair of this state conference until its formal organization the following year. He also participated in the organization of the General Conference in 1863, but his days as a conference chair had come to an end as younger men rose to the fore.

His seventy-plus years slowed Bates down only slightly, although most of his activity from this point on was limited to the state of Michigan. Anderson writes that "he was involved in about 130 meeting days with the local Michigan churches during 1864" and that "throughout most of the year 1865 Bates continued very actively to visit churches and hold meetings in his adopted state."[35] In 1868 he attended and spoke at the first official Adventist camp meeting, which took place in Wright, Michigan. As late as 1871 he held more than 100 meetings in eleven months and gave a personal testimony at a health convention in Battle Creek.

The passage of time took its toll, however. In 1865, as noted previously, Bates's son died at sea; five years later his wife passed away. His reports in the *Review and Herald* ended in November 1871, although he wrote a strong letter to Ellen White in February of the next year defending his dietary practices and refuting a report that his daughter and her son, who had been living with him for some time, were starving. On March 19, 1872, Bates died at the Adventist Health Reform Institute in Battle Creek. The cause was listed as putrid erysipelas—a form of shingles—and diabetes, which in the nineteenth century had imprecise meaning. His obituary in the *Review and Herald* stated that "having for many years faithfully endeavored to live the life of the righteous, his last end was such as those alone can expect who have sedulously endeavored to preserve a conscience void of offense toward God and man."[36]

## Bates's Contributions to Seventh-day Adventism

As suggested in the foregoing biographical sketch, Joseph Bates played a key role in the development of the Seventh-day Adventist Church. Bates's most important contribution, as George Knight argues in his recent biography, lay in defining Sabbatarian Adventist theology,[37] for without that system of thought there would have been no movement centered around the doctrines of the Sanctuary, the Sabbath, and the Second Coming of Jesus. In the series of tracts that Bates wrote between 1846 and 1850, he integrated these ideas into a theological system that gave the Sabbatarian Adventists their dynamic missionary thrust.

Bates's *Seventh Day Sabbath, A Perpetual Sign* (1846) argued that the Sabbath was instituted at creation as recorded in Genesis, that a change of the Sabbath from Saturday to Sunday appears nowhere in the Bible, and that the Sabbath is still binding on Christians. In his expanded 1847 edition of this tract, Bates added several elements. Using the phrase "Present Truth," which Millerites had earlier applied to the doctrine of the Second Coming, Bates connected the Sabbath doctrine to eschatology by suggesting that the opening of the heavenly sanctuary's Most Holy Place, where the ark which contained the Ten Commandments was located, drew end-time attention to the Sabbath. He further applied the three angels' messages of Revelation 14:6-11 to recent Adventist history: the first angel (verses 6 and 7) represented the Millerite movement, the second (verse 8) referred to Adventist preachers who announced the fall of Babylon, and the third (verses 9-11) found expression in the Millerite call to come out of Babylon (p. 58).[38] After the Great Disappointment, some of those who had come out of Babylon began preaching the Sabbath (verse 12), a doctrine that according to this prophecy would be restored before the end of time. Finally, Bates introduced what has become known as "great controversy theology," in which God's faithful remnant—those who keep the seventh-day Sabbath—are at war with the beast whose mark or sign is Sunday observance. "The two pages [pp. 58-59] in which Bates developed the great controversy theology...," Knight argues, "are two of the most influential in Sabbatarian Adventist history."[39] Although revision in this understanding would occur, Bates provided the basic structure out of which Sabbatarian Adventist theology developed.

Bates wrote *A Vindication of the Seventh-day Sabbath and the Commandments of God* (1848) in response to Sunday-observing Adventist attacks on the Sabbath doctrine. Among other things, he reiterated his identification of Sabbath observers with the remnant of Revelation 12:17 who were opposed by the beast. This argument indicated that the distinction between Sabbatarians and other Adventists was becoming ever more clear. A year later, Bates published *A Seal of the Living God* (1849), in which he developed further a theme he had introduced in his *Vindication* tract. He identified the sealing of the 144,000 (Revelation 7:1-4 and 14:1) with observance of the seventh-day Sabbath, thereby giving the doctrine further eschatological significance. According to Bates, Sabbath observers who remained faithful to God's commands would experience increasing persecution before the end of time from those who despised God's law.

As Bates studied the prophetic role of the Sabbath, he developed an expanded sense of purpose. For a time after the Great Disappointment he had been a hard-line advocate of the "Shut Door" theory, believing that probation had closed for Christians on October 22, 1844.[40] But now, as he thought about the sealing of the 144,000, he began advocating the conversion of those outside North America who had never had the chance to hear the Millerite message. By identifying the Sabbath as an end-time message, Bates sowed the seeds of Adventism's missionary thrust.

In developing this distinctive theology, Bates also contributed to Sabbatarian Adventist self-understanding by identifying the movement's role in history. In *The Opening Heavens* (1846), he sought to correct those "spiritualizers" who believed that Jesus had come in some mystical form in 1844. Advocating the cleansing of the heavenly sanctuary interpretation of October 22, developed by Hiram Edson and O. R. L. Crosier, he suggested that those who kept all of God's commandments, including observance of the seventh day as the Sabbath, would preserve belief in the literal second coming of Jesus and guide the Advent believers through the myriad false doctrines that purported to explain the Great Disappointment. He developed this idea further in *Second Advent Waymarks and High Heaps* (1847) in which he argued that God had providentially guided the Advent movement through a series of steps from Miller's first preaching of Christ's coming to the Sabbatarians' call to keep all of the commandments of God. In Bates's view, the Sabbatarian Adventists were a people of destiny, ordained by God to restore to the world the observance of the Sabbath in light of the knowledge that Christ had ushered in the last phase of history when he entered the Most Holy Place of the heavenly sanctuary on October 22, 1844.

This sense of the eschatological importance of the Sabbatarian message led Bates to not only publish tracts but also to seek out former Millerites and present to them this expanded understanding of Adventist belief. By the early 1850s he had made his way to Michigan. There, in an event that indicates a softening of his "Shut Door" convictions, Bates met with David Hewitt, who apparently had never previously accepted Millerite teaching, and encouraged him to do. As Bates gradually moved away from the limitations of a "Shut Door" understanding, he contributed to Adventism's growth through his constant itinerating which expanded Sabbatarian Adventism beyond its New England-New York roots. "He was a trailblazer, opening up new areas, such as Michigan, a dozen years after it had achieved statehood,…" Anderson wrote. "He was the first Adventist Sabbatarian preacher in several states, including Wisconsin,

Iowa, and Minnesota."[41] As he pursued this missionary activity, Bates influenced many of those who would become the early Sabbatarian Adventist leaders. In addition to convincing James and Ellen White of the importance of observing the seventh day, Bates also led Stephen N. Haskell, Merritt E. Cornell, John Byington, Annie Smith, and R. F. Cottrell to Sabbatarian Adventism.

Probably too much an activist to ever be comfortable with administration, Bates nonetheless guided the Sabbatarians as they moved toward formal organization in the 1850s and early 1860s, chairing nearly all of the conferences that made important organizational decisions. Also, while he did not push his health reform ideas on others, he provided an example of healthful living and at times made connections between health reform and faithfulness to God's end-time message, such as in his tract *A Seal of the Living God*. His work prepared the way for Ellen White's vigorous advocacy of the theme in the 1860s and after. This "Pioneer of the Pioneers among Seventh-day Adventists" was indeed the "real founder" of Seventh-day Adventism, shaping its theology, formulating its sense of history and mission, giving the movement its first expansive thrust, and pointing it toward a concern with both spirit and body.

## The *Autobiography*

Most people would agree that Joseph Bates led an interesting and sometimes exciting life. Thus, it is no surprise that his friends and associates urged him to record his memories. Finally responding to these requests at the age of sixty-six, he wrote the story of his life for the Seventh-day Adventist publication, *The Youth's Instructor*, where it appeared in fifty-one articles between November 1858 and May 1863. The first installment gave no indication that it was to be part of a series. Entitled "Sailing,"[42] it contained three paragraphs on his first voyage through Hurl Gate on Long Island Sound, and two paragraphs drawing a Christian moral from the story. Two months later Bates published a second installment, this time entitled "Incidents of My Past Life No. 2,"[43] that clearly indicated the story was part of a larger series. From that time on, Bates's accounts appeared in nearly every issue of *The Youth's Instructor* for the next four and a half years.[44] The last installment carried Bates's story through the Millerite disappointment of the spring of 1844. He then explained why he was ending his account at that point:

I have now reached a point in my history, the most trying in all my Christian experience. From the spring of 1844 to the present time, has been a scene of exaggeration and misrepresentation on the part of our opponents respecting the manner and time to proclaim the second advent of our Lord and Saviour Jesus Christ....

I now find it very difficult to write without assuming much more than I should be able to prove without referring to circumstances, books, and papers, a great portion of which would be considered uninteresting for a paper like yours. I deem it duty, therefore, to say that the present number, 51, is the last of my series of articles for the Instructor, and leave whatever part of the history of the advent movement for the last twenty years, which may yet be required to be written, for abler pens than mine.[45]

When these articles were combined into a book in 1868, probably with the help of James White, Bates added to the beginning of the first chapter about one and a half pages on his family and early life. Approximately four other pages were added between the descriptions of the Hurl Gate passage and his fall overboard. Further, he reorganized the fifty-one *Youth's Instructor* articles into twenty-six chapters. Minor changes were made, such as dropping some of the moral lessons he had attached to his first few articles and revising some of the language marking transitions between chapters. He also added a twenty-seventh chapter briefly describing the second disappointment of October 22, 1844, and the emergence of Sabbatarian Adventism. He apparently had written a longer account of this period of his life which was cut "for want of room."[46] Announcing the volume in the *Review and Herald*, James White suggested that purchase of the volume would help alleviate Bates's financial situation and strongly urged church members to buy a copy:

> This is...one of the most interesting books in our country....It is one of the best books in the world. It is especially adapted to the youth. It should be in every family. The old friends of Father Bates should all take a special interest in this book. We have all been blest with the labors of this good man. Let none be too stingy to purchase a copy of his good book. When the printer and binder are paid, what remains from the sale of the book will go for the benefit of this pioneer of the cause, whom we all love....Turn out some of those worthless books from the library, and let good ones take their places. Read good books, and let the youth and children have the benefit of them.[47]

Nine years later the *Autobiography* appeared in a new printing, this time with a new title and James White listed as editor,[48] a role he had probably played in the 1868 edition. In a preface White noted that the book had been out of print for about a year but that "the call for it continues."[49] White also contributed an introduction in which he recommended the book for its potential moral influence:

> That which makes his [Joseph Bates's] early history intensely interesting
> to his personal friends is the fact that he became a devoted follower of
> Christ, and a thorough practical reformer, and ripened into glorious man-
> hood a true Christian gentleman, while exposed to the evils of sea-faring
> life, from the cabin-boy of 1807, to the wealthy retiring master of 1828, a
> period of twenty-one years.[50]

In addition, White added some "Remarks by the Editor" at the end of
the volume. In these comments, the editor briefly discussed Bates's health
reform practices, which by the late 1870s the Adventists were generally
advocating, and then described the fifty-four-year-old former sea captain
as he had looked at their first meeting in 1846:

> His countenance was fair, his eye was clear and mild, his figure was erect
> and of fine proportions, and he was the last man to be picked out of the
> crowd as one who had endured the hardships and exposure of sea life, and
> who had come in contact with the physical and moral filth of such a life
> for more than a score of years. He had been from the seas the period of
> eighteen years, and during that time his life of rigid temperance in eating,
> as well as in drinking, and his labors in the pure sphere of moral reform,
> had regenerated the entire man, body, soul, and spirit, until he seemed
> almost re-created for the special work to which God had called him.[51]

Clearly emphasizing Bates as a model for healthful living, White also
reproduced a speech Bates had made to a health reform convention at
Battle Creek, Michigan, in 1871. He then quoted from an obituary and
from a September 1872 resolution passed by the Michigan Conference of
Seventh-day Adventists which stated, "while we deeply mourn our loss,
we will remember his counsels, imitate his virtues, and endeavor to meet
him in the kingdom of God."[52] Other than these changes and additions,
the 1878 volume was the same as that published in 1868.

The *Autobiography* next appeared in 1927 when C. C. Crisler, who
had served as a secretary to Ellen G. White and a missionary in China,
provided a shortened version. Crisler said that he had first read the book
in 1886 at the age of nine and had reread it several times thereafter. But
when he had recently begun asking his friends if they had read the book,
he found to his "surprise that only a few had had this privilege. Several
had never heard of the book."[53] While traveling by sea, Crisler prepared
the volume for "republication in abridged form," bringing it "into as
brief a form as seems consistent with the preservation of the Captain's
quaint and racy style."[54] Crisler divided the chapters into shorter lengths,
producing forty-six chapters in his version compared to twenty-seven in
the original. He also replaced Bates's several-line chapter descriptions

with titles such as "Collision with an Iceberg," "Doubling Cape Horn," and "Uniting with the Adventist People."

Although he mostly kept Bates's original language, Crisler deleted many details. For instance, he cut out all of Bates's description of his first passage through Hurl Gate in 1807.[55] He also sometimes altered Bates's original wording. Where Bates stated regarding the poem entitled "The Hour of Death" that "the lines mentioned in the last chapter did arrest my attention," Crisler, who placed this statement in the same chapter as the poem, rendered Bates's comments as "these lines seriously arrested my attention."[56] While this change in wording is small, it suggests that readers should regard the Crisler volume as both an abridgement and a slightly modernized revision. After the Crisler version, Bates's *Autobiography* did not appear again until the 1868 edition was reprinted in 1970.[57]

In writing the autobiography, Bates stated that he "had no manuscripts or anything definite in mind, only what occurred to it as I passed along in my history."[58] James White said something very similar, noting that Bates had written "much of the book from memory, without the help of any sort of memorandum."[59] Recently, both Jerry E. Daly and George R. Knight, who have studied Bates's surviving logbook, have concluded that he appears to have used that document while composing his *Autobiography*.[60] A reproduction of the Hemans poem; Bates's own "A Solemn Covenant with God" (October 4, 1824); and an 1828 letter to John Carroll regarding a financial error suggest that he had a few documents to assist his memory.[61] To illustrate various points that he makes regarding social developments, particularly in relation to reform and religious movements, Bates also quotes a number of public documents, among them the constitution of the American Colonization Society, Sylvester Graham, newspapers, and Millerite papers.[62] In general, however, Bates appears to have relied on his memory. In those places where it can be corroborated, the *Autobiography* seems to be fairly accurate, although Knight notes that the logbook suggests that the temperance ship may have had more problems than Bates described thirty to forty years later.[63]

Readers should recognize that autobiographies are a literary genre that arises from the author's attempt to understand his or her life.[64] As James Goodwin writes, "an autobiography represents the writer's effort, made at a certain stage of life, to portray the meaning of personal experience as it has developed over the course of a significant period of time *or* from the distance of that significant time period."[65]

Furthermore, Anne Hunsaker Hawkins argues that within this genre, spiritual autobiography—of which Bates's account is an example—has its own distinctive form.[66]

As we might expect from a former sea captain with no literary pretensions, Bates writes his autobiography in a matter-of-fact, chronological manner. After briefly describing his family, birth, and first voyage, however, he soon reveals to the reader that he is interpreting his story within a Christian framework. After telling the story of how his ship was stuck in the ice of the north Atlantic but eventually broke free, he comments, "In this state of suspense we were unable to devise any way for our escape, other than that God in his providence was manifesting to us, as above described. Praise his holy name!"[67] Then after quoting passages from the Psalms, Matthew, and Hebrews, he introduces his Adventist theological understanding by drawing an analogy between the ship and God's people being guided to the safety of the new earth. A few pages later, he judges strongly the British naval officers when they read from the prayer book, saying "Poor, wicked, deluded souls! how little their hearts were inclined to keep the holy law of God, when almost every other hour of the week, their tongues were employed in blaspheming his holy name."[68]

Of course, Bates at this point in his story was not yet a Christian, and the first two-thirds of his book moves on a trajectory from a period of no religious interest (chapters 1-10) to one of moral reform (chapters 11-14), which extends into the period of his conversion to Christianity (chapters 15-19). The account of his moral reform and conversion begins when Bates attributes the preservation of his ship during a terrific storm to the prayers of a black cook on the ship and a Methodist minister who was simultaneously visiting Bates's wife. A few pages later he reveals his awakening religious consciousness when he writes that "we felt thankful to God for preserving and sustaining us through the perilous scenes we had experienced."[69] He then tells the story of a drunkard, drawing a brief moral lesson which prepares the way thematically for him to discuss his decision to stop drinking "ardent spirits." The next thirty pages, while continuing to tell of his experiences in the maritime trade, largely revolve around his progressive steps in moral reform, which eventually led to complete abstinence from all alcoholic beverages, tobacco, and profanity. He seldom pursues any lengthy explanation of why he adopted these reforms, except to say such things as "I had become disgusted with its [alcohol's] debasing and demoralizing effects, and was well satisfied that drinking men were daily ruining themselves, and moving with rapid strides to a drunkard's grave."[70] Often, however, he simply states that he had "deep convictions" regarding tobacco and that he "resolved" or "decided" to no longer consume any of even what were regarded as lighter forms of alcohol such as wine or beer.[71]

Bates's account of his movement toward conversion is more laden with emotion than his description of moral reform. He first addresses his experience by noting that he had strayed from the example set by his parents but that he was trying to break himself of the habit of swearing and was beginning to read his Bible on Sundays. But after he reads Felicia Hemans's "Hour of Death" and deals with a dying sailor, his account becomes more introspective. "I longed to be a Christian; but the pride of my heart and the vain allurements of the wicked world, still held me with a mighty grasp," he wrote. "I suffered intensely in my mind before I decided to pray."[72] The emotional intensity of his story increases as he speaks of his strong sense of sin, lack of guidance in how to become a Christian, and an urge to jump overboard. While performing the religious service for the dead sailor, Bates "felt indeed that I was a sinner before God....I passed down into my praying place and vented my feelings in prayer for the forgiveness of all my sins....From thence I felt a sinking into the will of God."[73] Even though he did not yet understand that he was converted, Bates continues to write about his religious experience in subjective terms, saying at one point that "I enjoyed freedom in prayer beyond anything I had ever experienced before. It was indeed a heavenly place in Christ Jesus."[74] Finally, after hearing testimonies similar to his own experience at a revival meeting, he concludes that he is indeed converted, but describes this experience in a more objective manner than earlier. "I began to reason, and ask myself, Is this conversion from sin? Is this really it? Then I have experienced the same."[75]

From this point on (chapters 17-27), Bates largely returns to his matter-of-fact reporting of his experiences, although he occasionally offers expressions of praise to God such as "thanks to his holy name" and "by the blessing of God our boat returned in safety."[76] His Adventist perspective appears in the attention he devotes to the 1833 falling of the stars, which he describes as a "portentous" sign, and the space he gives to William Miller.[77] Regarding his acceptance of Miller's teaching that Jesus would return about the year 1843, however, Bates says only that his "mind was much enlightened"[78] and spends less than a page discussing the subject. Chapters 23 and 24 are largely about the Millerite movement rather than Bates's own experiences and appear to have apologetic intent in their emphasis on documented signs and wonders. Although he describes in considerable detail his preaching trip into Maryland with H. S. Gurney,

he says virtually nothing of a personal nature regarding the disappoint-
ments of April and October 1844. The first disappointment, he states,
left "those who felt the burden of the message…in deep trial and anguish
of spirit." Then in October, "another sad disappointment awaited the
watching ones…All were waiting in ardent expectation for the coming of
their Lord and Saviour. The day passed, and another twenty-four hours
followed, but deliverance did not come. Hope sunk and courage died
within them."[79]

In contrast to Bates's highly personal account of his movement toward
conversion, he says nothing in particular about his own disappointment
experience. Perhaps the memory was too painful. Neither does he say
anything about his experience of accepting the seventh-day Sabbath and
other elements of Sabbatarian Adventism other than making general
statements such as "we were also greatly cheered and strengthened by
the light which we received on the subject of the three angels' messages
of Rev. xiv, 6-12."[80] Instead, he presents about two pages summarizing
the argument for the Sabbath. As a consequence, Bates's autobiography
provides relatively little insight into either the Millerite movement or the
rise of Sabbatarian Adventism.

Nonetheless, the volume continues to be worthy of our attention.
As a record of a remarkable nineteenth-century individual, it offers a
unique perspective on such subjects as the War of 1812, American maritime trade, reform movements, and the Second Great Awakening, and
is of potential value to scholars. Although the volume spends most of
its pages on Bates's life prior to his acceptance of Adventism, because
it is written from his Adventist perspective it also offers insight into the
moral and religious elements of Bates's personality. We thereby better
understand why this early leader took his Adventist faith so seriously.
*The Autobiography of Elder Joseph Bates* should continue to attract
readers in the twenty-first century, whether they simply want to vicari-
ously relive the ages of sail, revival, and reform; are seeking to better
understand nineteenth-century American society; or want to encounter
directly the self-understanding of the "real founder" of the Seventh-day
Adventist Church.

1. C. Mervyn Maxwell, *Tell It to the World: The Story of Seventh-day
Adventists*, rev. ed. (Mountain View, Calif.: Pacific Press, 1977), 76; Godfrey T. Anderson, "Sectarianism and Organization, 1846-1864," in *Adventism in America: A History*, ed. Gary Land, rev. ed. (Berrien Springs, Mich.:
Andrews University Press, 1998), 31.

2. Everett N. Dick, *Founders of the Message* (Washington, D.C.: Review and Herald, 1938).

3. Everett N. Dick, "The Advent Crisis of 1843-1844," (Ph.D. diss., University of Wisconsin, 1930); Everett N. Dick, *The Sod-House Frontier, 1854-1890: A Social History of the Northern Plains from the Creation of Kansas and Nebraska to the Admission of the Dakotas* (New York: D. Appleton-Century, 1937).

4. Dick, *Founders*, 9. See also Gary Land, Foreword to Everett N. Dick, *William Miller and the Advent Crisis, 1831-1844* (Berrien Springs, Mich.: Andrews University Press, 1994), viii.

5. Joseph Bates, *The Autobiography of Elder Joseph Bates...* (Battle Creek, Mich.: Steam Press of the Seventh-day Adventist Publishing Association, 1868); John N. Loughborough, *Rise and Progress of the Seventh-day Adventists: With Tokens of God's Hand in the Movement and a Brief Sketch of the Advent Cause from 1831 to 1844* (Battle Creek, Mich.: General Conference Association of the Seventh-day Adventists, 1892); and John N. Loughborough, *The Great Second Advent Movement: Its Rise and Progress* (Washington, D.C.: Review and Herald, 1905). In his first volume Loughborough recounted the events surrounding the publication of Bates's first tract (110-14) and the conversion of Annie Smith (161-62). The second volume included these stories (251-55, 312-15) and added a story about Bates's acceptance of the divine inspiration of Ellen White's visions (255-60).

6. Dick, *Founders*, 105, 123, 141, and 145.

7. Ibid., 146.

8. Clarence Edwin Stenberg, "A Study of the Influence of Joseph Bates on the Denomination of Seventh-day Adventists" (master's thesis, Seventh-day Adventist Theological Seminary, 1950).

9. Ibid., 90, 92.

10. Virgil Robinson, *Cabin Boy to Advent Crusader* (Nashville, Tenn.: Southern Publishing Association, 1960; reprint, Hagerstown, Md.: Review and Herald, 1992).

11. J. O. Corliss, "Joseph Bates As I Knew Him," *The Advent Review and Sabbath Herald*, 16 August 1923, 7-8.

12. Robinson (1992), 187.

13. Godfrey T. Anderson, *Outrider of the Apocalypse: The Life and Times of Joseph Bates* (Mountain View, Calif.: Pacific Press, 1972).

14. Ibid., 60.

15. Ibid., 70.

16. Ibid., 93.

17. Jerry E. Daly, "Joseph Bates's Logbook of the Brig *Empress*" (master's thesis, Loma Linda University, 1981). See also Michael Ooley, "The Logbook (1827-1828) of Captain Joseph Bates of the Ship Empress," *Adventist Heritage: A Journal of Adventist History* 5 (Winter, 1978): 4-12.

18. George R. Knight, *Joseph Bates: The Real Founder of Seventh-day Adventism* (Hagerstown, Md.: Review and Herald, 2004). Knight kindly loaned me a photocopy of his manuscript prior to publication.

19. Ibid., 149.

20. Ibid., 168.

21. Ibid., 212.

22. The following biographical information is drawn primarily from Anderson, *Outrider of the Apocalypse.*

23. Bates, *Autobiography*, 35.

24. For discussion of impressments, see Donald R. Hickey, *The War of 1812: A Forgotten Conflict* (Urbana: University of Illinois Press, 1989), 11.

25. Bates, *Autobiography*, 174.

26. Ibid., 180. Although Bates reprints the poem, he provides no title and says only that the poet was "Mrs. Hemans." The poem was "Hour of Death" by a popular English poet of the day, Felicia Dorothea Browne Hemans (1793-1835). That the poem had considerable currency in the nineteenth century is illustrated by the fact that a recent exhibition of mourning and the arts in the nineteenth century took its title from the verse's first line, which in turn was taken from a reproduction of the poem on a period quilt in the exhibition. "'Leaves have their time to fall': Reflections of Mourning in Nineteenth-Century Decorative Arts" opened at the Georgia Museum of Art on July 19, 2003.

27. Ibid., 184.

28. Steven Mintz, *Moralists and Modernizers: America's Pre-Civil War Reformers* (Baltimore: The Johns Hopkins University Press, 1995), 28.

29. For the history of the Millerite movement, see Dick, *William Miller*, and George R. Knight, *Millennial Fever and the End of the World* (Boise, Idaho: Pacific Press, 1994).

30. Bates, *Autobiography*, 262.

31. David L. Rowe, *Thunder and Trumpets: Millerites and Dissenting Religion in Upstate New York, 1800-1850* (Chico, Calif.: Scholars Press, 1985), 91.

32. Bates, *Autobiography*, 294.

33. Ibid., 300.

34. Anderson, *Outrider*, 63.

35. Ibid., 107.

36. W. H. Littlejohn, "Obituary Notice," *The Advent Review and Herald of the Sabbath*, 16 April 1872, 143. It should be noted that the page numbers are printed out of order in this issue.

37. Knight, *Joseph Bates*, 210-11. The following summary of Bates's theology is drawn from Knight, 107-34.

38. James White revised this interpretation by seeing the Millerite movement as a fulfillment of the first and second angels' messages while the third angel's message referred to the Sabbatarian Adventist movements. Over time the Sabbatarian Adventists expanded White's interpretation as they came to understand that the "Third Angel's Message" included the first two messages as well.

39. Knight, *Joseph Bates*, 115.

40. Richard W. Schwarz and Floyd Greenleaf, *Light Bearers: A History of the Seventh-day Adventist Church*, rev. ed. (Nampa, Idaho: Pacific Press, 2000), 61.

41. Anderson, *Outrider*, 118-19.

42. Joseph Bates, "Sailing," *The Youth's Instructor*, November 1858, 84-85.

43. Joseph Bates, "Incidents of My Past Life, No. 2," *The Youth's Instructor*, January 1859, 4-5.

44. The only issues in which an installment did not appear were December 1858, February 1859, March 1863, and April 1863.

45. Joseph Bates, "Incidents of My Past Life, No. 51," *The Youth's Instructor*, May 1863, 34.

46. Joseph Bates to "Sister Harriet," 19 July 1868. Photocopied typescript of letter in collection of George R. Knight.

47. James White, "The Autobiography," *Review and Herald*, 17 November 1868, 248.

48. James White, ed., *The Early Life and Later Experience and Labors of Elder Joseph Bates* (Battle Creek, Mich.: Steam Press of the Seventh-day Adventist Publishing Association, 1878).

49. Ibid., vi.

50. Ibid., xv.

51. Ibid., 311.

52. Ibid., 320.

53. *Life of Joseph Bates: An Autobiography*, abridged and edited by C. C. Crisler (Washington, D.C.: Review and Herald, 1927), 9.

54. Ibid., 9.

55. Compare Bates, *Autobiography*, 18-19, with *Life of Joseph Bates*, 14.

56. Bates, *Autobiography*, 181; *Life of Joseph Bates*, 136.

57. *The Autobiography of Elder Joseph Bates...* (Nashville, Tenn.: Southern Publishing Association, 1970).

58. Bates, "Incidents of My Past Life, No. 51," 34.

59. White, "Autobiography," 248.

60. George R. Knight to Gary Land, 11 July 2003.

61. Bates, *Autobiography*, 180, 185, 224.

62. Ibid., 232, 234, 239-41, 245-49, 259, 270-76, and 295-96.

63. Knight, *Joseph Bates*, 45.

64. See Ray Pascal, *Design and Truth in Autobiography* (London: Routledge and Kegan Paul, 1960), 61-83; James Olney, *Metaphors of Self: The Meaning of Autobiography* (Princeton, N.J.: Princeton University Press, 1972); Paul John Eakin, *Fictions in Autobiography: Studies in the Art of Self-Invention* (Princeton, N.J.: Princeton University Press, 1985), 181-278; and Herbert Leibowitz, *Fabricating Lives: Explorations in American Autobiography* (New York: Alfred A. Knopf, 1989), 3-28.

65. James Goodwin, *Autobiography: The Self Made Text*, Studies in Literary Themes and Genres, no. 2 (New York: Twayne Publishers, 1993).

66. Anne Hunsaker Hawkins, *Archetypes of Conversion: The Autobiographies of Augustine, Bunyan, and Merton* (Lewisburg, Pa.: Bucknell University Press, 1985).

67. Bates, *Autobiography*, 31.

68. Ibid., 43.

69. Ibid., 125.

70. Ibid., 143.
71. Ibid., 168, 179.
72. Ibid., 181.
73. Ibid., 184.
74. Ibid., 193.
75. Ibid., 203.
76. Ibid., 219, 224.
77. Ibid., 238-48.
78. Ibid., 244.
79. Ibid., 294, 300.
80. Ibid., 301.

# THE AUTOBIOGRAPHY

## OF ELDER JOSEPH BATES.

*Yours in the blessed hope*

*Joseph Bates*

# AUTOBIOGRAPHY

— OF —

# ELDER JOSEPH BATES;

EMBRACING

## A LONG LIFE ON SHIPBOARD,

WITH SKETCHES OF

VOYAGES ON THE ATLANTIC AND PACIFIC OCEANS,
THE BALTIC AND MEDITERRANEAN SEAS;

— ALSO —

Impressment and Service on board British War Ships, Long Confinement In
Dartmoor Prison, Early Experience In Reformatory Movements;

## TRAVELS IN VARIOUS PARTS OF THE WORLD;

AND A BRIEF ACCOUNT OF

### The Great Advent Movement of 1840--44.

————————— •❖• —————————

STEAM PRESS
OF THE SEVENTH–DAY ADVENTIST PUBLISHING ASSOCIATION,
BATTLE CREEK, MICH.
————
1868.

# PREFACE.

I HAVE frequently been solicited by relatives and friends to write a brief history of my past life, but never felt seriously inclined to do so until the year 1858, when I was requested by my friends in the West to furnish a series of articles in relation to my past life, for a religious paper entitled, "The Youth's Instructor," published at Battle Creek, Mich. In compliance with their wishes, fifty-one numbers were issued and published in said paper, ending in May, 1863.

As these numbers are about exhausted, we again comply with the request of friends to furnish them, with additional numbers, for publication in book form.

JOSEPH BATES.

*Monterey, Mich., May* 1, 1868.

# TABLE OF CONTENTS.

# CHAPTER FOURTEEN.

# CHAPTER FIFTEEN.

# CHAPTER SIXTEEN.

## CHAPTER SEVENTEEN.

### PAGES 204–213.

## CHAPTER EIGHTEEN.

### PAGES 213–226.

## CHAPTER NINETEEN.

### PAGES 226–230.

## CHAPTER TWENTY.

### PAGES 230–241.

# LIFE OF JOSEPH BATES.

## Chapter One.

*Parentage—Birth—Residence—First Foreign Voyage —Hurlgate—London Water for Sailors—Mr. Loyd's Story—Mr. Moore and his Book—Sea Journal— Overboard—Shark.*

MY HONORED father and his forefathers were for many years residents in the town of Wareham, Plymouth county, State of Massachusetts. My mother was the daughter of Mr. Barnebas Nye, of the town of Sandwich, Barnstable County, both towns but a few hours' ride from the noted landing-place of the Pilgrim Fathers.

My father was a volunteer in the Revolutionary war, and continued in the service of his country during its seven-years' struggle. When Gen. Lafayette re-visited the United States, in 1825, among the many that were pressing to shake hands with him, at his reception rooms, in the city of Boston, was my father. As he approached, the General recognized him, and grasped his hand, saying, "How do you do, my old friend, Captain Bates?" "Do you remember him?" was asked. His answer was something like the following: "Certainly; he was under my immediate command in the American army," &c.

After the war, my father married and settled in Rochester, an adjoining town, in Plymouth county, where I was born, July 8, 1792. In the early part of 1793 we moved to New Bedford, some seven miles distant, where my father entered into commercial business.

During the war with England, in 1812, the town of New Bedford was divided, and the eastern part was called Fairhaven. This has ever been my place of residence, until I moved my family to Michigan, in May, 1858.

In my school-boy days my most ardent desire was to become a sailor. I used to think how gratified I should be if I could only get on board a ship that was going on a voyage of discovery round the world. I wanted to see how it looked on the opposite side. Whenever I thought of asking my father's consent to let me go to sea, my courage failed me for fear he would say, No. When I would endeavor to unburden my mind to my mother she would try to dissuade me, and recommend some other occupation, till at last I was permitted to go a short trip with my uncle to Boston, &c., to cure me, but this had the opposite effect. They then complied with my wishes.

A new ship called the Fanny, of New Bedford, Elias Terry, commander, was about to sail for Europe, and he agreed with my father to take me on the voyage as cabin boy.

In June, 1807, we sailed from New Bedford, to take our cargo on board at New York city, for London, England. On our passage to New York city we sailed by the way of Long Island Sound. In this route, several miles from the city, is a very narrow and dangerous passage, bounded with rocks on the right, and a rock-bound shore on the left,

called "Hurl Gate." What makes it so dangerous
is the great rush of water that passes through this
narrow channel. As the tide ebbs and flows each
way, it rushes with such impetuosity that few dare
venture to sail through against it without a strong,
steady wind in their favor. For want of watchfulness and care many vessels have been whirled
from their course by this rushing foam, and hurled
against the rocks, wrecked and lost in a few moments of time. Sailors call it "Hell Gate."

As our gallant ship was bringing us in sight of
this dreadful place, the pilot took the helm, and
requested the captain to call all hands on deck.
He then stationed us in various parts of the ship,
for the purpose of managing the sails in case of an
emergency, according to his judgment. He then
requested us to remain silent while passing this
dangerous gateway, that we might the better understand his orders. In this way, every man and
boy at their post, with their eyes silently fixed on
the pilot waiting his orders, our good ship winged
her way through the hurling foam, and passed on
safely to her anchorage before the city.

The experienced and thorough knowledge of our
pilot, in guiding our gallant ship safely through
that dangerous gateway, with the stillness and
breathless attention of her crew, were stamped
deeply in my mind. Promptness and exertion in
perilous times on the ocean, has, with the blessing
of God, saved thousands of souls from a watery
grave.

Our good ship was deeply laden with choice
wheat, in bulk, even into her hatchways. It was
feared that she would sink under her heavy burden. On the eve of our departure, Mr. S. Eldridge,
then our chief mate, was coming on board the ship

in the dark night with a lighted lantern in his hand, when he fell from the plank into the river, between the ship and the wharf, where the tide was running from three to five miles an hour. Mr. Adams threw a coil of rope under the wharf at a venture; fortunately he caught it, and after some struggle, he was hauled up on the ship's deck. When he began to breathe freely, he lamented the loss of the new lantern. Said Mr. A., "Why, you have got it in your hand." If it had been a cannon ball it would most likely have carried him to the bottom, for drowning persons hold on with a deadly grasp to whatever is in their hands.

We had a pleasant run across the Atlantic ocean. In our passage up the British Channel, between France and England, we discovered a number of kegs floating on the top of the sea. The main-top-sail was laid to mast, and a boat lowered with a crew, which soon returned to the ship deeply laden with gin and brandy. The duties on such articles are so high, from France to England, that smugglers can afford to lose a whole cargo sometimes, and yet make their business profitable. But if they are caught by their revenue cutters, or war ships, while thus defrauding their government in her revenue laws, the penalty about ruins them for life. They sling and fasten them with ropes and buoys, so that by diligently hunting for them, they find them again after their pursuers are out of sight.

On our safe arrival in the London dock, the English officers who came to inspect our cargo, on opening the hatches, expressed their surprise to see the clean and dry wheat, up into the hatchway, as fresh as when we left New York. When we hauled out of the dock into the river Thames, and commenced filling our water-casks for our homeward voyage with the river water that was passing us, finding its way to the great ocean, I thought, how could a person drink such filthy water. Streaks of green, yellow, and red muddy water, mixed up with the filth of thousands of shipping, and scum and filth of a great portion of the city of London. After a few days it becomes settled and clear, unless it is stirred up from the bottom of the water-casks. Some four years after this, being then an impressed seaman in the British service attached to the Rodney, seventy-four gun ship, in the Mediterranean sea, we were emptying out all our old stock of fresh water; the ground tier was full of the same river water from the Thames, only a little further down from London, and had been bunged up tight for about two years. On starting the bung and applying our lighted candle, it would blaze up a foot high, like the burning of strong brandy. Before stirring it up from the bottom, some of the clear was exhibited among the officers in glass tumblers, and pronounced to be the purest and best of water, only about two years from London. I admit that it looked clear and tasted good, but from my former knowledge of its origin, I confess I had a little rather quench my thirst from some of the pure springs from the Green Mountains of Vermont, or granite hills in New Hampshire.

Among our passengers to New York was a Mr. Loyd, chief mate of a Philadelphia ship that was detained in London. He, in a very serious manner, related a very singular incident that occurred some few years previous, while he was a sailor from Philadelphia. He said that he never had dared to tell his mother or sisters of it. I will try to relate it in his own words. Said he, " I was lodging away from my home one night in another part of the city, when the house was beset by the police. For fear of being identified with those that were disturbing the peace, I fled from my bed into the street with nothing but my night-dress on, and finally secreted myself in the market place, while a friend that was with me went back to obtain my clothes. About midnight a gang of men, passing through the market place, discovered me, and after a few inquiries of who I was, &c., they said, 'Drive this fellow on before us.' My pleading was in vain; they continued to keep me before them until we entered the Cemetery, about two miles out of the city. We here came to a large flat stone with an iron hook in it. They placed a stout rope in the hook, which they brought with them, with which they swayed the stone up. This was opening a family vault, where a Jewish lady of distinction had been deposited that day. The jewelry upon her person was what they were after. The exciting question now was, who among them would go down into the vault and get the jewels? Said one, '*Here is the fellow.*' I begged and entreated them, for the Lord's sake, not to require me to commit such a dreadful deed. My entreaties were disregarded; they crowded me down into the vault, ordering me to go and strip off her jewels. I tried, and then returned to the open place, and stated that her fingers were so swollen that I could not get her rings off. 'Here is a knife,' said one, 'take it and cut her fingers off.' I began to plead again, but they gave me to understand there was no alternative; I must either do it or stay where I was. Almost dead with fear, I laid hold of her hands and cut her fingers off, and when I came to the open place, they bid me hand them up. As soon as they got hold of them, they dashed down the slab and ran away.

"I felt overwhelmed at my hopeless condition, doomed to die a most horrible death, and fearing every moment that the mangled corpse would lay hold of me. I listened to the rumbling sound of these robbers, until all was silent as death. The stone over me I could not move. After a little I heard a distant rumbling of the ground, which continued to increase until I heard strange voices over the vault. I soon learned that this was another gang, most likely unbeknown to the first, and they were placing their rope to swing up the same stone slab. I at once decided what to do to save myself. As the slab came up, I leaped out of the vault in my white night-dress, or shirt. Horror-stricken, they all fled back toward the city, running with such speed that it was difficult for me to keep up behind them, and yet I feared if they should stop, I should be discovered and taken. Before reaching the city, I had drawn up some nearer the two hinder ones, when one of them cried out to his companion, ' *Patrick! Patrick!! the old woman is close to our heels!*' Onward they raced through the market and fled away from me, for I stopped here to hide myself. After a while my friend, having obtained my clothes, found me, and I returned home."

Before sailing on our voyage, a good-looking man, about twenty years of age, came on board, stating that he had come from Philadelphia, Pennsylvania, to get a passage to London. He stated that he had no means nor way to pay his passage. He also stated that his only object in going to L. was to obtain a certain book, (the title I have forgotten), which could not be obtained at any other place. He finally shipped for a green or new hand before the mast.

This was rather new among sailors, for a man, having no desire to be a sailor, to be willing to endure the hardships of a seven-months' voyage, with no other object but to get one book, and no certainty about that.

But on our arrival in London the captain advanced him some money, and before night he returned from the city rejoicing that he had found the book. I have often regretted that our acquaintance ended with that voyage, for I have often thought, if his life was spared, he was destined to occupy some important position among men.

On recovering from my sea-sickness, I commenced my sea journal, to keep the run of the ship, and the daily occurrences of the voyage. This and other journals which I afterward endeavored to keep, would have been of much value to me when I commenced this work, but they were all used up, or destroyed, after my last voyage.

One circumstance occurred on our homeward voyage, some eighteen days after departing from Land's End, of England, which I will here relate:

In the morning (Sunday) a large shark was following us. A large piece of meat was fastened to a rope and thrown over the stern to tempt him to come up a little nearer, that we might fasten to him with a barbed iron made for such purposes; but no inducement of ours seemed to affect him. He maintained his position, where he could grasp whatever fell from either side of the ship.

On such occasions the old stories about sharks are revived; how they swallow sailors alive, and at other times bite them in two, and swallow them at two mouthfuls, &c. They hear so much about them that they attribute more to their sagacity than really belongs to them. It is said that sharks have followed vessels on the ocean for many days when there were any sick on board, that they may satiate their voracious appetites on the dead bodies that are cast into the sea. Sailors are generally brave and fearless men; they dare meet their fellows in almost any conflict, and brave the raging storms of the sea; but the idea of being swallowed alive, or even when dead, by these voracious creatures, often causes their stout hearts to tremble. Still they are often credulous and superstitious.

Toward the evening of the day referred to, when we had ceased our fruitless labors to draw the shark away from his determined position astern of the ship, I ascended to the main-top-gallant mast-head, to ascertain if there was any vessel in sight, or anything to be seen but sky and water. On my way down, having reached about fifty feet from the deck, and sixty from the water, I missed reaching the place which I designed grasping with my hand, and fell backward, striking a rope in my fall, which prevented my being dashed upon the deck, but whirled me into the sea. As I came up on the top of the waves, struggling and panting for breath, I saw at a glance that the ship, my only hope, was passing onward beyond my reach. With the incumbrance of my thick, heavy clothing, I exerted all my strength to follow. I saw that the captain, officers and crew had rushed toward the ship's stern. The first officer hurled a coil of rope with all his strength, the end of which I caught with my hand. He cried out, " Hold on!" I did so until they hauled me through the sea to the ship, and set my feet upon the deck.

To the question if I was hurt, I answered, "No."

Said another, "Where is the shark?" I began to tremble even as they had done, while they were in anxious suspense fearing he would grasp me every moment. The thought of the shark had never entered my mind while I was in the water. I then crossed over to the other side of the ship, and, behold, he was quietly gliding along his way with us, not far from the side of the vessel, seemingly unconscious of our gaze. And we did not disturb him in any way; for the sailors and passengers were all so glad that the cabin-boy was rescued, not only from a watery grave, but from his ferocious jaws, that they had no disposition to trouble him. He was soon missing, and we saw him no more. But the wonder to all was, how he came to change his position to a place where he could neither see nor hear what was transpiring on the other side and stern of the ship.

The following item from a public newspaper, illustrates the voracity of these creatures:

DESPERATE ENCOUNTER WITH A SHARK.

SOUTHOLD, L. I., September 9, 1865.

*To the Editor of the Herald:* A few days since the schooner Catharine Wilcox, of Lubec, Maine, George McFadden, master, being bound from New York to Eastport and Lubec, fell in, when opposite this place, with what is termed a "dead calm." The opportunity seeming propitious, the captain and a young man named Peter Johnson, who was formerly a member of the First Maine Heavy Artillery, and who was wounded in the neck at Spottsylvania, Virginia, determined to enjoy a salt-water bath.

Jumping into the water, it was not many minutes when, as young Johnson says, he saw something "all white," and in an instant he was carried under the surface to a depth of twenty feet. He now discovered that he was in the jaws of one of those voracious man-eater sharks. Struggling with all his strength, Johnson managed to break away and reach the surface again; but the shark was soon after him, and continued to bite him in various parts of the body, when the young man bethought him of the sailor trick of putting his fingers in the shark's eyes, which he did, and to his no small gratification soon saw the frenzied monster fleeing from him. Johnson now swam to the vessel, and, being taken on board, was found to have been fearfully torn about the abdomen—its lower section entirely off—both thighs and shoulder being terribly lacerated. There being no wind to get anywhere, the crew took him in the yawl and rowed him eight miles to the village of Greenport, where his wounds were sewed up and dressed by Drs. Kendall, Bryant and Skinner, and the young man made as comfortable under the circumstances as possible. He is growing worse hourly, and there is not much chance for his recovery.

The Sound is now full of these rapacious monsters, and if some of our New York sportsmen are fond of game worthy of their steel, this is the month to attack them. They are caught and landed with perfect safety by our villagers almost every day.

## Chapter Two.

*Shipwrecked in the Ice—An Attempt to Throw the Captain Overboard—Deliverance—Arrive in Ireland—Pursuing our Voyage—British Convoy—Part our Cable—Taken by Privateers—Nature of an Oath, and the Box—Ship Condemned—Voyage up the Baltic—Arrive in Ireland—Pressed into the British Service.*

PROCEEDING on another voyage from New York to Archangel, in Russia, about the middle of May, in the afternoon, we discovered a number of islands of ice, many of them appearing like large cities. This was an unmistakable sign that we were nearing the banks of Newfoundland, about one thousand miles on the mariner's track from Boston to Liverpool. These large masses, or islands of ice, are driven by wind and current from the ice-bound regions of the North, and strike the bottom more than three hundred feet from the surface of the sea, and in some seasons they are from two to three months dissolving and tumbling to pieces, which lightens them of their prodigious burdens, and they are driven onward over this deep water into the fathomless part of the ocean, and are soon dissolved in warm sea water.

A strong westerly gale was wafting us rapidly in our onward course, and as the night set in we were past this cluster. The fog then became so dense that it was impossible to see ten feet before us. About this time, while one W. Palmer was steering the ship, he overheard the chief mate expostulating with the captain, desiring him to round the ship to, and lay by until morning light. The captain decided that we were past all the ice, and said the ship must continue to run, and have a good lookout ahead. Midnight came, and we were relieved from our post by the captain's watch, to retire below for four hours. In about an hour from' this we were aroused by the dreadful cry from the helmsman, "*An island of ice!*" The next moment came the dreadful crash! When I came to my senses from the blow I received from being tossed from one side of the forecastle to the other, I found myself clinched by Palmer. The rest of the watch had made their escape on deck, and shut down the scuttle. After several unsuccessful attempts to find the ladder to reach the scuttle, we gave up in despair. We placed our arms around each other's necks, and gave up to die. Amid the creaking and rending of the ship with her grappled foe, we could once in a while hear the screams and cries of some of our wretched companions, on the deck above us, begging God

for mercy, which only augmented our desperate
feelings. Thoughts came rushing like the light,
that seemed to choke, and for a few moments block
up all way to utterance.

Oh, the dreadful thought! Here to yield up
my account and die, and sink with the wrecked
ship to the bottom of the ocean, so far from home
and friends, without the least preparation, or hope
of Heaven and eternal life, only to be numbered
with the damned and forever banished from the
presence of the Lord. It seemed that something
must give way to vent my feelings of unutterable
anguish!

In this agonizing moment the scuttle was thrown
open, with a cry, " Is there any one below?" In
a moment we were both on deck. I stood for a
moment surveying our position ; the ship's bow
partly under a shelf of ice, everything gone but
her stem. All her square sails filled with the
wind, and a heavy sea rushing her onward in closer
connection with her unyielding antagonist. Without some immediate change, it was evident that
our destiny, and hers, would be sealed up in a few
moments.

With some difficulty I made my way to the quarter-deck, where the captain and second mate were
on their knees begging God for mercy. The chief
mate, with as many as could rally around him,
were making fruitless efforts to hoist the long boat,
which could not have been kept from dashing
against the ice for two moments. Amid the crash
of matter and cry of others, my attention was arrested by the captain's crying out, " What are you
going to do with me, Palmer?" Said P., " I am
going to heave you overboard!" " For God's sake
let me alone," said he, " for we shall all be in eter-

nity in less than five minutes!" Said P., with a dreadful oath, "I don't care for that, you have been the cause of all this! It will be some satisfaction to me to see you go first!" I laid fast hold of him, and entreated him to let go of the captain and go with me and try the pump. He readily yielded to my request; and to our utter astonishment the pump *sucked*. This unexpected good news arrested the attention of the chief mate, who immediately turned from his fruitless labor, and after a moment's survey of the ship's crashing position, cried out with a stentorian shout, "Let go the top-gallant and the top-sail halyards! let go the tacks and sheets! haul up the courses! clew down and clew up the top-sails!" Perhaps orders were never obeyed in a more prompt and instantaneous manner. The wind thrown out of the sails relieved the ship immediately, and like a lever sliding from under a rock, she broke away from her disastrous position, and settled down upon an even keel broadside to the ice.

We now saw that our strongly-built and gallant ship was a perfect wreck forward of her foremast, and that mast, to all appearances, about to go too; but what we most feared was, the ship's yards and mast coming in contact with the ice, in which case the heavy sea on her other side would rush over her deck, and sink us in a few moments. While anxiously waiting for this, we saw that the sea which passed by our stern bounded against the western side of the ice, and rushed back impetuously against the ship, and thus prevented her coming in contact with the ice, and also moved her onward toward the southern extremity of the island, which was so high that we failed to see the top of it from the mast-head.

In this state of suspense we were unable to devise any way for our escape, other than that God in his providence was manifesting to us, as above described. Praise his holy name! "His ways are past finding out." About four o'clock in the morning, while all hands were intensely engaged in clearing away the wreck, a shout was raised, "Yonder is the eastern horizon, and *it's daylight!*" This was indication enough that we were just passing from the western side, beyond the southern extremity of the ice, where the ship's course could be changed by human skill. "Hard up your helm," cried the captain, "and keep the ship before the wind! Secure the foremast! clear away the wreck!" Suffice it to say, that fourteen days brought us safely into the river Shannon, in Ireland, where we refitted for our Russian voyage.

"They that go down to the sea in ships, that do business in great waters; these see the works of the Lord, and his wonders in the deep. . . . . Their soul is melted because of trouble, . . then they cry unto the Lord in their trouble, and he bringeth them out of their distresses. . . . Oh! that men would praise the Lord for his goodness, and for his wonderful works to the children of men." Ps. cvii.

Dear friends, whatever be your calling here, "Seek ye *first* the kingdom of God, and his righteousness," (Matt. vi, 33) and get your feet planted on board the gospel ship. The Owner of this majestic, homeward-bound vessel, shows the utmost care for every mariner on board; even to the numbering of the hairs of their heads. He not only pays the highest wages, but has promised every one who faithfully performs their duty an exceeding great reward. That all the perils of this voyage may be passed in safety, he has commanded his holy ones (Heb. i, 14,) to attend and watch over this precious company, who fail not to see through all the mist and fogs, and give warning of all the dangers in the pathway.　Moreover, he has invested his dear Son with all power, and given him for a Commander and skillful Pilot, to convey this good ship and her company into her destined haven.　Then he will clothe them with immortality, and give them the earth made new for an everlasting inheritance ; and make them kings and priests unto God, to "reign on the earth."

After repairing damages in Ireland, we sailed again on our Russian voyage, and in a few days we fell in with and joined an English convoy of two or three hundred sail of merchant vessels, bound into the Baltic Sea, convoyed by British ships of war, to protect them from their enemies. On reaching a difficult place called the "Mooner passage," a violent gale overtook us, which, in spite of our efforts, was driving us on a dismal, shelterless shore.　With the increasing fury of the gale, and darkness of the night, our condition became more and more alarming, until finally our commodore hoisted the "lighted lantern," a signal for all the fleet to anchor without delay.

The long-wished-for morning at length came, which revealed to us our alarming position.　All that were provided with cables were contending with the boisterous seas driven against us by the furious gale.　It seemed almost a miracle to us that our cables and anchors still held.　While watching one after another as they parted their cables and were drifting toward the rocks to be dashed in pieces, our own cable broke !　With all haste we crowded what sail we dared on the ship, and she being a fast sailer, we found by the next day that we had gained some distance in the offing. Here a council was called, which decided that we should make sail from the convoy and take a lone chance through the sound, by the coast of Denmark.

Not many hours from this, while we were congratulating ourselves respecting our narrow escape from shipwreck, and for being out of reach of the commodore's guns, two suspicious-looking vessels were endeavoring to cut us off from the shore. Their cannon balls soon began to fall around us, and it became advisable for us to round to and let them come aboard. They proved to be two Danish privateers, who captured and took us to Copenhagen, where ship and cargo were finally condemned, in accordance with Bonaparte's decrees, because of our intercourse with the English.

In the course of a few weeks, we were all called to the court house to give testimony respecting our voyage. Previous to this, our supercargo and part owner had promised us a handsome reward if we would testify that our voyage was direct from New York to Copenhagen, and that we had no intercourse with the English. To this proposition we were not all agreed. We were finally examined separately, my turn coming first. I suppose they first called me into court because I was the only youth among the sailors. One of the three judges asked me in English if I understood the nature of an oath. After answering in the affirmative, he bade me look at a box near by (about 15 inches long, and 8 high), and said, "That box contains a machine to cut off the two fore-fingers and thumb of every one who swears falsely here. "Now," said he, "hold up your two fore-fingers and thumb on your right hand." In this manner I was sworn to tell the truth, and regardless of any consideration, I testified to the facts concerning our voyage. Afterward, when we were permitted to go aboard, it was clear enough that the "little box" had brought out the truthful testimony from all; viz., that we had been wrecked by running against an island of ice fourteen days from New York; refitted in Ireland, after which we joined the British convoy, and were captured by the privateers. After this, some of our crew, as they were returning from a walk where they had been viewing the prison, said that some of the prisoners thrust their hands through the gratings, to show them that they had lost the two fore-fingers and thumb of their right hand. They were a crew of Dutchmen, who were likewise taken, and had sworn falsely. We now felt thankful for another narrow escape by telling the truth.

> "We want the truth on every point,
> We want it too, to practice by."

With the condemnation of our ship and cargo, and loss of our wages, in company with a strange people who had stripped us of all but our clothing, ended our Russian voyage. But before winter set in, I obtained a berth on board a Danish brig, bound to Pillau, in Prussia, where we arrived after a tedious passage, our vessel leaking so badly that it was with difficulty we kept her from sinking until we reached the wharf. In this extremity I obtained a berth on an American brig from Russia, bound to Belfast, Ireland.

Our voyage from Prussia to Ireland was replete with trials and suffering. It was a winter passage down the Baltic Sea, and through the winding passages of the Highlands of Scotland, under a cruel, drunken, parsimonious captain, who denied us enough of the most common food allowed to sailors. And when, through his neglect to furnish such, we were in a famishing condition and almost exhausted with pumping to keep us from sinking, he would swear and threaten us with severer usage if we failed to comply with his wishes. Finally, after putting in to an island and furnishing a fresh supply of provisions, we sailed again for Belfast, in Ireland, where the voyage ended. From thence two of us crossed the Irish Channel to Liverpool, to seek a voyage to America. A few days after our arrival, a "press-gang" (an officer and twelve men) entered our boarding house in the evening and asked to what country we belonged. We produced our American protections, which proved us to be citizens of the United States. Protections and arguments would not satisfy them. They seized and dragged us to the "rendezvous," a place of close confinement. In the morning we were examined before a naval lieutenant, and ordered to join the British navy. To prevent our escape, four stout men seized us, and the lieutenant, with his drawn sword, going before, we were conducted through the middle of one of the principal streets of Liverpool like condemned criminals ordered to the gallows. When we reached the river side, a boat well manned with men was in readiness, and conveyed us on board the Princess, of the royal navy. After a rigid scrutiny, we were confined in the prison room on the lower deck, with about sixty others who claimed to be Americans, and impressed in like manner as ourselves. This eventful epoch occurred April 27, 1810.

# Chapter Three.

*Attempt to Escape—Flogging—Ship St. Salvadore—*
*Attempt to Swim Away—Rodney 74—Spanish War*
*Ship—A Levanter—Image Worship—Another At-*
*tempt for Freedom—Battle—Storm—Shipwreck—*
*Blockading Squadron—Church Service on Board a*
*King's Ship—Port Mahon—Subterranean Passage*
*—Holy-Stone—Wash Days—Threatened Punish-*
*ment—Storm—New Station.*

ON board of this ship, one feeling seemed to
pervade the minds of all who claimed to be Americans, viz., that we were unlawfully seized without any provocation on our part, hence, any way
by which we could regain our liberty, would be
justifiable. In a few days the greater portion of
the officers and crew took one of their number on
shore to be buried. It was then suggested by
some that this was a favorable time for us to break
the iron bars and bolts in the port-hole, and make
our escape by swimming in the strong current that
was rushing by us. In breaking the bars we suc-
ceeded beyond our expectation, and when all ready
to cast ourselves overboard, one after another, the
boats came along side with the officers, and our
open place was discovered. For this, they began
by taking one after another and whipping them on
their naked backs in a most inhuman manner.
This dreadful work was in progress for several
hours, and ceased about nine o'clock at night, in-
tending to finish next day. But they did not
have time to carry out their cruel work, for orders were given to tranship us all on board a frig-

ate near by, that was weighing her anchors to put to sea.

In a few days we came to Plymouth, where we were re-examined, and all such as were pronounced in good condition for service in the British navy, were transferred to one of their largest-sized stationary ships, called the "Saint Salvadore Del Mondo." On this monstrous floating castle were fifteen hundred persons in the same condition as myself.

Here, in conversation with a young man from Massachusetts, we agreed to try to make our escape if we perished in the attempt. We prepared us a rope, and closely watched the soldiers and sailors on guard till they were being relieved from their posts at midnight. We then raised the "hanging port" about eighteen inches, and put the "tackle fall" in the hands of a friend in the secret, to lower it down when we were beyond the reach of the musket balls. Our rope and blanket, about thirty feet long, reached the water. Forbes, my companion, whispered, "Will you follow?" I replied, "Yes." By the time he reached the water, I was slipping down after him, when the alarm ran through the ship, "A man overboard." Our friend dropped the "port" for fear of being detected, which left me exposed to the fire of the sentinels. But I was soon in the water, and swam to a hiding place under the "accommodation ladder," by the time the boats were manned, with lanterns, to hunt us out. We watched for an opportunity to take an opposite direction from our pursuers, who were repeatedly hailed from the ship to know if they had found any one. We had about three miles to swim with our clothes on, except our jackets and shoes; these I had fastened on the back of my neck to screen me from a chance shot from the ship. An officer with men and lanterns descended the accommodation ladder, and sliding his hand over the "slat" he touched my hand, and immedately shouted, "Here is one of them! Come out of that, you sir! Here is another! Come out, you sir!" We swam round to them, and were drawn upon the stage. "Who are you?" demanded the officer. "An American." "How dare you undertake to swim away from the ship? Did you not know that you were liable to be shot?" I answered that I was not a subject of King George, and had done this to gain my liberty. "Bring them up here!" was the order from the ship. After another examination we were put into close confinement with a number of criminals awaiting their punishment.

After some thirty hours of close confinement, I was separated from my friend, and hurried away with about one hundred and fifty sailors (all strangers to me), to join His Majesty's ship, "Rodney," of 74 guns, whose crew numbered about seven hundred men. As soon as we had passed our muster on the quarter-deck of the Rodney, all were permitted to go below and get their dinners but *Bates*. Commander Bolton handed the first lieutenant a paper, on reading which he looked at me and muttered, "scoundrel." All the boats' crews, amounting to more than one hundred men, were immediately assembled on the quarter-deck. Said Capt. Bolton, "Do you see that fellow?" "Yes sir." "If ever you allow him to get into one of your boats, I will flog every one of the boat's crew." "Do you understand me?" "Yes sir, yes sir," was the reply. "Then go down to your dinners, and you may too, sir."

I now began to learn something of the nature of my punishment for attempting in a quiet and peaceable manner to quit His Majesty's service. In the commanding officer's view this seemed to amount to an unpardonable crime, and never to be forgotten. In a few hours, the Rodney, under a cloud of sail, was leaving Old Plymouth in the distance, steering for the French coast to make war with the Frenchmen. "Hope deferred makes the heart sick;" thus my hope of freedom from this oppressive state, seemed to wane from my view like the land we were leaving in the distance.

As our final destination was to join the British squadron in the Gulf of Lyons, in the Mediterranean sea, we made a stop at Cadiz in Spain. Here the French troops of Napoleon Bonaparte were bombarding the city and British and Spanish ships of war in the harbor. These comprised a part of the Spanish fleet that finally escaped from the battle of Trafalgar, under Lord Nelson, in 1805, and were now to be refitted by their ally, the English, and sail for Port Mahon in the Mediterranean. Unexpectedly, I was one of fifty, selected to refit and man one of them, the "Apollo." A few days after passing the Straits of Gibraltar, we encountered a most violent gale of wind, called a "levanter," common in those seas, which caused our ship to labor so excessively that it was with the utmost exertions at the pumps that we kept her from sinking. We were finally favored to return back to Gibraltar and refit.

A number of Spanish officers with their families still belonged to the ship. It was wonderful and strange to us to see how tenaciously these people hung around their images, surrounded with burning wax candles, as though they could save them in this perilous hour, when nothing short of our continual labor at the pumps, prevented the ship from sinking with us all.

After refitting at Gibraltar, we sailed again, and arrived safely at the Island of Mahon. Here I made another attempt to regain my liberty with two others, by inducing a native to take us to land in his market boat. After some two days and nights of fruitless labor to escape from the island by boats or otherwise, or from those who were well paid for apprehending deserters, we deemed it best to venture back. Our voluntary return to the ship was finally accepted as evidence that we did not design to desert from the service of King George III. Thus we escaped from being publicly whipped.

Our crew was now taken back to Gibraltar, to join the Rodney, our own ship, who had just arrived in charge of another Spanish line-of-battle ship for Port Mahon, having a crew of fifty of the Rodney's men. In company with our Spanish consort, we sailed some eighty miles on our way to Malaga, where we discovered the combined armies of the English and Spanish in close engagement with the French army on the seaboard. Our ship was soon moored broadside to the shore. As the orders for furling the sails were not promptly obeyed by reason of the Frenchmen's shot from the fort, all hands were ordered aloft, and there remained exposed to the enemy's shot until the sails were furled. This was done out of anger. While in this condition, a single well-directed shot might have killed a score, but fortunately none were shot till all had reached the deck. Our thirty-two pound balls made dreadful havoc for a little while in the enemy's ranks. Nevertheless, they soon managed to bring their enemies between us, and thereby check our firing. Then, with a furious onset they drove them to their fortress; and many seeing our boats near the shore, rushed into the sea, and were either shot by the French, or drowned, except what the boats floated to our ship. This work commenced about 2 P. M., and closed with the setting sun. After disposing of the dead, and washing their blood from the decks, we sailed away with our Spanish consort for Port Mahon. Just before reaching there, another levanter came on so suddenly that it was with much difficulty that we could manage our newly-built ship. Our Spanish consort, unprepared for such a violent gale, was dashed to pieces on the rocks on the Island of Sardinia, and nearly every one of the crew perished.

After the gale we joined the British fleet consisting of about thirty line-of-battle ships, carrying from eighty to one hundred and thirty guns apiece, besides frigates and sloops of war. Our work was to blockade a much larger fleet of French men-of-war, mostly in the harbor of Toulon. With these we occasionally had skirmishes or running fights. These were not prepared, neither disposed, to meet the English in battle.

To improve our mental faculties, when we had a few leisure moments from ship duty and naval tactics, we were furnished with a library of two choice books for every ten men. We had seventy of these libraries in all. The first book was an abridgment of the life of Lord Nelson, calculated to inspire the mind with deeds of valor, and the most summary way of disposing of an unyielding enemy. This, one of the ten men could read, when he had leisure, during the last six days of each week. The second was a small church-of-England prayer book, for special use about one hour on the first day of the week.

## CHURCH SERVICE ON BOARD A KING'S SHIP.

As a general thing, a chaplain was allowed for every large ship. When the weather was pleasant, the quarter-deck was fitted with awnings, flags, benches, &c., for meeting. At 11 A. M., came the order from the officer of the deck, "Strike six bells there!" "Yes sir." "Boatswain's mate!" "Sir." "Call all hands to church! Hurry them up there!" These mates were required to carry a piece of rope in their pocket with which to start the sailors. Immediately their stentorian voices were heard sounding on the other decks, "Away up to church there—every soul of you—and take your prayer books with you!" If any one felt disinclined to such a mode of worship, and attempted to evade the loud call to church, then look out for the men with the rope! When I was asked, "Of what religion are you?" I replied, "A Presbyterian." But I was now given to understand that there was no religious toleration on board the king's war ships. "Only one denomination here—away with you to church!" The officers, before taking their seats, unbuckled their swords and dirks, and piled them on the head of the capstan in the midst of the worshiping assembly, all ready to grasp them in a moment, if necessary, before the hour's service should close. When the benediction was pronounced, the officers clinched their side arms, and buckled them on for activ eservice. The quarter-deck was immediately cleared, and the floating bethel again became the same old weekly war ship for six days and twenty-three hours more.

Respecting the church service, the chaplain, or in his absence, the captain, reads from the prayer book, and the officers and sailors respond. And when he read about the law of God, the loud response would fill the quarter deck, " *O Lord, incline our hearts to keep thy law.*" Poor, wicked, deluded souls! how little their hearts were inclined to keep the holy law of God, when almost every other hour of the week, their tongues were employed in blaspheming his holy name; and at the same time learning and practicing the way and manner of shooting, slaying, and sinking to the bottom of the ocean, all that refused to surrender, and become their prisoners; or who dared to oppose, or array themselves in opposition to a proclamation of war issued from their good old Christian king.

King George III not only assumed the right to impress American seamen to man his war ships, and fight his unjust battles, but he also required them to attend his church, and learn to respond to his preachers. And whenever the band of musicians on shipboard commenced with " *God save the king!*" they, with all his loyal subjects, were also required to take off their hats in obeisance to his royal authority.

At that time I felt a wicked spirit toward those who deprived me of my liberty, and held me in this state of oppression, and required me in their way to serve God, and honor their king. But I thank God who teaches us to forgive and love our enemies that through his rich mercy, in Jesus Christ, I have since found forgiveness of my sins;

that all such feelings are subdued, and my only wish is, that I could teach them the way of life and salvation.

The winter rendezvous of the Mediterranean British squadron was in the Isle of Minorca, harbor of Port Mahon. Sailing, after the middle of the seventh month, is dangerous. See St. Paul's testimony, Acts xxvii, 9, 10.

While endeavoring to escape the vigilance of our pursuers, after we stepped out of the Spaniard's market boat, as before narrated, away beyond the city, at the base of a rocky mountain, we discovered a wooden door, which we opened; and away in the distance it appeared quite light. We ventured on through this subterranean passage till we came to a large open space, where the light was shining down through a small hole wrought from the top of the mountain down through the dome. This subterranean passage continued on in a winding direction, which we attempted to explore as far as we dared to for the want of light to return to the center. On both sides of this main road we discovered similar passages all beyond our exploration. Afterward, we were told that this mountain had been excavated in past ages for the purpose of sheltering a besieged army. In the center or light place was a large house chiseled out of a rock, with doorway and window frames, designed undoubtedly for the officers of the besieged, and rallying place of the army.

After a close survey of this wonderful place, we became satisfied that we had now found a secure retreat from our pursuers, where we could breathe and talk aloud without fear of being heard, or seized by any of the subjects of King George III. But alas! our joy soon vanished, when we thought again that there was nothing here for us to eat.

When we ventured to a farm house to seek for bread, the people eyed us with suspicion, and fearing they would seize us, and hand us over to our pursuers, we avoided them, until we became satisfied that it was in vain to attempt an escape from this place, and so returned to the ship. The stone of this mountain is a kind of sandstone, much harder than chalk, called "*holy-stone*," which is abundant on the island, and made use of by the British squadron to scour or holy-stone the decks with every morning to make them white and clean.

In the mild seasons, the sailor's uniform was white duck frocks and trowsers, and straw hats. The discipline was to muster all hands at nine o'clock in the morning, and if our dress was reported soiled or unclean, then all such were doomed to have their names put on the "black list," and required to do all kinds of scouring brass, iron, and filthy work, in addition to their stated duty, depriving them of their alloted time for rest and sleep in their morning watch below. There was no punishment more dreaded and disgraceful to which we were daily liable.

If sufficient changes of dress had been allowed us, and sufficient time to wash and dry the same, it would have been a great pleasure, and also a benefit to us, to have appeared daily with unsoiled white dresses on, notwithstanding the dirty work we had to perform. I do not remember of ever being allowed more than three suits at one time to make changes, and then only one day in the week to cleanse them, viz., about two hours before daylight once a week, all hands (about 700) called on the upper decks 'to wash and scrub clothes. Not more than three-quarters of these could be accommodated to do this work for themselves at a time; but no matter, when daylight came at the expiration of the two hours, all washed clothes were ordered to be hung on the clothes-lines immediately. Some would say, I have not been able to get water nor a place to wash mine yet. "I can't help that! clear out your clothes, and begin to holystone and wash the decks." Orders were most strict, that whoever should be found drying his clothes at any other but this time in the wash-day, should be punished.

To avoid detection and punishment, I have scrubbed my trowsers early in the morning, and put them on and dried them. Not liking this method, I ventured at one time to hang up my wet trowsers in a concealed place behind the maintop-sail: but the sail was ordered to be furled in a hurry, and the lieutenant discovered them. The maintop men (about fifty) were immediately ordered from their dinner hour to appear on the quarter deck. "All here, sir," said the under officer that mustered us. "Very well, whose trowsers are these found hanging in the maintop?" I stepped forward from the ranks, and said, "They are mine, sir." "Yours, are they? you ―― ――!" and when he had finished cursing me, he asked me how they came there? "I hung them there to dry, sir." "You ―― ―― see how I will hang you, directly. Go down to your dinner, the rest of you," said he, "and call the chief boatswain's mate up here." Up he came in great haste from his dinner. "Have you got a rope's end in your pocket?" He began to feel, and said, "No, sir." "Then away down below directly and get one, and give that fellow there one of the —— floggings he ever had." "Yes, sir, bear a hand."

Thus far I had escaped all his threats of punishment, from my first introduction into the ship. I had often applied for more clothes to enable me to muster with a clean dress, but had been refused. I expected now, according to his threats, that he would wreak his vengeance on me by having the flesh cut off my back for attempting to have a clean dress, when he knew I could not have it without venturing some way as I had done.

While thoughts of the injustice of this matter were rapidly passing through my mind, he cried out, "Where is that fellow with the rope? why do n't he hurry up here?" At this instant he was heard rushing up from below. The lieutenant stopped short and turned to me, saying, "If you do n't want one of the —— floggings you ever had, do you run." I looked at him to see if he was in earnest. The under officer, who seemed to feel the injustice of my case, repeated, "Run!" The lieutenant cried to the man with the rope, "Give it to him!" "Aye, aye, sir." I bounded forward, and by the time he reached the head of the ship, I was over the bow, getting a position to receive him near down by the water, on the ship's bobstays. He saw at a glance it would require his utmost skill to perform his *pleasing* task there. He therefore commanded me to come up to him. "No," said I, "if you want me, come here."

In this position, the Devil, the enemy of all righteousness, tempted me to seek a summary redress of my grievances, viz., if he followed me and persisted in inflicting on me the threatened punishment, to grasp him and plunge into the water. Of the many that stood above look-

ing on, none spake to me, that I remember, but
my pursuer.   To the best of my memory, I remained in this position more than an hour.   To
the wonder of myself and others, the lieutenant
issued no orders respecting me, neither questioned
me afterward, only the next morning I learned
that I was numbered with the black-list men for
about six months.   Thanks to the Father of all
mercies for delivering me from premeditated destruction by his overruling providence in that
trying hour.

Ships belonging to the blockading squadron in
the Mediterranean Sea, were generally relieved
and returned to England at the expiration of three
years;  then the sailors were paid their wages,
and twenty-four hours' liberty given them to spend
their money on shore.   As the Rodney was now
on her third year out, my strong hope of freedom
from the British yoke would often cheer me while
looking forward to that one day's liberty, in the
which I was resolving to put forth every energy
of my being to gain my freedom.   About this time
the fleet encountered a most dreadful storm in the
gulf of Lyons.   For awhile it was doubted whether
any of us would ever see the rising of another sun.
These huge ships would rise like mountains on the
top of the coming sea, and suddenly tumble again
into the trough of the same, with such a dreadful
crash that it seemed almost impossible they could
ever rise again.   They became unmanageable, and
the mariners were at their wit's end.   See the
Psalmist's description, Ps. cvii, 23–30.

On our arrival at Port Mahon, in the Island of
Minorca, ten ships were reported much damaged.
The Rodney was so badly damaged that the com-
mander was ordered to get her ready to proceed

to England. Joyful sound to us all! "Homeward bound! Twenty-four hours' liberty!" was the joyous sound. All hearts glad. One evening after dark, just before the Rodney's departure for England, some fifty of us were called out by name and ordered to get our baggage ready and get into the boats. "What's the matter? Where are we going?" "On board the Swiftshore, 74." "What, that ship that has just arrived for a *three years' station?*" "Yes." A sad disappointment indeed; but what was still worse, I began to learn that I was doomed to drag out a miserable existence in the British navy. Once more I was among strangers, but well known as one who had attempted to escape from the service of King George III.

---

## Chapter Four.

*Impressing American Seamen—Documents of Citizenship—War—Voluntary Surrender as Prisoners of War—Preparation for a Battle—Unjust Treatment —Close Confinement—Relieved—British Fleet Outgeneraled—Prisoners sent to England—London Newspaper—Another Movement—Without Bread.*

THE Swiftshore was soon under way for her station off Toulon. A few days after we sailed, a friend of my father's arrived from the United States, bringing documents to prove my citizenship, and a demand for my release from the British Government.

One of the most prominent causes of our last war with England, in 1812, was her oppressive and unjust acts in impressing American seamen on sea or land, wherever they could be found. This was denied by one political party in the United States. The British government also continued to deny the fact, and regard the passports or protection of American citizens of but little importance. Such proofs of American citizenship were required by them as were not very readily obtained. Hence their continued acts of aggression until the war. Another additional and grievous act was, that all letters to friends were required to be examined by the first lieutenant before leaving the ship. By accident I found one of mine torn and thrown aside, hence the impossibility of my parents learning even that I was among the living. With as genuine a protection as could be obtained from the collector of the custom house at New York, I nevertheless was passed off for an Irishman, because an Irish officer declared that my parents lived in Belfast, Ireland.

Previous to the war of 1812, one of my letters reached my father. He wrote to the President of the United States (Mr. Madison), presenting him with the facts in my case, and for proof of his own citizenship referred him to the archives in the War Department for his commissions returned and deposited there after his services closed with the Revolutionary war. The President's reply and documents were satisfactory. Gen. Brooks, then Governor of Massachusetts, who was intimately acquainted with my father as a captain under his immediate command in the Revolutionary war, added to the foregoing another strong document.

Capt. C. Delano, townsman and friend of my father, preparing for a voyage to Minorca, in the Mediterranean, generously offered his services as bearer of the above-named documents, and so sanguine was he that no other proof would be required, that he really expected to bring me with him on his return voyage.

On his arrival at port Mahon, he was rejoiced to learn that the Rodney, 74, was in port. As he approached the R. in his boat, he was asked what he wanted. He said he wished to see a young man by the name of Joseph Bates. The lieutenant forbid his coming alongside. Finally one of the under officers, a friend of mine, informed him that I had been transferred to the Swiftshore, 74, and that she had sailed to join the British fleet off Toulon. Capt. D. then presented my documents to the United States consul, who transmitted them to Sir Edward Pelew, the commander-in-chief of the squadron. On the arrival of the mail, I received a letter from Capt. D., informing me of his arrival, and visit to the R., his disappointment, and what he had done, and of the anxiety of my parents. I think this was the first intelligence from home for over three years.

I was told that the captain had sent for me to see him on the quarter-deck. I saw that he was surrounded by signal men and officers, replying by signal flags to the admiral's ship which was some distance from us. Said the captain, "Is your name Joseph Bates?" "Yes sir." "Are you an American?" "Yes sir." "To what part of America do you belong?" "New Bedford, in Massachusetts, sir." Said he, "The admiral is inquiring to know if you are on board this ship. He will probably send for you," or something of the like import. "You may go below." The news spread throughout the ship that Bates was an American, and his government had demanded his release, and the commander-in-chief was signalizing our ship about it, &c. What a lucky fellow he was, &c.

Weeks and months rolled away, however, and nothing but anxious suspense and uncertainty in my case, till at length I received another letter from Capt. D. informing me that my case was still hanging in uncertainty, and it was probable war had commenced, and he was obliged to leave, and if I could not obtain an honorable discharge, I had better become a prisoner of war.

It was now the fall of 1812. On our arrival at port Mahon to winter, the British consul sent me what money I then needed, saying that it was Capt. D.'s request that he should furnish me with money and clothing while I needed. Owing to sickness in the fleet, it was ordered that each ship's company should have 24 hours' liberty on shore. I improved this opportunity to call at the offices of the British and American consuls. The former furnished me with some more money. The latter said that the admiral had done nothing in my case, and now it was too late, for it was ascertained that war was declared between the United States and Great Britain.

There were about two hundred Americans on board the ships in our squadron, and twenty-two on board the Swiftshore. We had ventured several times to say what we ought to do, but the result appeared to some very doubtful. At last some six of us united and walked to the quarter-deck with our hats in hand, and thus addressed the first lieutenant:

"We understand, sir, that war has commenced between Great Britain and the United States, and we do not wish to be found fighting against our own country; therefore it is our wish to become prisoners of war." "Go below," said he. At dinner hour all the Americans were ordered between the pumps, and not permitted to associate with the crew. Our scanty allowance was ordered to be reduced one third, and no strong drink. This we felt we could endure, and were not a little comforted that we had made one effectual change, and the next would most likely free us from the British navy.

From our ship the work spread, until about all the Americans in the fleet became prisoners of war. During eight dreary months we were thus retained, and frequently called upon the quarter-deck and harangued, and urged to enter the British navy. I had already suffered on for thirty months an unwilling subject; I was therefore fully decided not to listen to any proposal they could make.

A few months after our becoming prisoners of war, our lookout ships appeared off the harbor, and signalized that the French fleet (which we were attempting to blockade) were all out and making the best of their way down the Mediterranean. With this startling information orders were immediately issued for all the squadron to be ready to proceed in pursuit of them at an early hour in the morning. The most of the night was spent preparing for this expected onset. The prisoners were invited to assist. I alone refused to aid or assist in any way whatever, it being unjustifiable except when forced to do so.

In the morning the whole fleet was sailing out of the harbor in line of battle. Gunners were ordered to double-shot the guns, and clear away for action. The first lieutenant was passing by where

I stood reading the Life of Nelson. (One of the library books.) "Take up that hammock, sir, and carry it on deck," said he. I looked off from the book and said, "It's not mine, sir." "Take it up." "It's not mine, sir." He cursed me for a scoundrel, snatched the book from me, and dashed it out of the gun-port, and struck me down with his fist. As soon as I got up, said he, "Take that hammock [some one's bed and blankets lashed up] on deck." "*I shall not do it, sir!* I am a prisoner of war, and hope you will treat me as such." "Yes, you ——— Yankee scoundrel, I will. Here," said he to two under officers, "take that hammock and lash it on to that fellow's back, and make him walk the poop deck twenty-four hours." And because I put my hands on them to keep them from doing so, and requested them to let me alone, he became outrageous, and cried out, "Master-at-arms! take this fellow into the gun-room and put him double legs in irons!" "That you can do, sir," said I, "but I shall not work." "When we come into action I'll have you lashed up in the main rigging for a *target*, for the Frenchmen to fire at!" "That you can do, sir, but I hope you will remember that I am a prisoner of war." Another volley of oaths and imprecations followed, with an inquiry why the master-at-arms did not hurry up with the irons. The poor old man was so dismayed and gallied that he could not find them.

He changed his mind, and ordered him to come up and make me a close prisoner in the gun-room, and not allow me to come near any one, nor even to speak with one of my countrymen. With this he hurried up on the upper gun-deck where orders were given to throw all the hammocks and bags into the ship's hold, break down all cabin and berth partitions, break up and throw overboard all the cow and sheep pens, and clear the deck fore and aft for action. Every ship was now in its station for battle, rushing across the Mediterranean for the Turkish shore, watching to see and grapple with their deadly foe.

When all the preparation was made for battle, one of my countrymen, in the absence of the master-at-arms, ventured to speak with me through the musket gratings of the gun-room, to warn me of the perilous position I should be placed in when the French fleet hove in sight, unless I submitted, and acknowledged myself ready to take my former station (second captain of one of the big guns on the fore-castle), and fight the Frenchmen, as he and the rest of my countrymen were about to do. I endeavored to show him how unjustifiable and in-inconsistent such a course would be for us as prisoners of war, and assured him that my mind was fully and clearly settled to adhere to our position as American prisoners of war, notwithstanding the perilous position I was to be placed in.

In the course of a few hours, after the lieutenant had finished his arrangements for battle, he came down into my prison-room. "Well sir," said he, "will you take up a hammock when you are ordered again?" I replied that I would take one up for any gentleman in the ship. "You would, ha?" "Yes sir." Without inquiring who I considered gentleman, he ordered me released. My countrymen were somewhat surprised to see me so soon a prisoner at large.

The first lieutenant is next in command to the captain, and presides over all the duties of the ship during the day, and keeps no watch, whereas

all other officers do. As we had not yet seen the
French fleet, the first lieutenant was aware that
my case would have to be reported to the captain;
in which case if I, as an acknowledged prisoner of
war, belonging to the United States, were allowed
to answer for myself, his unlawful, abusive, and
ungentlemanly conduct would come to the captain's knowledge. Hence his willingness to release
me.

The British fleet continued their course across
the Mediterranean for the Turkish coast, until they
were satisfied that the French fleet was not to the
west of them. They then steered north and east
(to meet them), until we arrived off the harbor of
Toulon, where we saw them all snugly moored, and
dismantled in their old winter quarters; their officers and crews undoubtedly highly gratified that the
ruse they had practiced had so well effected their
design, viz., to start the British squadron out of
their snug winter quarters to hunt for them over
the Mediterranean sea. They had remantled, and
sailed out of their harbor, and chased our few
lookout ships a distance down the Mediterranean,
and then, unperceived by them, returned and dismantled again.

After retaining us as prisoners of war about
eight months, we, with others that continued to
refuse all solicitation to rejoin the British service,
were sent to Gibralter, and from thence to England,
and finally locked up on board an old sheer-hulk,
called the Crown Princen, formerly a Danish 74-
gun ship, a few miles below Chatham dock-yard,
and seventy miles from London. Here were many
others of like description, many of them containing
prisoners. Here about seven hundred prisoners
were crowded between two decks, and locked up

every night, on a scanty allowance of food, and in crowded quarters. Cut off from all intercourse except floating news, a plan was devised to obtain a newspaper, which often relieved us in our anxious, desponding moments, although we had to feel the pressing claims of hunger for it. The plan was this: One day in each week we were allowed salt fish; this we sold to the contractor for cash, and paid out to one of our enemies to smuggle us in one of the weekly journals from London. This being common stock, good readers were chosen to stand in an elevated position and read aloud. It was often interesting and amusing to see the perfect rush to hear every word of American news, several voices crying out, " Read *that* over again, we could not hear it distinctly;" and the same from another and another quarter. Good news from home often cheered us more than our scanty allowance of food. If more means had been required for the paper, I believe another portion of our daily allowance would have been freely offered rather than give it up.

Our daily allowance of bread consisted of coarse, brown loaves from the bakery, served out every morning. At the commencement of the severe cold weather, a quantity of ship biscuit was deposited on board for our use in case the weather or ice should prevent the soft bread from coming daily. In the spring, our first lieutenant or commander, ordered the biscuit to be served out to the prisoners, and directed that one-quarter of the daily allowance should be deducted, because nine ounces of biscuit were equal to twelve ounces of soft bread. We utterly refused to receive the biscuit, or hard bread, unless he would allow us as many ounces as he had of the soft. At the close

of the day he wished to know again if we would
receive the bread on his terms. "No! no!" "Then
I will keep you below until you comply." Hatchways unlocked in the morning again. "Will you
come up for your bread?" "No!" At noon again,
" Will you have your meat that is cooked for you?"
" No!" " Will you come up for your water?" " No,
we will have nothing from you until you serve us
out our full allowance of bread." To make us comply the port holes had been closed, thus depriving
us of light and fresh air. Our president had also
been called up and conferred with (we had a president and committee of twelve chosen, as we found
it necessary to keep some kind of order). He told
the commander that the prisoners would not yield.

By this time hunger, and the want of water, and
especially fresh air, had thrown us into a state of
feverish excitement. Some appeared almost sav-
age, others endeavored to bear it as well as they
could. The president was called for again. After
awhile the port where he messed was thrown open,
and two officers from the hatchway came down on
the lower deck and passed to his table, inquiring
for the president's trunk. "What do you want
with it?" said his friends. "The commander has
sent us for it." "What for?" He is going to send
him on board the next prison ship." "Do you drop
it! He shall not have it!" By this time the officers became alarmed for their safety, and attempted
to make their escape up the ladder to the hatchway.
A number of the prisoners, who seemed fired with
desperation, stopped them, and declared on the
peril of their lives that they should go no further
until the president was permitted to come down.
Other port holes were now thrown open, and the
commander appeared at one of them, demand-
ing the release of his officers. The reply from within
was, " When you release our president we will release your officers." " If you do not release them,"

said the commander, " I will open these ports [all of them grated with heavy bars of iron,] and fire in upon you."  " Fire away !" was the cry from within, " we may as well die this way as by famine ; but, mark, if you kill one prisoner we will have two for one as long as they last."  His officers now began to beg him most pitifully not to fire, "for if you do," said they, " they will kill us ; they stand here around us with their knives open, declaring if we stir one foot they will take our lives."

The president being permitted to come to the port, begged his countrymen to shed no blood on his account, for he did not desire to remain on board the ship any longer, and he entreated that for *his* sake the officers be released. The officers were then released.

Double-plank bulkheads at each end of our prison rooms, with musket holes in them to fire in upon us if necessary, separated us from the officers, sailors and soldiers. Again we were asked if we would receive our allowance of bread. " No." Some threats were thrown out by the prisoners that he would hear from us before morning. About ten o'clock at night, when all were quiet but the guard and watch on deck, a torch-light was got up by setting some soap grease on fire in tin pans. By the aid of this light, a heavy oak stanchion was taken down, which served us for a battering-ram. Then, with our large, empty, tin water cans for drums, and tin pails, kettles, pans, pots, and spoons for drum-sticks, and whatever would make a stunning noise, the torch-lights and battering-ram moved onward to the after bulkhead that separated us from the commander and his officers, soldiers and their families. For a few moments the ram was applied with power, and so successfully that consternation seized the sleepers, and they fled, crying for help, declaring that the prisoners were breaking through upon them. Without stopping for them to rally and fire in upon us, a rush was made for the forward bulkhead, where a portion of the ship's company, with their families, lived. The application of the battering-ram was quite as successful here, so that all our enemies were now as wide awake as their hungry, starving prisoners, devising the best means for their defense. Here our torch-lights went out, leaving us in total darkness in the midst of our so-far-successful operations. We grouped together in huddles, to sleep, if our enemies would allow us, until another day should dawn to enable us to use our little remaining strength in obtaining, if possible, our full allowance of bread and water.

The welcome fresh air and morning light came suddenly upon us by an order from the commander to open our port-holes, unbar the hatchways, and call the prisoners up to get their bread. In a few moments it was clearly understood that our enemies had capitulated by yielding to our terms, and were now ready to make peace by serving us with our full allowance of bread.

While one from each mess of ten was up getting their three days' allowance of brown loaves, others were up to the tank filling their tin cans with water, so that in a short space of time, a great and wonderful change had taken place in our midst. On most amicable terms of peace with all our keepers, grouped in messes of ten, with three days' allowance of bread, and cans filled with water, we ate and drank, laughed and shouted immoderately over our great feast and vanquished foe. The wonder was that we did not kill ourselves with over-eating and drinking.

The commissary, on hearing the state of things in our midst, sent orders from the shore to the commander, to serve out our bread forthwith.

# Chapter Five.

*Cutting a Hole through the Ship—Perilous Adventure of a Narragansett Indian—Hole Finished—Eighteen Prisoners Escape—Singular Device to Keep the Number Good—Drowning Man Saved—Night Signals for Relief—Another Hole Cut and Discovered —Letter from the Escaped Prisoners—U. S. Government Clothe their Prisoners—Prisoners Sent to Dartmoor—Cheering News of Peace.*

OUR keepers were in the habit of examining the inside of our prison every evening before we were ordered up to be counted down, to ascertain whether we were cutting through the ship to gain our liberty. We observed that they seldom stopped at a certain place on the lower deck, but passed it with a slight examination. On examining this place, a number of us decided to cut a hole here if we could effect it without detection by the soldier who was stationed but a few inches above where we must come out, and yet have room above water.

Having nothing better than a common table-knife fitted with teeth, after some time, we sawed out a heavy three-inch oak plank, which afterward served us successfully for a cover when our keepers were approaching. We now began to demolish a very heavy oak timber, splinter by splinter. Even this had to be done with great caution, that the soldier might not hear us on the outside. While one was at work in his turn, some others were watching, that our keepers should not approach and find the hole uncovered. About forty

were engaged in this work. Before the heavy
timber was splintered out, one of our number obtained the cook's iron poker. This was a great
help to pry off small splinters around the heavy
iron bolts. In this way, after laboring between
thirty and forty days, we reached the copper on
the ship's bottom, some two to three feet from the
top of our cover, on an angle of about 25° downward. By working the poker through the copper,
on the upper side of the hole, we learned to our
joy that it came out beneath the stage where the
soilder stood. Then on opening the lower side of
the hole, the water flowed in some, but not in sufficient quantities to sink the ship for some time,
unless by change of wind and weather, she became
more unsteady in her motion, and rolled the hole
under water, in which case we should doubtless
have been left to share her fate. The commander
had, before this, stated that if by any means the
ship caught fire from our lights in the night, he
would throw the keys of our hatchways overboard,
and leave the ship and us to burn and perish together. Hence we had chosen officers to extin-
guish every light at 10 P. M.

Sunday afternoon, while I was at work in my
turn, enlarging the hole in the copper, a shout of
hundreds of voices from the outside so alarmed me
for fear that we were discovered, that in my hurry
to cover up the hole, the poker slipped from my
hands, through the hole, into the sea. The hole
covered, we made our way with the rushing crowd,
up the long stairway to the upper deck, to learn
the cause of the shouting. The circumstances
were these : Another ship like our own, containing
American prisoners, was moored about one-eighth
of a mile from us. People from the country, in their

boats, were visiting the prison ships, as was their custom on Sundays, to see what looking creatures American prisoners were. Soldiers with loaded muskets, about twenty feet apart, on the lower and upper stages outside of the ship, were guarding the prisoners' escape. One of the countrymen's boats, rowed by one man, lay fastened to the lower stage, at the foot of the main gangway ladder, where also one of these soldiers was on guard. A tall, athletic, Narragansett Indian, who, like the rest of his countrymen, was ready to risk his life for liberty, caught sight of the boat, and watching the English officers who were walking the quarter-deck, as they turned their backs to walk aft, he bolted down the gangway ladder, clinched the soldier, musket and all, and crowded him under the thwarts, cleared the boat, grasped the two oars, and with the man (who most likely would have shot him before he could clear himself) under his feet, he shaped his course for the opposite, unguarded shore, about two miles distant!

The soldiers, seeing their comrade, with all his ammunition, snatched from his post, and stowed away in such a summary manner, and moving out of their sight like a streak over the water, by the giant power of this North-American Indian, were either so stunned with amazement at the scene before them, or it may be with fear of another Indian after them, that they failed to hit him with their shot. Well-manned boats, with sailors and soldiers, were soon dashing after him, firing and hallooing to bring him to; all of which seemed only to animate and nerve him to ply his oars with herculean strength.

When his fellow-prisoners saw him moving away from his pursuers in such a giant-like manner, they shouted, and gave him three cheers. The prisoners on board our ship followed with three more. This was the noise which I had heard while working at the hole. The officers were so exasperated at this, that they declared if we did not cease this cheering and noise they would lock us down below. We therefore stifled our voices, that we might be permitted to see the poor Indian make his escape.

Before reaching the shore, his pursuers gained on him so that they shot him in his arm (as we were told), which made it difficult to ply the oar; nevertheless he reached the shore, sprang from the boat, and cleared himself from all his pursuers, and was soon out of the reach of all their musket balls. Rising to our sight upon an inclined plane, he rushed on, bounding over hedges and ditches like a chased deer, and, without doubt, would have been out of sight of his pursuers in a few hours, and gained his liberty, had not the people in the country rushed upon him from various quarters, and delivered him up to his pursuers, who brought him back, and for some days locked him up in the dungeon. Poor Indian! he deserved a better fate.

The prisoners now understood that the hole was completed, and a great many were preparing to make their escape. The committee men decided that those who had labored to cut the hole should have the privilege of going first. They also selected four judicious and careful men, who could not swim, to take charge of the hole, and help all out that wished to go.

With some difficulty, we at length obtained some tarred canvas, with which we made ourselves small bags, just large enough to pack our jacket, shirt and shoes in, then a stout string about ten feet long fastened to the end, and the other end made with a loop to pass around the neck. With hat and pants on, and bag in one hand, and the other fast hold of our fellow, we took our rank and file for a desperate effort for liberty. At the given signal (10 P. M.), every light was extinguished, and the men bound for liberty were in their stations.

Soldiers, as already described, above and below, were on guard all around the ship with loaded muskets. Our landing-place, if we reached it, was about half a mile distant, with a continued line of soldiers just above high-water mark. The heads of those who passed out, came only a few inches from the soldiers' feet, i. e., a grating stage between.

A company of good singers stationed themselves at the after port-hole where the soldier stood that was next to the one over the hole. Their interesting sailor and war songs took the attention of the two soldiers some, and a glass of strong drink now and then drew them to the port-hole, while those inside made believe drink. While this was working, the committee were putting the prisoners through feet foremost, and as their bag string began to draw, they slipped that out also, being thus assured that they were shaping their course for the shore. In the mean time, when the ship's bell was struck, denoting the lapse of another half hour, the soldier's loud cry would resound, " All's well!" The soldier that troubled us the most, would take his station over the hole, and shout, " All's well!" Then when he stepped forward to hear the sailors' song, the committee would put a few more through, and he would step back and cry again, " All's well!" It surely was most cheering to our friends while struggling for liberty in the watery element, to hear behind and before them the peace-and-safety cry, " All's well !

Midnight came;  the watch was changed, the cheering music had ceased.  The stillness that reigned without and within, retarded our work. At length it was whispered along the ranks that the few that had passed out during the stillness, had caused great uneasiness with the soldiers, and they judged it best for no more to attempt to leave for fear of detection.  It was also near daylight, and we had better retire quietly to our hammocks.

Edmond Allen and myself, of New Bedford, covenanted to go, and keep together.  We had been hold of each other during the night, and had advanced near the hole when it was thought best for no more to go.  In the morning the cover was off, and E. A. was among the missing.

The committee reported seventeen, and E. A. made eighteen, that had passed out during the night.

The prisoners were greatly elated at the last night's successful movement, and took measures to keep the hole undiscovered for another attempt at 10 P. M.

We were confined between two decks, with no communication after we were counted down at night and locked up.  During the day some tools were obtained, and a scuttle was cut through the upper deck, and covered up undiscovered.  Word was then circulated among the prisoners to go up from the upper deck as soon as the soldiers ordered the prisoners up to be counted down for the night.  But those on the lower deck were to move tardily, so that those on the upper deck might be counted down before the lower deck was cleared.

This was done, and eighteen that had just been counted, slipped through the scuttle unperceived by the soldiers, mingled with the crowd up the lower-deck ladder, and were counted over again. At 10 P. M., the lights were again extinguished, and the ranks formed for another attempt to escape.

On taking our stations at 10 P. M., it was whispered along our ranks that two men not of our number were waiting at the hole, insisting that they would go first or they would raise a cry and prevent any one from going. They had been drinking, and would not be reasoned with. It was finally settled to let them go. The first was put through very quietly, saying to his drunken companion, "I will hold on to the ship's rudder-rings until you come." The second man, being not much of a swimmer, sank like a log, and rose up under the stage, splashing and struggling for life. Said the soldier to his next companion, "Here's a porpoise." "Put your bayonet into him," replied he. "I will," said the first, "if he comes up again." We were by this time all listening with almost breathless attention, fearing our chance for liberty was about gone. Up he came again. We heard the rush, and then the cry, "Don't kill me! I'm a prisoner." "Prisoner? prisoner? where did you come from?" "Out of a hole in the ship." The soldier cried, "Here's a prisoner overboard! Prisoners are getting out of the ship!" "Prisoners are getting out of the ship!" was the quick response of all the watchmen. All hands came rushing on the deck. In a few moments our vigilant commander came running from his bed, frantically inquiring, "Where?" and hearing the sound outside, he rushed down the accommodation ladder, crying out, "How many have gone?" One of the prisoners, who felt disposed to quicken our chief captain's speed, put his face to the grating hole, and cried out, "About forty, I *guess*."

In quick succession, the night signals of distress brought well-manned boats to pick them up. "Where shall we pull?" "Here, there, all around." "Do you find any?" "No sir, no sir."

Orders were now given to land a body of men, and surround Gelingham forest, where they supposed the "forty" must have escaped, explore it in the morning, and take them on board. We were much amused to see what full credit the commander gave to the prisoner's "guess."

After making these arrangements, they got the drowning man on deck, and demanded of him to state the facts; but he was so far gone with the large draughts of salt water which he had swallowed, somewhat mixed up with his rum, and the dreadful fear of being harpooned with a soldier's bayonet, that he failed to satisfy them, only that there was a hole in the ship, from which he passed out. One of the boats at length found it, pushed a long iron rod inside, and remained there watching until morning.

When we were permitted to come on deck in the morning, poor Johnson was lying, tied to a stake floating in the water, near the beach. All that we could learn was, that the string of his bag was fast around his left wrist, below which his hand was nearly cut off. Some of his friends knew that he had a sharp knife in the pocket of his pants, which was missing when found floating near the shore. Fastening his bag on his wrist instead of his neck, was doubtless a great hindrance to his getting away from the boats. In attempting to cut this string, we supposed he cut his wrist, and thus bled to death by the time he reached the shore.

We were kept on deck all day, without food, mustered by name, and strictly examined, to see if we answered to our original descriptions. When it was clearly ascertained that eighteen living men had escaped the night previous to the discovery of the hole, and the full number of prisoners still reported on board, the British officers were arrested for making a false report, but released again on our president's declaring how the affair was managed.

The following day, the king's carpenters, from Chatham, were sent on board with their tools and a heavy stick of timber to plug up the hole. While they were busy, cutting and pounding in our midst, some of the prisoners picked up a few of their loose tools and began, the opposite side of the ship, to cut out another hole, equally as good as the first, and finished it before the carpenters had closed up the other. The soldiers outside ascribed the noise to the king's carpenters.

That night a number of us stationed ourselves at this hole to watch for an opportunity to escape, and remained there until about four o'clock in the morning. The copper being cut off in a great hurry, ragged and sharp points were left. To prevent these points from mangling our flesh, we fastened a woolen blanket to the lower side to slip out on. Besides the vigilant guard, a boat was pulling around the ship during the night, with one man in the centre, sounding the side of the ship, under the lower stage, with a long iron rod. The rod continued to strike on each side of the hole during the night, but failed to find the place they were punching for.

Before daylight, one of our number ventured to slip out, just after the boat passed, to ascertain whether the night was light, or dark enough to escape detection by swimming astern of the ship before the boat could get round. After pulling him in, he said the night was clear, and he could see a great distance on the water. We therefore concluded to wait until the following night. By negligence of our committee, the blanket was left with the end floating in the water. This was discovered by the boatmen soon after daylight. "Here's another hole on this side of the ship!" and in came the iron rod, blasting all our hopes of escape from this quarter. To repair these damages, a portion of food was deducted from our daily allowance, and continued for some time.

Our boasting commander began to be sorely troubled for the safety of himself and family. It seemed almost certain that these audacious, daring Yankees would yet sink their prison-ships or gain their liberty. I was told that he declared he would sooner take charge of six thousand French prisoners than six hundred Yankees.

After all their search for the eighteen who had escaped, a letter came from London, directed to the commander of the Crown Princen prison-ship, informing him of the happy escape of every one of them, and of their safe travel, seventy miles, to the city of London; and that it would be useless for him to trouble himself about them, for they were on the eve of sailing on a foreign voyage. They gave him to understand that they should remember his unkind treatment.

From this, the British government began to talk

of sending us all to Dartmoor prison, a dreary waste some fifteen miles inland from Old Plymouth harbor, where we should find some trouble in getting outside the massy stone walls and dungeons that were so strongly fortified.

In 1814 the American prisoners continued to pour in from Halifax, the West India Islands, and other parts of the world. Their state was miserable indeed for want of proper and decent clothing, especially the soldiers. It was distressing to see them in their tattered rags, many of them having their dirty woolen blanket wrapped around them to shield them from the cold storms. Statements were sent to the United States, which at length aroused the government to take measures to provide their prisoners with suitable clothing.

Mr. Beasley, acting agent for the United States in London, was empowered to attend to this matter for his suffering countrymen. He sent a London Jew with his boxes of ready made or basted clothing, and a stripling of a clerk to deal them out to us according to his judgment; so that some who were not needy got supplied with a whole suit, while others were turned away, who were much in want. The prisoners remonstrated with Mr. B. by letter, but he justified his agent, and paid little or no attention to our grievances.

After remaining a prisoner over a year, the British government condescended to pay us our small pittance of wages, which enabled me to furnish myself with clothing and some extra food as long as it lasted. My father was favored with an opportunity to send to an agent in London to furnish me with means from time to time. The agent sent me twenty dollars, which were most gladly received. Soon after this the American prisoners were sent off to Dartmoor, and I heard no more from him.

It was in the summer of 1814, that we were sent in large drafts by sea to Plymouth, and from thence to Dartmoor. Soon we numbered, as we were told, six thousand. The double stone walls, about fourteen feet high, broad enough for hundreds of soldiers to walk on guard, formed a half moon, with three separate yards containing seven massy stone buildings, capable of holding from fifteen to eighteen hundred men each. The center one was appropriated to the colored prisoners.

These buildings were located on the slope of a hill, fronting the east, affording us a prospect of the rising sun ; but it was shut out from our view long before sunset. A large number of similar buildings lay above us, on the west, separated by heavy iron palings, occupied for barracks, store and dwelling houses for our keepers, and a hospi-. tal. On these three sides, one of the most dreary wastes, studded with ledges of rocks and low shrubs, met our view, as far as the eye could reach. Surely, it was rightly named *Dartmoor*.

The prisons were three story, with a flight of stone steps at each end, open in the center. There was one iron-grated port-hole on each gable end. We were guarded by a barrack of six hundred soldiers, counted out in the morning, and driven in at sunset. It was quite a sight, when the sun shone, to see those who desired to keep themselves decent, seated in groups about the yard, clearing their blankets and beds from vermin. On hearing of a fresh arrival, the prisoners would crowd up to the gates, and make a lane for all to pass through ; and as they passed along, some of them would recognize their friends. "Halloo ! Sam. Where did you come from?" "Marblehead." "Any more left?" "No; I was the last one." And in this way all were recognized. It was often stated that nearly all the Marblehead sailors were prisoners.

During the winter, agent Beasley's men appeared again to supply us with clothing, which was done much more to our satisfaction.

Religious meetings were held in the colored prison about every Sunday, and some professed to be converted, and were baptized in a small pool of water in the yard, supplied from a reservoir on the hill, which was generally used by the prisoners in washing their clothes.

December, 1814, brought us the cheering intelligence that a treaty of peace between the United States and Great Britain was signed by the Plenipotentiaries at Ghent, on the continent of Europe. Those who were never doomed to imprisonment in this dark and most dreary spot can appreciate nothing respecting our feelings. Yet we were held in suspense while a frigate was dispatched across the ocean to obtain President Madison's signature. In February, 1815, she returned with the treaty ratified. Shoutings of rapturous joy rang through our gloomy dungeons, such as most likely will never be heard there again. What! about to be liberated, go to our native country, and gather around the paternal fireside once more? Yes, this hope was in us, and it seemed sometimes as though we were almost there.

It was supposed that there were about two hundred of us in Dartmoor who came there from the British navy. This was a tacit acknowledgment on their part, of our impressment. Some of these had served them from twenty to thirty years. As we had not taken up arms against them, we sent up a respectful petition to the British Parliament, asking a mitigation of our sufferings, or an honorable release. This was strongly objected to by the noble lords, on the ground that they had trained us in their naval tactics, and if we were liberated before the close of the war, we would, as a matter of course, enter the United States navy, and teach them how we learned to fight. That, said they, will be putting sticks into their hands, wherewith to break our heads.

## Chapter Six.

*Subterranean Passage—A Traitor—Ratification of Peace—American Consul Hung in Effigy—Bread Withheld for Two Days—Prisoners Demand and Obtain their Bread—Inhuman Massacre of Prisoners—English Soldier Liberated—Court of Inquiry—Arrival of a Cartel—Liberated from Prison—Display of Flags Respecting the Massacre.*

ABOUT this time the prisoners in one of the prisons had commenced the herculean task of opening a subterranean passage to the outside of the prison walls, to obtain their liberty. To accomplish this, one of the large, heavy flagging stones on the ground floor was raised, and the work begun of scratching the dirt into small bags, and packing it snugly away under the flight of stone steps which reached up to the third loft, planked up on the back side. To effect this, one of the planks had to be removed, but carefully replaced, and also the flagging stone, before morning, subject to the critical inspection of the turn-keys after all the prisoners were counted out.

The length of the passage from under the foundation of the prison to the first wall across the prison-yard (as near as I can remember,) was about one hundred feet; from thence to the outer wall about twenty feet more. These walls, we were told, were fourteen feet high, and two feet below the surface of the earth; broad enough for the soldiers on guard to pass and re-pass on the top.

A friend of mine, Capt. L. Wood, of Fairhaven, Mass., who lived in this prison, with whom I had frequent intercourse, informed me about the work, and how difficult it was to enter that stifled hole after they had progressed some distance, and return with a small bag of dirt. Said he, "Their faces are almost black, and they are nearly exhausted for want of breath;" but still another would rush onward, and presently return with a full bag. In this manner they continued their night work, undiscovered, until they reached and dug under the foundation of the first, and the second, or outer wall. Many now prepared themselves with knives and such deadly weapons as they could defend themselves with, determined to fight their way at the risk of their lives, to the sea coast, and seize on the first vessel or boats, and steer for the coast of France.

Before they broke the ground outside of the outer wall for as many as desired to pass out, one following the other in the darkness of the night, one of the prisoners, being acquainted with their proceedings, informed on them. Suddenly armed soldiers and officers came into the prison-yard with their informer in their midst, who pointed to the place over the dark passage, which they soon broke in, and thus in a few moments it was filled with stones and dirt from the stone-paved yard, and the traitor carefully conveyed out under guard for fear the prisoners would seize him and tear him in pieces. " What is his name ?" " Who is he ?" " What State does he belong to ?" was the inquiry. Those who knew him replied that he belonged to New Hampshire. The governor gave him his liberty, and we heard no more about him.

On the arrival of the frigate from the United States, bringing the ratified treaty of peace between us and Great Britain, we learned that Mr. Beasly had resumed his functions as United States consul in London, and was instructed by our government to procure suitable ships to convey the American prisoners from England to the United States. After waiting a suitable time, Mr. B. was addressed in behalf of the Dartmoor prisoners, to know why the ships did not come. His reply was very unsatisfactory. Again we expressed our surprise at his seeming neglect of us, when nearly two months had expired since the treaty of peace was ratified, and no relaxtion of our sufferings. His reply was far from relieving us. At length the prisoners became so exasperated at his willful neglect of them, that they erected a gallows in the prison-yard, and hung and then burned Mr. B. in effigy. As the English periodicals began to herald this matter, Mr. B. began to wake up and expostulate with us for daring to take such liberties with his character. We gave him to understand that he was instructed to relieve and release us from imprisonment, and we were still waiting for the event.

Our governor, who bore a commission as post

captain in the British navy, also undertook to take advantage of us, by ordering that the prisoners consume the hard ship-bread, that had been stored for them in the winter, in case soft bread could not be procured. This was not objected to, provided they gave us as many ounces of hard as we had been receiving of the soft bread. This governor Shortland objected to, and said we should not have so much by one-third. This was what the commander of the prison-ship attempted to do with us the year before, and failed, as we have before shown. We unhesitatingly objected to Governor S.'s proposals. He said we should have that or none. We claimed our full allowance or none. We continued thus two days without bread, with a threat if we did not yield, our water would be withheld also.

It was now the fourth of April, 1815. Governor S. left the depot that day on a visit for a few days, thinking that probably by the time he returned we should be hungry enough to accede to his terms. But before sunset, or the time came for turning us in to be locked up for another dismal night, a great portion of the prisoners were becoming so exasperated with their down-trodden and starving condition, that when the soldiers and turnkeys came to order us in to be locked up, we refused to obey, until they gave us our bread. " Go into your prisons!" they cried. " No, we will not until we get our bread!" Soldiers were called to arms, and with their colonel and second in command, arranged above the great iron gateway, above the great public square containing the hospital and store-houses where our bread was stored. On the lower side of this square was another iron fence and locked-up iron gateway, which was the line of demarkation between us and our keepers. Here was a narrow pass-way of about ten feet wide and thirty long, where all the prisoners, when out of their prisons, were continually passing and re-passing into yards Nos. 1, 4 and 7, containing the seven prison-houses prepared to accommodate about ten thousand prisoners.

About dark the excitement had become general on both sides, and the narrow passway became so crowded that it was difficult to pass. The pressure at length became so heavy that the lock of the great folding gateway broke, and the gates flew open. In a few moments, the prisoners, unarmed and without any preconcerted plan, were treading on forbidden ground, filling up the public square, and crowding up to the great iron gateway on the opposite side of the square, on the other side of which stood the colonel in command, with his regiment of armed soldiers, commanding the prisoners to retire or he should fire upon them. "Fire away!" cried the prisoners, as they crowded in front of the soldiers, "we had as lief die by the sword as by famine." The colonel, still more unwilling to fire, wished to know what we wanted. "We want our bread, sir." "Well, retire quietly to your respective prisons, and something shall be done about it." "No, sir, we shall not leave until we get our full allowance of bread." The colonel ordered the contractor to serve the prisoners with their full allowance of soft bread. About nine in the evening the various messes had all received their bread. The prisoners then quietly entered their respective prisons and commenced satiating their appetites on the coarse brown loaves and cold water, commending in the highest terms the cool, courageous and gentlemanly manner in which the colonel received us, and granted our request.

Two days after this, viz, April 6, 1815, Governor S. returned to his station. On learning what had transpired on the evening of the 4th, he declared (as we were told) that he would be revenged on us. On this 6th day, P. M., some of the prisoners were playing ball in No. 7 yard. Several times the ball was knocked over the wall, and was as often thrown back by the soldiers when kindly asked so to do. Presently one of the prisoners cried out in quite an authoritative manner, "Soldier, throw back that ball." And because it failed to come, some of the ball-players said, "We will make a hole in the wall and get it." Two or three of them began by pecking out the mortar with small stones. A sentinel on the wall ordered them to desist. This they did not do until spoken to again. I was walking back and forth by the place during the time, with others, but did not suppose they could make a hole with the stones they were using, or that anything touching that matter was of much or any importance. Aside from this trifling affair, the prisoners were as orderly and as obedient as at any time in the past.

At sunset the turnkeys, as usual, ordered the prisoners to turn in. To effect this and get to their respective prisons, the narrow passway was so densely crowded that the folding gateway, which had not been repaired since the 4th, and was very slightly fastened, burst open, and some few were necessarily and without design crowded into the square. It appeared that Governor S., with a regiment of armed soldiers, had stationed himself above the square, watching for a pretext to come upon us. The bursting open of the folding gates,

though unintentional, seemed sufficient for his purpose ; for he advanced with his soldiers and ordered them to fire. His orders were promptly obeyed, the soldiers rushing in among the fleeing
prisoners, and firing among them in all directions.
One poor fellow fell wounded, and a number of
soldiers surrounded him. He got on his knees
and begged them to spare his life, but their answer
was, "No mercy here!" They then discharged
the contents of their muskets into him and left
him a mangled corpse. Others, fleeing for the doors
of their respective prison, that always before had
been left open at turning-in time, found them shut,
and while endeavoring to gain the opposite door,
found themselves subject to the cross fire of the
soldiers. This was further proof that this work
was premeditated.

As I was crowding my way down the flight of
stone steps to ascertain respecting the uproar, and
report of muskets, a number of soldiers came rushing to the doorway (while the remnant outside
were wedging themselves in), and discharged their
musket-shot upon us. One man fell dead, another
fell just before me with the loss of his leg, and
one English soldier, against his will, was crowded
in, and the door shut against those most cowardly,
murderous soldiers who discharged their muskets
on those who had not been outside of their prisons.

The greatest confusion and excitement now prevailed throughout the different prisons. The most
we could learn was that some, while fleeing from
these murderers, said they passed the dead and
dying all along in their way to the prison. We
hailed the next prison to our own, and they said
about two hundred of their number were missing.

We thought this was about the number missing in ours. Judging thus, we supposed a great many must have been massacred. Fathers, sons and brothers were missing, and a most intense excitement prevailed in our prison. Suddenly we heard the boatswain's whistle from the daily crier. All was silent on the upper floor. He now began to read like the following: "There is an English soldier found among us on the lower floor, and a number of prisoners have a rope around his neck, and the other end over the beam, urging him to say his prayers, for they are about to hang him. Two of the committee have prevailed on them to hold on until they get the mind of the prisoners. *What shall be done with him?*" "Hang him! hang him! hang him! cried some; others, "No, no; let him go!" Second loft and lower floor, about the same. The crier reported the majority for hanging him. The committee, with others, begged them to hold on until they tried the vote once more. The prisoners were too much excited, and therefore judged too hastily. The poor soldier was still begging for his life, expecting to be swung up the next moment. When the crier passed around the second time, it was difficult to decide, but many more were in favor of sparing the life of their enemy. This opened the way for a third trial, which was decidedly in favor of releasing him. During this interval, the dead and dying had been gathered out of the yards, and conveyed to the hospital. A guard of soldiers then came to our door for the dead and wounded prisoners. "Have you any here?" "Yes, here are two; and here is also one of *your own soldiers*, take him along with you."

When the court of inquiry that set on this mur-

derous affair adjourned, (which will be referred to
presently,) the English periodicals were loud in
their applause of the honorable and merciful act
of the Dartmoor prisoners, under such aggravating circumstances, in sparing the life of the English soldier.

It was late in the morning before the doors of
our prison were opened ; for it required some time
to wash away the blood of our murdered companions, which our enemies were very unwilling for us
to see.   When we got out into the yard, many
found their lost friends : for during the massacre,
to escape the fire of the soldiers, several fled to
the nearest prisons, and remained in them until the
morning, while others sought and found theirs in
the hospital, among the murdered and wounded.
After much inquiry, we learned that seven were
killed and sixty wounded.   What made this the
more aggravating was, that the two governments were on the most amicable terms, and
many of our ships and countrymen were already
negotiating their business in England, while,
as already shown, instead of relaxing their rigor
over us, they were drawing our cords tighter
and stronger; and this they even did for seven
weeks after the ratification of the treaty of peace
between Great Britain and the United States.   If
Mr. B., our consul in London, had promptly obeyed the instructions of our government, he might
have saved us the trouble of hanging and burning
him in effigy, and Governor Shortland also the
gratification of murdering us in such an unwarrantable manner, by furnishing ships, or satisfying us that he was doing what he could to release
us from our dismal confinement.

A court of inquiry was now instituted to investigate this matter. John Quincy Adams, late Secretary of the American Legation at Ghent, on the part of the United States, and one of the experienced Admirals from Plymouth, on the part of Great Britain, with their retinue.

A place was fitted for the court on the top of the walls over the narrow passage and place of demarkation between the prisoners and their keepers, so that the court could be addressed by the prisoners on the left, and by their keepers on the right, the walls being between us. The statement of Governor Shortland and his party, with respect to the attempt of making a hole in the wall, and the bursting open the broken locked gates, to justify his attack upon us in the manner already described, seemed to have but little weight. It was settled with us at the time of the massacre, that his plan was preconcerted. The British Admiral seemed intent on questioning the prisoners with regard to their allowance of food, and whether they had not had all that was allowed them, &c. The reply was, that our grievance was not then about our allowance of food, but the inhuman manner in which our countrymen had been massacred. Finally, in the settlement of this grievous question, the massacre at Dartmoor was *disavowed* by the British Government, and compensation made to the widows of the sufferers. (See *D. Haskel's Leading Events of Universal History.*)

Three weeks after the massacre the long-looked-for news came, viz., that a cartel had arrived in Plymouth for a draft of prisoners. As I was among the first on the prisoner's list at this time, I was called out and mustered with a draft of about two hundred and fifty. Many of this number, as we were mustered before Gov. S. and his armed soldiery, bore white flags on long poles with mottoes in large black letters like the following, viz : " *Massacre of American prisoners in Dartmoor prison, April 6th, 1815.*" " *The bloody 6th of April!*" And others had flags with Shortland's name as the murderer of American prisoners. Some of the prisoners openly declared that they would kill him if they could get near him. He seemed to be aware of these threats, and kept himself at a safe distance while we were being mustered in the upper yard near his and his officers' dwellings, preparatory to our final departure. We also expected that he would command us to strike our flags while we remained under his immediate inspection, or his armed regiment of soldiers that guarded us from thence to Plymouth harbor, (a distance of fifteen miles,) but he did not for they continued to wave them until we passed through Plymouth to our place of embarkation.

We were liberated from the Dartmoor prison on the morning of the 27th of April, 1815, just five years to a day from the time I was impressed in Liverpool, in England. About two years and a half in actual service in the British navy, and two years and a half their prisoner of war. The western gate of our dreary and bloody place of confinement was at length thrown open, and the soldiers ordered to march out with the prisoners. As we ascended the heights of Dartmoor, we turned to look back on that dark and massy pile of stone buildings where we had suffered so many privations, and then forward to the western horizon which could now for the first time since our confinement be seen stretching away in the distance toward our native country, where were our paternal homes and dear friends. Our mingled emotions of oppressive bondage on the one hand, and unbounded liberty on the other were more easily felt than described. With an old pair of worn-out shoes, I stooped to re-lash them on my feet, and felt myself competent to perform what to us, in our weak state, was a tedious journey. But the joyful feelings of liberty and the pleasing anticipation of soon greeting our dear friends, though an ocean of three thousand miles in width divided us, cheered us onward to the city of old Plymouth. The people stared at us, and no marvel, for I presume they had never seen so motley a company of men with such singular flags flying, pass through their city before.

## Chapter Seven.

*Embarkation for the United States—Ocean Larks— Excitement Respecting our Port of Destination— Banks of Newfoundland—Perils of the Ocean— Threatened Mutiny—Islands of Ice—Mutiny on the High Seas—Speak an American Ship—Joyful News —Land in Sight—A Prize Taken—Safe Arrival at New London, Ct.—Sail Again for Boston.*

BOATS were waiting, and before night we were embarked on board the cartel. This was an English merchant-ship of 400 tons burden, called the Mary Ann, of London, commanded by Capt. Carr, with temporary berths between decks to accommodate about two hundred and eighty persons. Some officers that had been on parole joined us at P.,

which swelled our number to two hundred and
eighty.

Here, *past* scenes were brought to remembrance.
Away some three miles, in the upper harbor, were
moored a fleet of old sheer hulks (ships of war un-
seaworthy and dismantled), where some five years
before I had been sent, after I was impressed, to
be held in readiness for actual service in the British navy.   Rather than submit to such unwarrantable oppression, at the midnight hour I lowered myself from the gun-port hole of the middle
deck of the St. Salvadore del Mondo (an old Spanish three-decker), into the sea, thinking to swim
these three miles, and possibly land somewhere
near the place where I was now, through the providence and mercy of God, embarking for my own
native country.   From this desperate effort for
liberty I was prevented, as already shown, and
sent away among strangers, with my character
branded as a runaway from His Majesty's service.
This side of that dark spot of dismantled ships lay
moored the Swiftshore, 74, recently returned from
her three years' station in the Mediterranean—
the same ship to which I was drafted on her arrival in the Mediterranean from the Rodney, 74,
when she was about returning from thence to England ; the same ship in which I spent my first six
months' imprisonment, where I was threatened, if
I would not comply with the urgent request of the
first lieutenant, that I should be lashed in the main
rigging, a target for the French fleet to fire at.
As I was transferred to this ship because I had
attempted to gain my liberty (as stated above—so
I was informed), I should be transferred when she
was relieved, at the expiration of some three years
more, and thus I was doomed to remain in a for-

eign country, deprived of the privileges allowed in
their service, such as paying their seamen their
wages, and granting them twenty-four hours' liberty on shore, &c. But my sufferings in their
prisons had now gained for me what they were not
disposed to grant, viz., entire freedom and liberty
from the service of King George III.

England and America have done, and still are
doing, much by way of compensation for such as
have labored and suffered in their service. Millions of dollars were expended to carry on the war
of 1812. Americans demanded and fought for
"free trade and sailors' rights." England acknowledged the justice of their claim : first, by
permitting hundreds, who requested to become
prisoners of war rather than remain in their service, so to do. It was often stated that about two
hundred of this class of American prisoners were
confined in Dartmoor ; second, by treaty of peace
in 1815. But no remuneration was ever allowed
for depriving us of our liberty, and unjustly retaining us to fight their battles, except the small
allowance of wages which they were disposed to
grant. I was required to do the duty of an able
seaman the last part of my service, and was told
that I was so rated, where I was stationed in the
maintop. While a prisoner of war in 1813, the
navy agent paid me £14, 2s. 6d., or $62.71. This,
including my coarse, cheap wearing apparel (for a
mild climate), served me from what the officers
call the sailors' " slop chest," was all the compensation England allowed me for my services for
some two years and a half. After which they
held me a prisoner of war two and a half years
longer, treating and regarding me in the same way
and manner, without any mitigation or favor, as

those of our countrymen that were taken in privateers or in battle. But if England feels disposed at this late hour of my sojourn here to do me justice, it will be very acceptable.

Our berths on board the cartel were much crowded together, and were prepared for both sleeping and eating, with a narrow passway, just wide enough to admit of our passing up on deck, and down, rank and file. The next morning we weighed our anchor and passed out of the harbor under a cloud of sail, with a fair wind. Very soon we took our departure from old England, and were glad enough to find ourselves on the wide ocean steering westward. Nothing worthy of note occurred on board until we reached the eastern edge of the celebrated banks of Newfoundland, except the little sea larks which came fluttering in our wake, seemingly overjoyed to find another ship and her company on the ocean, from which they could obtain their daily allowance of food. How they rest in the night, if they do at all, is the marvel! Sailors call them "Mother Carey's chickens," perhaps in honor of a good old lady by that name, for her kind care and sympathy to poor sailors.

When a few days out, we learned from the captain that Mr. Beasly, our consul at London, had chartered this ship to land us at City Point (a long distance up the James River, Va.), and load with tobacco for London. We considered this a cruel and unwarrantable act of Mr. B.'s, for only about six of our number would be accommodated, while the rest would have to pass hundreds of miles to reach their homes in New York and New England, if they could beg their way. We expostulated with the captain, but he declared he would not deviate from his charter to land us at any other place. The prisoners declared, on the other hand, that his ship should never carry us to City Point; whereupon arrangements were soon made among us in a private manner, in case of a revolution in our floating castle, who the captain and officers should be.

As we approached the eastern edge of the banks of Newfoundland, about two-thirds of the distance across the Atlantic Ocean, I found we were in the place where I was shipwrecked by the ice several years before, as related in a previous chapter. As this perilous place became the topic of conversation, we learned that a number among us had experienced like difficulties in passing over these banks in the spring season of the year. Capt. Carr said he had made fifteen voyages to Newfoundland and never had seen any ice, and he did not believe there was any in our way. In the afternoon we saw a large patch of sheet-ice. We asked the captain what he called that? He acknowledged that it was ice. As the night set in the wind increased to a gale from the east. Capt. Carr, unmindful of all that had been said to him respecting the danger of ice in our track, still kept the ship scudding before the gale under a close-reefed main-top-sail and foresails, determined to have his own way rather than lay by until morning, as suggested by some of the prisoners. Some thirty of us, unwilling to trust to the captain's judgment, took our position on the bow and bowsprit of the ship to look out for ice. At midnight the ship was driving furiously before the gale and storm, evidently without any hope of our having time to avoid ice if we should see it; and in danger of being dashed in pieces without a moment's warning. We also felt a marked change in the air. In this dilemma we decided to take the ship from the captain and heave her to. We found him at the quarter-deck cunning* the ship. We briefly stated our dangerous position, and told him that about three hundred souls were at the mercy of his will; and now, if he did not round his ship to, *we would do it for him.* Seeing our determination to act in this matter immediately, he cried out to his crew, "Round in the larboard main brace! Put the helm a-starboard!" This laid the main-top-sail to the mast, and let the ship come by the wind.

This being done, the onward progress of the ship was stayed until the dawn of the morning, which showed us how narrowly we had escaped with our lives. Large islands of ice lay right in our track, and if we had continued to run before the gale we should have been in the midst of them, in imminent danger of being dashed in pieces. The willfulness of Capt. Carr was now evident to all, and the course we pursued in requiring him to heave the ship to was also justifiable. And after the ship was again turned on her onward course, and passing these huge islands of ice, we were all stirred to watch until we had passed the banks and were again safe in the fathomless ocean. These bodies of ice had the appearance of large cities in the distance, and had it not been for our forethought, would in all probability have been the cause of our immediate destruction.

Moreover, a large majority of us were satisfied that this was the best time to take the ship from

---

* Cunning: In seamen's language, guiding or directing a vessel by orders to the steersman.

the captain and proceed to New York or Boston, from whence we could more readily reach our homes. For we had decided and declared, as before stated to Capt. Carr, that his ship should never take us to City Point, Va., where his charter party required him to land us. Having passed beyond all danger from ice, the most difficult point for us to decide was, which of the two ports we should steer for, if we took the ship. Suddenly, and unexpectedly, one of our company placed himself amid-ships upon the main hatchway, and with a stentorian voice cried out, "All you that are for New York go on the starboard side of the ship, and all that are for Boston go on the larboard side!" Sides were immediately taken, when it was declared that the greatest number were on the starboard side; hence the ship was for New York. Capt. Carr stood in our midst, near by the man at the wheel, gazing at this unlooked-for and strange movement, when suddenly one of our number took the wheel from the helmsman. Capt. Carr demanded that he should leave it immediately, and ordered his man to take the helm again. A number of us also urged our friend to take the helm and we would protect him. At this Capt. C. became very much enraged, saying what he would do with us if he had a crew able to cope with us. But he saw that resistance was vain; we had taken possession of the helm, the ship therefore would no longer be steered by his direction. Seeing what was done, he called us a "rabble," "roughally," &c., for taking his ship from him on the high seas, and wished to know what we were going to do with her, and who was to be the captain? Capt. Conner, of Philadelphia, was lifted up by those who stood near him, and placed with his feet on the head of the capstan (a cylinder four feet high, with levers to weigh the anchors, &c.). "There is our captain!" cried the multitude. Said Capt. Carr, "Are you going to take charge of my ship, Capt. Conner?" "No, sir," was the reply. "Yes, you shall!" was the unanimous cry. "I don't want anything to do with her," said Capt. Conner. "You shall," was the loud cry, " or we will throw you overboard!" "You hear what they say, Capt. Carr. What shall I do?" "Take her, take her, Capt. Conner," said the English commander. This being settled, Capt. Carr began to call us hard names again. Some that stood near him advised him to cease and get down into his cabin as soon a possible, out of the way of danger. He did so, and order was soon restored. Capt. Conner took charge of the ship, and named three officers for mates. A number of us volunteered as sailors to man the ship, and we were divided into three watches, that every advantage might be taken to urge our ship onward for the port of New York under all the sail she could bear.

Capt. Carr and crew had their liberty, and were treated kindly, but not allowed to interfere with the sailing of the ship. He declared that if the vessel ever arrived in the States he would have us all arraigned before the United States Court for taking his ship from him on the high seas. The idea of being deprived of our liberty and arraigned before our country for trial in this case, on our arrival, troubled us some; nevertheless, we were resolved to keep charge until we arrived.

A ship was seen bearing down toward us with American colors flying. We hoisted English colors. It was a rare sight to see one of our own country's ships with the stars and stripes floating at her peak. As she came riding triumphantly within speaking distance by our side, the cry was given, "What ship is that?" "Where are you from?" and, "Where bound to?" Answer: "From the United States, bound to Europe." "What ship is that?" &c. Answer: "The Mary Ann, of London, a cartel with American prisoners from Dartmoor, England, bound to the United States." A few more inquiries, and as each ship filed away for their onward voyage, we gave them three loud cheers, so glad were we to see the face of some one from our native country afloat on the wide ocean.

About ten days after the revolution, or time we took the ship, we saw the land looming in the distance before us. As we drew near the coast we learned to our great joy that it was Block Island, R. I., about forty miles from our home. Sail boats were now pushing out from the land to get the first opportunity to pilot us in. Some of our number thought this would be a rare chance for them to go on shore in their boats, and so got up their hammocks and bags, waiting to jump aboard when they should come along. A heavy squall was now rising out of the north-west, so the topsails were clewed down, and many hands were on the yards reefing them. As the boats came sheering up to our side, the men on the topsail yards cried out, "Do n't you come here! for we have got the plague on board!" The men that were in waiting for them declared that we had nothing of the kind, and bid them come along side. A multitude of voices from the topsail yards was again saying, "Yes, we have got the plague on board, too!" Do n't you come here!" The boats immediately hauled their wind, and steered for the land. Nothing that we had would induce one of them to come on board, for they knew that a bare report of their doing so would subject them to a tedious quarantine. The *plague* we had on board was this: We were expecting that Capt. Carr would (as he had threatened) have us arraigned before the United States Circuit Court for piracy on the high seas. Therefore we were unwilling to part with them until we learned more about the matter.

The wind died away during the night, and the next morning we perceived that a heavy swell and current was setting us in between the east end of Long Island and Block Island into Long Island Sound. We now concluded if we could get a pilot we would pass up the Sound to New York. From some one of the many fishing smacks in sight we hoped to find one. At length, one of the smacks was induced to come along side. In less than five minutes she was taken possession of, while the captain and crew retreated away to the stern in amazement at the strange work that was going on. We judged that nearly one hundred of our company began throwing their bags and hammocks on board of her, and themselves after them in quick succession. They then cast off from the ship, gave us three cheers, and bore away for Newport, R. I., before we could learn their object. They had no idea of being brought to trial for piracy by Capt. Carr.

As the wind was now unfavorable to proceed to New York, we concluded to go to New London, Ct., at which port we arrived the next forenoon, and anchored off the wharf before the town, six weeks from Plymouth, in England. A great number of us now crowded aloft for the purpose of furling all the sails at the same time. We then stood on our feet on the yards, and gave three cheers to the gazing multitude on the wharfs in New London. In a few moments more, boat loads of our joyous company, with their bags and hammocks, were crowding for the shore, leaving their captured ship and Capt. Carr to find his way from thence for his load of tobacco at City Point, Va., as best he could, or even to find us the next twenty-four hours, if he still felt disposed to prosecute us for our so-called piratical proceedings on the ocean. Doubtless, he was so wonderfully relieved at the departure of such a rebellious crew that he had no particular desire to come in collision with them again.

The good people on the land seemed about as glad to see and welcome us on shore as Capt. Carr was to get rid of us. But neither party were half as glad as we were. It seemed almost too much to believe that we were actually on our own native soil once more as freemen, free from British warships and their gloomy, dismal prisons. After our joyful feelings in a measure subsided, we were inquiring our ways home. Within twenty-four hours a great portion of our company took passage in a packet for New York city. Four of us, by fair promises, without money, chartered a fishing smack at two dollars per head, to carry twenty-two of us around Cape Cod into Boston, Mass. This placed us beyond the reach of Capt. Carr, or ever hearing from him again.

# Chapter Eight.

*Arrival Home—Voyage to Europe—Singular Rock in
the Ocean—Sudden Commencement of Winter—Voyage Ended—Another Voyage—Perilous Situation in
the Chesapeake Bay—Criterion in Distress—Wrecked
in a Snow Storm—Visit to Baltimore—On Board
the Criterion Again—Cargo Saved—Another Voyage
—Hurricane—Voyage Ended—Married—Another
Voyage—Captain Reefing Topsails in his Sleep.*

THE purser of the cartel allowed each of us about
a week's amount of provision for our voyage. We
were highly favored with good weather, and arrived
in Boston the third day from New London, when
we sold our remaining stock of provisions for enough
to pay our passage money and redeem our clothing.
A friend and neighbor of my father (Capt. T. Nye,)
being in Boston on business, lent me thirty dollars
on my father's account, which enabled me to purchase some decent clothing to appear among my
friends. The next evening, June 14 or 15, 1815,
I had the indescribable pleasure of being at my
parental home (Fairhaven, Mass.), surrounded by
mother, brothers, sisters, and friends, all overjoyed
to see me once more in the family circle ; and all
of them exceedingly anxious to hear a relation of
my sufferings and trials during the six years and
three months that I had been absent from them ;
for my position on board the British war-ships, and
in prison for the past five years, rendered it extremely difficult, as I have before shown, for any
of my letters to reach them. It was well known
that for my six-and-a-quarter years' suffering and

labor I had nothing to show but a few old, worn garments, and a little canvas bag which I have had no use for since I was prevented from swimming away from the prison-ship in 1814, except my experience,—the relation of which caused the tears to flow so freely around me that we changed the subject for that time.

My father had been told by those who thought they knew, that if ever I did return home I would be like other drunken man-o'-war sailors. He was away from home on business when I arrived, but returned in a few days. Our meeting quite overcame him. At length he recovered and asked me if I had injured my constitution. "No, father," I replied, "I became disgusted with the intemperate habits of the people I was associated with. I have no particular desire for strong drink," or words to this effect, which very much relieved his mind at the time. I now renewed my acquaintance with my present companion in life, which had commenced at an early age.

In a few weeks after my return an old schoolmate of mine arrived at New Bedford in a new ship, and engaged me for his second mate to perform with him a voyage to Europe. Our voyage was to Alexandria, D. C., and load for Bremen, in Europe, and back to Alexandria. On our passage out we sailed round the north side of England and Ireland. Sailors call it "going north about." This passage is often preferred to going on the south side of these islands through the English Channel. In this passage, north-west of Ireland, some over two hundred miles from land stands a lone rock rising some fifty feet above the level of the sea, called by navigators, "Rockal." Its form is conical, having the appearance of a sugar-loaf, or light-house, in the distance. We had been running for it, and when we got our observation at meridian, we were drawing close up with this singular rock in the ocean. Our ship being under good headway, with a steady, flowing breeze, our captain ventured to run the ship close by it. The sea was rushing up its glassy sides, as it probably had been doing ever since the deluge, which had given it the appearance of a glassy polish on all its sides. This rock has always been a terror to the mariner when in its vicinity during a storm. What a tragic story could it tell, if it were intelligible, of the ten thousand terrific storms, and ten thousand times ten thousand raging seas rushing on all its sides; and how hundreds of heavy-laden ships, with one bound in a driving storm, dashed in pieces, and the poor heart-stricken mariners, unwarned and unprepared, engulfed at its base— their sad and tragic story never to be known until the resurrection of the dead! And yet it stands as unmoved and undisturbed as when it was first fashioned by its Creator.

After a prosperous passage we anchored in the river Weser, about thirty miles below Bremen. Winter commenced before we had discharged all our cargo, so that we were embargoed there until the spring. The closing up of these rivers often occurs in one night, and a long winter commences. It is astonishing also to see how rapidly ice will increase in the short space of a six-hour flood tide, even from fifteen to twenty feet thick along its banks. Up to this time we had seen no ice. We were enjoying a very pleasant day; the wind had changed to the east with a clear setting sun. Our captain and a pilot came on board to have the ship moored, and placed between "the slangs"—a kind

of wharf running out from "the dyke" to the deep
water for the purpose of breaking and turning the
ice into the channel from vessels that take shelter
there. The inhabitants had predicted ice in the
river before morning. A few hours after dark, ice
began to make, and increase so fast that with all
our square sails filled with a strong wind, and all
hands at the windlass, the ship could not be moved
toward her anchor, during the flood tide against
the running ice. In the morning at sunrise it was
deemed advisable to cut the cable at the windlass
and press her in between the slangs to save her
from being cut to pieces by the ice, and ourselves
from inevitable destruction. Fortunately she took
the right sheer, and in a few moments the tide and
ice bore her between the slangs to the shore along
side of the dyke. Dykes are embankments thrown
up to prevent the sea from overflowing the low
lands. One end of our cables were immediately
carried into the meadows and secured to sunken
timber to hold us clear of the ice at the flowing
and ebbing of the tide. At this time we judged
the ice was twenty feet high inside of us on the
shore, all of which had accumulated during the
night. During the winter our ship was very much
damaged by the ice. After repairing her thoroughly, we returned to Alexandria in the summer
of 1816.

I sailed again from Alexandria, chief mate of
the brig Criterion, of and for Boston, Mass. From
thence we loaded and sailed for Baltimore, where
we discharged our cargo, and loaded again and
sailed for New Orleans, in January, 1817. In
this month commenced one of the severest cold
winters known for many years. I will here relate
one circumstance as proof of this. A ship from

Europe with a load of passengers anchored in the Chesapeake Bay, about forty miles below Baltimore. Her passengers traveled on the ice to the harbor and city of Annapolis, distant about two miles. I was in the city of Annapolis at the time, endeavoring to procure cables and anchors to relieve the Criterion from her perilous situation, as I shall further show.

As we sailed out of the harbor and down the river in the afternoon, we saw the ice was making around us so fast that we were in danger of being seriously injured by it. As we came to the mouth or entrance of the river, the pilot gave orders to prepare to anchor until daylight. The captain and myself objected, and endeavored to persuade him to keep under way and get out of the way of the ice. But he judged otherwise, and anchored in the Chesapeake, at the mouth of the Patapsco river, some sixteen miles below Baltimore. The tide was so low that we grounded on the bank. In this situation the ice cut through our plank before the rise of the tide. All hands were hard at work from early in the morning carrying out anchors and heaving the Criterion over the bank. At the top of the flood-tide we concluded we could sail over the bank, if we could save our anchor. While we were getting the anchor up with the long boat, the tide turned and the ice began to press so heavily upon us that we dropped it again and made our way for the vessel. As we came on the lee side, and were in the act of reaching to get hold of the vessel, the ice suddenly broke away from where it had been held for a few moments on the windward side, and crowded us away from her into a narrow space of clear water, which was made by the breaking of the ice against her broadside, and passing by her bow and stern. By the time we got our oars out to pull up to the vessel, we had drifted several rods to leeward, and the clear place of water so narrowed up that the oars lapped over on the ice and rendered them useless. We then laid hold of the broken edge of the ice to haul her up, but the ice broke in our hands so fast that we could not hold her. The captain and pilot were doing what they could by thrusting oars, and various floating things, and ropes, toward us, but we drifted as fast as the things did, so that in a few moments we were thoroughly enclosed in a vast field of ice that was hurrying us away from our vessel down the Chesapeake Bay as fast as the ebb tide and a strong north-west gale could move us.

We were all thinly clad in our working-dress, and but little room to move about to keep ourselves from freezing. We had now been in the boat from about two o'clock in the afternoon. At the going down of the sun we looked every way to learn how we should direct our course, if the sea should break up the ice that bound us. We judged ourselves from twelve to fifteen miles distant from our vessel as she was waning from our view. The distant shores to leeward appeared unapproachable on account of ice. The prospect of deliverance before another day seemed hopeless, even if any one of us should survive the cheerless, bitter cold night before us. A few scattered lights to windward on the western shore of Maryland, some seven or eight miles distant, still gave us a ray of hope, though they were at the time unapproachable. About nine o'clock in the evening the ice began to break away from us, and soon left us in the open sea. We manned our oars and pulled for one of the above-named lights on the windward shore, all of which were extinguished in a few hours.

After about six hours' incessant rowing against the wind and sea, the boat struck the bottom about an eighth of a mile from the shore, so loaded with ice that had made from the wash of the sea, both outside and in, that she filled with water soon after we left her, and froze up, leaving the shape of her gunwale level with the ice.

The second mate waded through the water and ice to the shore to look for a house, while we were preparing to secure the boat. He soon returned with the joyful news that there was one not far off, and the family were making a fire for us. It was now three o'clock in the morning, and we had been about thirteen hours in the boat, with hardly any cessation from laboring and stirring about to keep from freezing, except the last fifteen or twenty minutes.

I now requested all to get out of the boat. The acute pain on getting into the water, which was about three feet deep, was indescribable, while the frost that was in us was coming to the surface of our bodies. I called again to get out of the boat, when I saw that "Tom," my best man, was at the side of the boat so fast asleep, or dying with the frost, that I could not wake him. I hauled him out of the boat into the water, keeping his head up until he cried out, "Where am I?" and got hold of the boat. One I saw was still in the boat. "Stone!" said I, "why don't you get out of the boat?" "I will," said he, "as soon as I get my shoes and stockings off!" He was so bewildered he was not aware that his feet (as well as those of all the rest of us) had been soaking in water and ice all night. We got him out, and all of us started together. By the time we had broken our way through the newly-made ice to the shore, we were so benumbed that we could not crawl up the cliff. I directed the sailors to follow the shore to the first opening, and I would come along with Stone as soon as I could get his shoes on.

On entering the house I perceived there was a great fire, and the men lying with their feet to it, writhing in agony from their swollen limbs and acute pain. I requested them to remove from the fire. As in the good providence of God we were now all in a place of safety, and I was relieved from my almost overwhelming anxiety and suspense, I moved to the opposite corner of the room, and sank down with exhaustion. As soon as I was relieved by our kind host and his companion, feeling still faint, I got out of the house on the deep snow, where it appeared to me I could hardly survive the excruciating pain which seemed to be racking my whole frame, and especially my head, caused by the frost coming out of my whole body. Thus the Lord delivered and saved me. Thanks to his name.

By keeping away from the hot fire until the frost came out of my body, I was the only one that escaped from frozen limbs and protracted sickness. Many years after this I fell in with "Tom," in South America. He told me how much he had suffered, and was still suffering, since that perilous night.

Captain Merica and his companion (for this was the name of our kind friends,) provided us with a warm meal, and very kindly welcomed us to their home and table. After sunrise, by the aid of a glass, we saw that the Criterion was afloat, drifting in the ice down the bay toward us, showing a signal of distress—colors flying half mast. It was not possible, however, for any human being to approach them while they were in the floating ice. We expected they were in a sinking condition, as she was cut through with the ice before we were separated from her. As the Criterion passed within four miles of the shore where we were, we could see the captain and pilot pacing the deck, watching to see what would be their destiny. We hoisted a signal on the cliff, but they appeared not to notice it. We saw that the Criterion was careened over to starboard, which kept the holes made by the ice on her larboard side out of the water. Before night the Criterion passed us again, drifting up the bay with the flood tide, and so continued to drift about for two days, until in a violent northeast snow storm, she was driven to her final destination and burying-place.

When the storm abated, with the aid of a spyglass, we saw the Criterion lying on Love Point, on the east side of the Chesapeake Bay, distant about twelve miles. As there was no communication with the sufferers only by the way of Baltimore, and thence around the head of the bay, across the Susquehanna, I decided to proceed to Baltimore and inform the consignees and shippers of her situation. Captain Merica said it was about thirty miles distant, and a good part of the way through the woods, and bad roads, especially then, as the snow was about one foot deep. Said he, "If you decide to go I will lend you my horse." Said his companion, "I will lend you a dollar for your expenses." After a fatiguing journey from morning until about nine in the evening, I reached Baltimore. The consignees furnished me with money to pay our board on shore as long as we were obliged to stay, and orders to merchants in

Annapolis for cables and anchors, if we needed them, to get the Criterion afloat again.

Some two weeks from the time we were separated from the Criterion, the weather moderated and became more mild, and the drifting ice much broken. Captain Merica, with some of his slaves, assisted us to cut our boat out of the ice and repair her. With our crew somewhat recovered, and two stout slaves of Captain M.'s, we run our boat on the ice until we broke through into deep water, and climbed into her. Then with our oars and borrowed sail we steered through the broken ice toward the Criterion. As we drew near her, we saw that she was heeled in toward the shore, and a strong current was hurrying us past her into a dangerous place, unless we could get hold of a rope to hold us. We hailed, but no one answered. I said to the men, "Shout loud enough to be heard!" The two slaves, fearing we were in danger of being fastened in the ice, set up such a hideous noise that the cook showed his head at the upper, or weather side, and disappeared immediately. We caught a hanging rope as we were passing her bow, which held us safely. The captain and pilot, in consternation, came rushing toward us, as I leaped on the deck of the Criterion to meet them. "Why," said Captain Coffin, as we grasped each other's hands, "where did you come from, Mr. Bates?" "From the western shore of Maryland," I replied. "Why," said he, "I expected all of you were at the bottom of the Chesapeake Bay! I buried you that night you passed out of our sight; not supposing it possible for you to live through the night."

The Criterion had parted her cables and lost her anchor in the violent storm that drove her to the shore. Her cargo was yet undamaged. The captain and pilot consented for me to take part of the crew and return back and procure cables and anchors from the city of Annapolis, which we accomplished, but were prevented from returning for several days, on account of another driving storm, in which the Criterion bilged and filled with water, and those on board abandoned her in time to save their lives.

During the winter, with a gang of hired slaves, (our men were on the sick list), we saved nearly all the cargo, in a damaged state. The men that were chosen to survey the Criterion, judged there was one hundred and seventy tons of ice on her hull and rigging, caused by the rushing of the sea over her and freezing solid. After stripping her, in the spring, she was sold for *twenty dollars !*

I returned to Baltimore and commenced another voyage as chief mate of the brig Frances F. Johnson, of Baltimore, for South America. Our crew were all black men, the captain's peculiar choice. I often regretted that we two were the only white men on board, for we were sometimes placed in peculiar circumstances, in consequence of being the minority.

With the exception of some dry goods, we disposed of our cargo in Maranham and Para. The last-mentioned place lies about one hundred miles up from the mouth of the river Amazon, the mouth of the river being on the equator. Here we took in a return cargo for Baltimore. On our homeward voyage we stopped at the French Island of Martinico. After taking our place among the shipping near the shore, and remaining a few days, the captain and myself were unexpectedly ordered on board by the commodore, who reprimanded us because we had failed to comply with a trifling point in his orders, for which he ordered us to leave the place in the morning. We considered this ungenerous and severe, and without precedent; but we obeyed, and had but scarcely cleared ourselves from the island when a dreadful hurricane commenced (which is common in the West Indies about the autumnal equinox), which caused such devastation among the shipping and seamen that about one hundred vessels in a few hours were dashed in pieces and sunk with their crews at their moorings, and some driven to sea in a helpless condition, leaving but two vessels saved in the harbor in the morning!

It was with much difficulty we cleared ourselves from the island during the day, because of the sudden changing of the wind from almost every quarter of the compass. We were pretty well satisfied that a violent storm was at hand, and made what preparations we deemed necessary to meet it. We fortunately escaped from the most violent part of it, with but little damage, and arrived safely at St. Domingo. A sloop from New York city came in a few days after us, the captain of which stated what I have already related respecting the storm and disaster at Martinico. Said he, "We arrived off the harbor of Martinico at the commencement of the hurricane, and as we were driven at the mercy of the storm, in the darkness of the night, while we were endeavoring to hold ourselves to the deck around our boat, which was lying bottom upwards, strongly lashed to ring-bolts in the deck, she was taken by the violence of the wind from our midst, and not one of us knew when, or how, or where she had gone." The miracle with them was that they survived the storm. But still more wonderful with us, that we, while attending to our lawful business, should in such an unexpected and unprecedented manner be driven from the place where none but the omniscient eye of Jehovah could tell of the terrible destruction that in a few hours was to come upon those we left behind. Surely, through his saving mercy and providential care, we were hurried out of that harbor just in time to be left still numbered among the living.

"God moves in a mysterious way,
His wonders to perform."

Capt. Sylvester here gave me the command of the F. F. Johnson, to proceed to Baltimore with the homeward cargo, while he remained in St. Domingo to dispose of the balance of the outward cargo. At the time of sailing I was sick, and fearing my disease was the yellow fever, I had my bed brought upon the quarter-deck, and remained exposed to the open day and night air, and soon recovered my health. We arrived safely in Baltimore, the beginning of January, 1818. From thence I returned to my father's in Fairhaven, Mass., having been absent some two years and a half. Feb. 15, 1818, I was united in marriage to Miss Prudence M., daughter of Capt. Obed Nye, my present wife.

Six weeks subsequent to this I sailed on another voyage, chief mate of the ship Frances, Captain Hitch, of New Bedford. We proceeded to Baltimore, Md., where we loaded with tobacco for Bremen, in Europe. From thence we proceeded to Gottenberg in Sweden, where we loaded again with bar iron for New Bedford, Mass.

I will here relate an incident which occurred on our passage from Bremen to Gottenberg, to show how persons are wrought upon sometimes in their sleep. We were passing what is called "the Scaw," up the Cattegat, not a very safe place in a gale, in company with a large convoy of British merchantmen bound into the Baltic Sea. Capt. H., unusual for him, remained on deck until midnight, at which time the larboard watch was called. The night was uncommonly light, pleasant, and clear, with a good, wholesale, flowing breeze,—all the convoy sailing onward in regular order. Capt. H. requested me to follow a certain large ship, and be particular to keep about so far astern of her, and if we saw her in difficulty, we could alter our course in time to avoid the same. Before my four-hours' watch was out, Captain H. came up to the gangway, saying, "Mr. Bates, what are you about, carrying sail in this way? Clew down the topsails and reef them! Where is that ship?" "Yonder," said I, "about the distance she was when you went down below!" I saw his eyes were wide open, but still I could not believe he was in his right mind in addressing me in the peremptory manner he did. Said I, "Capt. Hitch, you are asleep!" "Asleep!" said he! "I never was wider awake in my life! Clew the topsails down and reef them!" I felt provoked at this unusual arbitrary treatment without the least cause, and cried out at the top of my voice, "Forward there? Call all hands to reef the topsails!" This waked up the captain, inquiring, "What's the matter?" Said I, "You have been giving orders to reef the topsails!" "Have I? I did not know it. Stop them from doing so, and I will go down again out of the way."

As Capt. H. was part owner of the ship, with the prospect of making a few thousand dollars with a cargo of iron, he loaded the ship very deep, but did not seem to apprehend any particular danger until we encountered a snow-storm as we entered the North Sea, which determined us to go "north about," and brought us in the vicinity of "Rockal" in a violent storm in the night, which aroused our feelings and caused deep anxiety until we were satisfied we were past all danger from it.

## Chapter Nine.

*Allowance of Water—Casting Cargo into the Sea—Allowance of Provisions—Dreadful Storm—Gulf Stream—Dead Calm and Rushing Hurricane—Silent Agony—Wallowing between the Seas—Singular Coincidence in relation to Prayer—More respecting the Gale—Leak Increasing—Supply of Provisions and Water-Council—Bear up for the West Indies—Reported—Safe Arrival in the West Indies.*

OUR heavy cargo of iron, and prevailing westerly gales, caused our ship to labor so incessantly that she began to leak very freely. We got up about twenty tons of iron and secured it on the upper deck. This eased her laboring some, but still the westerly gales prevailed, and we gained westward but slowly. At length said Capt. Hitch, "We must come on an allowance of water;" and asked how much I thought we could begin with? I answered, "Two quarts per day." "Two quarts of water per day!" said he, "why, I never drank two quarts of water a day in my life. I drink two cups of coffee in the morning, and two cups of tea at night, and two or three glasses of grog during the day [temperance societies were not known then], and that is about all I drink." Said he, "I have been following the sea for about thirty years, and never have yet been put on an allowance." I had not been so fortunate, but had been on an allowance of food five years, and several months on a short allowance of water. I said to Capt. H., "The very idea of being on an allowance of water will increase your desire for more." Well, he knew nothing about that, but said, "We will wait a little longer, for I don't believe I ever drank two quarts a day."

As we were still hindered in our progress, and the ship increasing her leak, Capt. H, said, "It is your morning watch to-morrow, I think you had better begin and measure out the water, and fasten up the water casks." "Very well, sir," said I, "but how much shall I measure for each man?" "Well, begin with two quarts." This was done, and the captain's two quarts taken to the cabin. As I was walking the deck about 7 o'clock in the evening, the after hatchway being open, I heard Capt. H., in the dark, say in a loud whisper, "Lem! you got any water?" (Lemuel T. was a nephew of Capt. H., and messed in the steerage.) "Yes, sir." "Give me a drink, will you?" In a few moments I heard the captain gurgling the water down out of "Lem's" bottle as though he was very thirsty, and yet it was but twelve hours since his two quarts had been measured out. At the breakfast table next morning, said I, "Capt. Hitch, how did you make out for water last night?" He smiled, and acknowledged he was mistaken. "The thought of being on an allowance (as you said) makes one feel thirsty. I never tried it before."

After encountering another heavy gale, Capt. H. became seriously alarmed, fearing the Frances was too deeply laden to cross the Atlantic in safety. A council was held, which decided to relieve the ship of part of her burden by casting the twenty tons of iron overboard. In a few hours this work was accomplished, and the long bars of iron were gliding swiftly to their resting place some five or more miles below us, into what the sailors call, "Davy Jones's Locker."

Twenty tons more were taken on deck. This change relieved the ship very perceptibly, and enabled her to make better progress. But still the captain was fearful of carrying a press of sail for fear her leak would increase, and carry us all down to the bottom.

Our stock of provisions getting low, we came on a stated allowance of beef and bread, our small stores being about exhausted. We all began to feel anxious to get to our destined haven. When the captain was asleep, we would venture sometimes to crowd on a little more sail. After a westerly storm, the wind had come round to the east during the night. To improve this favorable wind, by the time the morning watch was called, we had all the reefs out of the top-sails, top-mast and lower studding sails set with a good top-gallant breeze, but rather a heavy head-beat sea. Capt. H. came on deck and looked around a few moments, and said, "Mr. Bates, you had better take in the main-top-gallant sail. Also the lower and top-mast studding sails. Now we will double and single reef the top-sails." This done, he concluded the ship would get along much easier, and almost as fast.

At length, the winds favored us, and we were making rapid progress. The last three days the wind had been increasing from the south-east, and according to our reckoning, if it continued, we should reach New Bedford in three days more, making our passage in seventy days from Gottenberg. In this we were sadly disappointed, for by the third day at midnight, the gale had increased to a dreadful height. The raging elements seemed to set at defiance every living creature that moved above the surface of the sea. In all my experience I had never witnessed such portentous signs of a dreadful, devastating storm in the heavens. The sea had risen to such an awful height, it seemed sometimes that it would rush over our mast-heads before our heavy-laden ship would rise to receive its towering, foaming top, and the howling, raging wind above it, straining every stitch of sail we dared to show, and then dash us headlong again into the awful gulf below. All the canvas we dared to show was a close-reefed main-top-sail and reefed foresail. We needed more to hurry the ship off before the foaming sea, but were in great fear that the heavy gusts of wind would wrench them from the bolt-ropes and leave us in the power of the next sea to be overwhelmed, and sink with our iron cargo to the bottom of the sea.

We charged the watch that were going below not to lay off any of their clothing, but be ready at a moment's warning. We considered ourselves in the eastern edge of the Gulf Stream, one of the most dreaded places for continual storms on the American coast, or any other coast in the world. Cross it somewhere we must to reach our home.

I entered the cabin for a moment to inform Capt. H. of the increasing storm. He was unwilling to see it, but said, "Mr. Bates, keep the ship dead before the sea!" That was our only hope. Our tiller had been broken off within four feet of the rudder-head, a short time previous, by a violent sea that struck us on the bow. We had spliced it, and now with tiller-ropes and relieving tackles it required four experienced men, with our utmost skill in "cunning" them, to manage the helm, to keep the ship running directly before the foaming, mountainous seas. Our continual work was something like the following: "Starboard your helm!" "Starboard, sir," was the reply. "Steady, here comes another dreadful sea!" "Steady," was the reply. "How do we head now?" "N. W.," was the reply. "Steady, keep her head just so. That was well done!" If the ship had not answered her helm as she did, it appeared that that fearful sea would have rushed over our quarter, and swept us all by the board. "Port your helm! here comes another on the larboard side! Steady now, the sea is square on our stern," &c.

With the dawn of the morning the rain came down upon us in such torrents that it was with much difficulty that we could see the shape of the sea until it was rushing upon us. This rain was ominous of a change more dreadful (if possible) than our present situation. My short experience had taught me that the Gulf Stream* was more

---

*The Gulf Stream is caused by a large body of water issuing from the Gulf of Mexico, flowing north-easterly from the southeast point of the coast of Florida, in some places passing close in with the land, widening as it flows onward by our northern coast, where it branches off toward the banks of Newfoundland, where it is sometimes found to be several hundred miles in width, nar-

dangerous for navigators on this account than any other navigable sea.

Between seven and eight o'clock in the morning, without a moment's warning, the wind suddenly struck us from the opposite quarter, and our sails were struck against the mast. The simultaneous cry was uttered, "The ship's aback!" "Hard aport your helm!" "Quick! quick!" It seemed as though I touched the deck but twice in getting some thirty feet to the mainmast, where the weather forebraces were belayed, and whirled them from the pins, and shouted, "All hands on deck in a moment!" Descending from the top of the sea, the ship answered her helm; her head paid off to the N. E. The foresail filled again, or we should inevitably have gone down stern foremost, from the overpowering rush of the next sea. The wind came furiously from the west for a few moments, and suddenly died away, leaving us in a *dead calm.* "Lash your helm to the starboard!" "Call the captain, one of you!" "Clew up the main-top-sail!" "Haul up the foresail!" "All hands aloft now, and furl the main-top-sail." "Make haste, men, and secure it to the yard as fast as you can!"

The ship was now *unmanageable.* The sea described above, was now on our lee beam, and seemed as though it would either run over our mast-heads or roll us bottom upward to windward. As the captain came up from the cabin and saw our situation, he cried out, " *Oh, my grief!*" and for a

---

rowing and widening as influenced by the heavy winds. This current sweeps along our southern coast sometimes at the rate of three miles per hour. In passing from or approaching the coast of the United States, mariners always find the water much warmer in this stream than on either side of it. Also, changeable, tempestuous, stormy weather, such as is not found elsewhere.

while was silent. The ship was now writhing and wrenching some like a person in perfect agony. Her tumbling in such a tumultuous and violent manner, made it very difficult for the men to get aloft. Before they reached the topsail-yard, the wind came rushing upon us like a tornado, from the W. S. W. This was what we feared, and why we hurried to save our storm-sails if we could. It was some time before the men could secure the sails. When this was done, and the ship pumped after a manner, the crew were all clustered on the quarter-deck, except Lemuel T. and George H., the captain's nephew and son, who, by the captain's orders, were fastened below for fear they would be swept from the deck; also one passenger. Said the captain, " Cook, *can you pray with us ?*" The cook knelt down where he could secure himself, the rest of us holding on upon our feet, and prayed most fervently for God to protect and save us from the dreadful, raging storm. This was the first prayer that I ever heard uttered in a storm upon the ocean. Sinners as we were, I believe it was remembered by Him whose ear is not closed to the distressed mariner's cry; for the Scriptures testify that " he commandeth and raiseth the stormy wind, which lifteth up the waves thereof. They mount up to the heaven, they go down again to the depths: their soul is melted because of trouble. They reel to and fro, and stagger like a drunken man, and are at their wit's end. Then they cry unto the Lord in their trouble, and he bringeth them out of their distresses." Ps. cxii, 25–28.

We seemed to be placed in the very position the Psalmist speaks of. After we had done all we could to save our lives from the raging elements of the past night, until our ship was rendered unmanageable, our sails secured and the helm lashed a-lee, then we were at our "wit's end," and prayed to the Lord for help, and secured ourselves to the mizzen-rigging and quarter-deck, there in deep contemplation and utter silence to wait the issue of our case. Captain H. doubtless felt that he had neglected his duty in commending us to God daily, during our long voyage, and now in this perilous hour, when we were at our "wit's end," his confidence failed him. Himself and the cook were the only professors of religion on board. They both belonged to the Close-Communion Baptist Church, in New Bedford, Massachusetts. The cook was the only colored man on board. I have always believed that the Lord specially regarded his prayer. Once only during the voyage I heard the captain pray. I had become almost exhausted from extreme labor in some of the storms I have before mentioned, and was losing two hours of my evening watch to get some rest, when I overheard Captain H., in a dark part of the cabin, praying the Lord to raise me to health and strength. In saying this I mean no disrespect to Captain H., for he was a gentlemanly, good-hearted man, and treated his officers and men with kindness and respect.

After the cook's prayer I secured myself to the weather foremost mizzen shroud, to watch the furious, raging storm. Captain H. was next behind me, the second mate and crew all ranged along the weather side of the quarter-deck, waiting in silence the decision of our case. The wind was so unabating in its fury that it would whirl the top of the contending seas over us, and drench us like pouring rain from the clouds. The labor of the ship seemed to be more than she could long endure. The marvel was that she had held together so long. It seemed sometimes, when she was rushing from the top of some of those mountain seas, broadside foremost, that she would either turn clear over or rush down with such impetuosity that she never would rise again. After a while the sea became furious from the west, and the two seas would rush together like enemies contending for victory. We had remained in silence about three hours, when I said, " Our ship can stand this but a little longer." " So I think," replied the captain. I said, " It appears to me that our only hope is to loose the wings of the foresail, and drive her between these two seas on a N. E. course." " Let us try it," said Captain H.

Soon our good old ship was making her way through between these two tumbling mountains, being most severely buffeted, first on the right and then on the left. And when our hearts would almost sink for fear of her being overwhelmed, she would seem to rise again above it all, and shake herself as though some unseen hand was girding her from beneath, and with her *two little, outstretched wings*, filled to overflowing with the howling, raging wind, she would seem to move onward again with more than mortal energy. Thus she wallowed along until midnight between these tumbling seas, trembling, wrenching and groaning, with her heavy iron load and precious living souls that she was laboring to preserve, in answer to the poor negro sailor's prayer, that had passed from her upper deck, away from amidst the *distracting hurricane and dreadful storm*, to the peaceful mansions of the Governor of Heaven, and earth, and seas.

My wife was visiting one of our relatives, a few miles distant from home, where a Methodist minister called in to visit the family. He asked why she appeared so sober? He was told that the ship her husband sailed in was out of time, and much fear was entertained for her safety, and particularly at that time, as there was a violent raging storm. Said the minister, "I want to pray for that ship's company." His prayer was so fervent, and made so deep an impression on my wife, that she noted down the time. When the ship came home, her log-book was examined, which proved it was the same storm.

Somewhere about midnight, as the wind had veered round to the north and west, and the furious sea from that quarter had become very dangerous, and was continuing to subdue and overpower the one that had been so dangerous from the S. E., we deemed it for our safety to still bear away and head the ship on to the S. E. sea, and give her the whole of her reefed foresail to drive her from the irregular, furious cross sea, that was raging from the west. Thus for four days, by the furious hurricane we were driven onward to save ourselves from what we considered a more dangerous position than lying to under bare poles, exposing the ship to the irregular cross seas that might render her unmanageable, and wrench her in pieces. First steering N. W. before a most violent S. E. gale, and in a moment of time our sails all aback with the gale from the N. W., then in a few moments a dead calm for about fifteen minutes, rendering the ship unmanageable; and then a raging hurricane from the W. S. W., veering in four days round by the N. to the E., our course being N. E. between the seas; then E. and S. E.,

S. and S. W. In this manner, in about four days, we run three-quarters of the way round the compass, some hundreds of miles further from home than we were at the height of the storm. This was the most peculiar and trying storm in all my experience; neither have I read of the like in its nature and duration. The marvel with us was that our good old ship had weathered this most trying time. Her leak, however, had increased to twelve thousand strokes of the pump in twenty-four hours.

Again, by a unanimous decision, we launched another twenty tons of our iron cargo into the sea. We endeavored to steer in for a southern port, but the westerly winds continued to check our progress westward. Winter had now fairly commenced, and our provisions and water were getting so low that we were about to reduce our allowance, while our constant labor at the pumps was also reducing our strength. We saw vessels occasionally, but at too great a distance to approach them. We made an extra effort, and sailed for one until night-fall, and then, to induce her to approach us, we rigged a spar over our stern, on which we fastened a barrel with tar, and fired it, to make them believe we were on fire, and induce them to come to our relief, but to no purpose.

Soon after this, when things began to look more dubious, just at the close of a gale of wind, about midnight, we saw a vessel directly ahead steering toward us. She soon answered our signal by hoisting her "lanthorn," and soon we met within speaking distance. "Where are you from?" "New York," was the reply. "Where are you bound?" "South America." "Can you spare us some provisions?" "Yes, as much as you want; I am loaded with them." "Lay by us and we will send our boat." "Very well."

Captain Hitch's heart began to fail him as we began to clear away our small boat. Said he, the swell is so high the boat will be swamped, and I dare not have you go, Mr. Bates. To lose some of the crew now would be very discouraging, and how could the ship be saved in her leaky, sinking condition?" "But, Captain Hitch, we are in want of provisions, and can now get a supply." He still declared himself unwilling to command any one to attempt it. Said I, "Allow me then to call for volunteers." He continued irresolute. Fearing we should miss this opportunity, I inquired, "Who among you will volunteer to go with me in the boat?" "I will go for one, sir." "I will go;" "and I will go," said others. "That will do," said I, "three are enough." In a few moments we were almost out of sight of our ship, steering for the signal light. One sea boarded us, and about half filled the boat. With one hand bailing out the water, and the other two at the oars, we reached the brig. On account of the rough sea we could carry but a few barrels of bread and flour. I gave the captain a draft on our owners in New Bedford. "Your name is Bates," said he; "are you related to Dr. Bates, of Barre, Massachusetts?" "He is my brother." "Well, I am his near neighbor; I left there a few weeks ago. Don't you want some more?" "No, sir. Only if you will fill away and tow us up to the windward of our ship we will be much obliged." This done, we reached the ship in safety, and soon had our supply of bread and flour safely landed on deck. Our boat was stowed away, and each vessel filled away on their course. Captain H. was almost overjoyed at our safe return with a supply of provisions to carry us into port. The westerly winds, however, prevailed, and our ship's bottom had become so foul with grass and barnacles that she moved very slowly. We prepared a scraper, with which we were enabled in a calm to scrape some of it off. Bushels of barnacles, as large as thimbles, and green grass, two feet long, would rise under our stern as we hauled the scraper under her bottom, all of which had accumulated during our passage. Again we met with a vessel from the West Indies, which supplied us with three casks of water ; after which a ship from Portland supplied us with potatoes from her cargo. These were very acceptable, not only for a change of diet, but also to check the scurvy, which is common with those seamen who are obliged to subsist on salted provisions. In a few weeks we obtained another short supply, and were animated with the hope of reaching some port on the coast in a few days. But our buoyant hopes would sink again with the increasing westerly gales, and we would wish that we had taken a larger supply of provisions. Thus we continued to toil on, gaining sometimes a considerable distance westward, and then in one gale losing almost as much distance as we gained in a week before.

Three times after this we obtained a supply of what could be spared from different vessels we met with, making in all seven different times. And it had become a common saying with us, that the very time we needed relief, it came. Wicked as we still were, we could but acknowledge the hand of a merciful God in it all. Finally, we began to despair, contending with the almost-continual westerly winds in our disabled condition, and called all hands in "council," to determine whether, in our perilous position to preserve our lives, we should change the voyage and run for a port in distress. It was decided unanimously that we bear up for the West Indies. After running about two days south, the wind headed us from that quarter. As the ship was now heading westward, Captain H. concluded he could reach a southern port in the United States. But the wind changed again, which cut off this prospect. Captain H. now regretted that he had taken it upon him to deviate from the decision of the council, and wished me to call another, and see if it would be decided for us to bear up again for the West Indies. The whole crew expressed themselves in favor of adhering to our previous decision, to steer for the West Indies, but what was the use in deciding? Captain H. would turn back again as soon as the wind came fair to steer westward. I stated if he did I should oppose him, and insist on abiding by the decision we then made in council. It was a unanimous vote to bear up in distress for the West Indies. Captain H. was not present.*

Shortly after we changed our course we met a schooner from the West Indies, bound to New York. We requested him to report the ship Frances, Hitch, one hundred and twenty-two days from Gottenberg, in Sweden, bound to St. Thomas, in the West Indies, in distress.

As letters had reached our friends, advising

---

*When a deviation from a policy of insurance is made in a vessel's voyage, it is required to be done by the majority or whole crew in council, that they do so for the preservation of lives, or vessel and cargo; this transaction being recorded in the daily journal or log-book of said vessel, that the owners may lawfully recover their insurance, if a loss occurs after deviation. The same is required when casting cargo overboard to preserve life.

them of our sailing from Gottenberg for New
Bedford, some four months previous, one-third of
the time being sufficient for a common passage,
various conjectures were afloat respecting our destiny. Few, if any, believed that we were numbered among the living.

As the New York packet was leaving the wharf,
for New Bedford and Fairhaven, the schooner
arrived and reported us. In about twenty-four
hours the New York packet touched at Fairhaven
wharf with the report, one day in advance of the
mail. My wife, father, mother and sisters were
on a social visit at my sisters, near the wharf. Mr.
B., my sister's husband, left them a few moments
and was standing on the wharf with other citizens
of F., when the first item of intelligence from the
packet as she touched the wharf, was that a
schooner had arrived in New York from the West
Indies, which had fallen in with the ship Frances,
Hitch, in lat. ——, and long. ——, one hundred
and twenty-two days from Gottenberg, bound to
St. Thomas, "*in distress.*" With this unexpected
item of news, Mr. B. hurried back to the family
circle, declaring that the ship Frances was still
afloat, bound to the West Indies. In a moment
the scene was changed, and the news spread
throughout the village to gladden other hearts, for
there were other husbands and sons on board the
long-looked-for missing ship. On the arrival of
the mail the next day the news was confirmed. No
piece of intelligence for many years had caused
such universal joy in F. The principal owner of
the ship and cargo (Wm. Roach, of New Bedford,)
said it gave him more joy to hear that the crew
was all alive, than all his interest in the ship and
cargo. Owners and friends were exceedingly anx-

ious to hear particulars how we had been sustained such a length of time with only provisions and water for about half said time, also what had caused our delay.

We had a successful run and passage to St. Thomas, one of the Virgin Islands in the West Indies, belonging to Denmark. The night preceding our arrival, a schooner came in company with us, bound on the same course. By request of Captain H., she consented to keep our company during the night, as he professed to be well acquainted with that region. The night was delightful, with a fair wind. The schooner took in all her sail except her top-sail lowered on the cap. We were under a cloud of sail, lower, top-mast, and top-gallant steering sails, all drawing and filled with the pleasant gale. The captain of the schooner seemed out of all patience with us because we did not sail fast enough to keep up with him. About midnight he sheered up within speaking distance, and cried out, "Ship ahoy!" "Halloo!" replied Captain H. "Do you know what I would do with that ship if I commanded her?" "No," was the reply. "Well, sir," said he, "if I had charge of that ship I would scuttle her and send her to the bottom with all hands on board!" Our ship's bottom was so full of grass and barnacles that she sailed only half her speed with a clean bottom.

We arrived, however, the next day, and thought we felt thankful to God for preserving and sustaining us through the perilous scenes we had experienced. Even when our ship was safely anchored and our sails all furled, for a while we could hardly realize that we were safe in the harbor of St. Thomas. Careening our ship to clean the bottom, it was wonderful to behold the quantity of green grass, from two to three feet long, and large barnacles on the bottom. The "survey" decided that the ship could be repaired to proceed to the United States.

---

## Chapter Ten.

*A Spoiled Child—Passage Home from the West Indies —False Alarm—Arrival Home—Voyage in the Ship New Jersey—Breakers off Bermuda—Dangerous Position in a Violent Storm—Turk's Island—Stacks of Salt—Cargo of Rock Salt—Return to Alexandria, D. C.—Voyage in the Ship Talbot to Liverpool—Storm in the Gulf Stream—Singular Phenomenon on the Banks of Newfoundland—An old Shipmate.*

WHILE we were refitting in St. Thomas, Capt. H. was going to visit an acquaintance of his on Sunday, and I proposed to spend a few hours on shore to see the place. Said he, "George wants to go on shore; I wish you would take him with you, but don't let him go *out of your sight*." While I was conversing with an acquaintance, George was missing. When I returned to the boat in company with the mate of the vessel where Capt. H. was visiting, we saw George lying in the boat *drunk!* When we came to the vessel where his father was, he was exceedingly aggravated, and endeavored in several ways to arouse him from his stupor and induce him to pull at the oar, for his father arranged that we three alone would manage the boat, and leave the sailors on board. George was unable to do anything but reply to his father in a very disrespectful manner, so his father had to ply his oar to the ship.

After George had somewhat recovered from his drunken spell, he made his appearance on the quarter-deck, when his father began to reprove and threaten to chastise him, for disgracing himself and his father among strangers as he had done. A few more words passed, and George clinched his father and crowded him some distance toward the stern of the ship before he could check him and get him down with his knee upon him. He then turned to me, saying, "Mr. Bates, what shall I do with this boy?" I replied, "Whip him, sir!" Said he, "I will!" and slapped him a few times with the flat of his hand on his back saying, "There! take that now!" &c.

George was so vexed and provoked because his father whipped him, that he ran down into the cabin to destroy himself. In a few moments the cook came rushing up from thence, saying, "Captain Hitch! George says he is going to jump out of the cabin window and drown himself!" "Let him jump!" said I. He had become sober enough by this time to know better, for he was a great coward.

George Hitch was about thirteen years of age at this time, and when free from the influence of strong drink was a generous, good-hearted boy, and with right management would have proved a blessing instead of a reproach and curse as he did to his parents and friends. His father in unburdening his heart to me about him, said, "When he was a child, his mother and I were afraid that he would not be roguish enough to make a smart man, so we indulged him in his childish roguery, and soon he learned to run away from school and associate himself with wicked boys, and the like, which troubled his mother so exceedingly that she could not have him at home. This is why I have taken him with me."

His father was aware that he would drink liquor whenever he could get it, and yet he would have the liquor in the decanter placed in the locker where George could get it whenever he pleased in our absence. Sometimes his father would ask the cook what had become of the liquor in the decanter. He knew that neither the second mate nor myself had taken it, for neither of us used strong drink; hence he must have known that George took it.

Our merchant in Gottenberg had placed in the hands of Capt. H. a case of very choice cordial as a present to Mrs. H. After our small stores and liquors were used up during our long passage, I saw George with his arms around his father's neck one evening in the cabin. Capt. H. said to me, "What do you think this boy wants?" "I don't know, sir," I replied. "He wants me to open the cordial case of his mother's and give him some of it." The indulgent father yielded, and very soon the mother's cordial case was emptied. This thirst for liquor, unchecked by his parents, ripened with his manhood, and drove him from all decent society, and finally to a drunkard's grave in the midst of his days. His mother mourned and wept, and died sorrowing for her ruined boy before him. His father lived to be tormented, and threatened with death if he did not give him money to gratify his insatiable thirst that was hastening him to his untimely end, and went down to the grave sorrowing that he had been the father of such a rebellious, unnatural child. Another warning to surviving parents and children who fail to follow the Bible, in obedience to God's infallible rule. Prov. xxii, 6.

On our passage from St. Thomas to New Bedford, Mass., we met a very tempestuous storm in the gulf stream, off Cape Hatteras. During the midnight watch George came rushing into the cabin, crying, "Father! father! the ship is sinking!" The second mate, who had charge of the watch, followed, declaring the ship was going down. As all hands were rushing for the upper deck, I asked Mr. Nye how he knew the ship was sinking? " Because," said he, " she has settled two or three feet." We raised the after hatchway to see how much water was in the hole, and found no more than usual. The almost continual cracking thunder and vivid lightning in the roaring storm, alarmed and deceived them, for the whole watch on deck also believed the ship was sinking.

In about three weeks from St. Thomas we saw Block Island. In the morning we were about twenty-five miles from New Bedford, when the wind came out ahead from the north in a strong gale, threatning to drive us off our soundings. We clinched our cables round the mast and cleared our anchors, determined to make a desperate effort, and try the strength of our cables in deep water rather than be blown off the coast. Then with what sail the ship could bear we began to ply her head to windward for a harbor in the Vineyard Sound. As the sea and sprays rushed upon us it froze on the sails and rigging, so that before we tacked, which was often, we had to break off the ice from our sails, tacks and sheets, with hand-spikes. In this way we gained about ten miles to windward during the day, and anchored in Tarpau-lin Cove, about fifteen miles from New Bedford. Our signal was seen from the observatory in New Bedford just as we were passing into the Cove. When our anchor reached the bottom, the poor, half-frozen crew were so overjoyed that they gave three cheers for a safe harbor. After two days the gale abated, and we made sail and anchored in the harbor of New Bedford, Feb. 20, 1819, nearly six months from Gottenberg. So far as I have any knowledge of ship-sailing, this was one of the most providential and singular passages from Europe to America, in its nature and duration, that is on record.

This voyage, including also our passage to the West Indies, could in ordinary weather be performed by our ship, when in good sailing trim, in less than sixty days. Our friends were almost as glad to see us as we were to get safely home. The contrast between the almost continual clanking of pumps to keep our ship afloat, and howling winter storms which we had to contend with, and a good cheering fireside, surrounded by wives, children and friends, was great indeed, and cheered us exceedingly. We thought we were thankful to God for thus preserving our lives. This was the third time I had returned home during ten years.

"The Old Frances," as she was called, apparently ready to slide into a watery grave, was soon thoroughly repaired and fitted for the whaling business, which she successfully pursued in the Pacific and Indian Oceans for many years. Capt. L. C. Tripp and myself are now the only survivors.

After a pleasant season of a few months at home with my family, I sailed again for Alexandria, D. C., and shipped as chief mate on board the ship New Jersey, of Alexandria, D. C., D. Howland commander. We proceeded up James River near Richmond, Va., to load for Europe. From there to Norfolk, Va., where we finally loaded and sailed for Bermuda.

On our arrival at Bermuda, our ship drew so much water that it became necessary for us to anchor in open sea, and wait for a smooth time and fair wind to sail into the harbor. The captain and pilot went on shore expecting to return, but were prevented on account of a violent gale and storm which came on soon after they reached the shore, which placed us in a trying and perilous situation for nearly two days. We were unacquainted with the dangerous reefs of rocks with which the north and east sides of the island were bounded, but with the aid of our spy-glass from the ship's mast-head,

still many miles off in the offing I could see the
furious sea breaking mast-head high over the reefs
of rocks, east and north, and on the west of us the
Island of Bermuda, receiving the whole rake of the
beating sea against its rock-bound coast, as far as
the eye could extend to the south. From my place
of observation I saw there was a bare possibility
for our lives, if during the gale our ship should be
driven from her anchors, or part her cable, to pass
out by the south, provided we could show sail
enough to weather the breakers on the south end
of the Island. Our storm sails were now reefed,
and every needful preparation made if the cables
parted, to chop them off at the windlass, and crowd
on every storm-sail the ship could bear, to clear if
possible the breakers under our lee. As the gale
increased we had veered out almost all our cable,
reserving enough to freshen the chafe at the bow
which was very frequent. But contrary to all our
fearful forebodings, and those on shore who were
filled with anxiety for our safety, and especially
our captain and pilot, our brow-beaten ship was
seen at the dawn of the second morning still contending with her unyielding foe, holding to her
well-bedded anchors by her long, straitened cables,
which had been fully tested during the violent
storm which had now begun to abate. As the sea
went down, the captain and pilot returned, and the
ship was got under way and safely anchored in the
harbor, and we discharged our cargo.

We sailed from Bermuda to Turk's Island for a
cargo of salt. In the vicinity of this island is a
group of low, sandy islands, where the inhabitants
make large quantities of salt from the sea water.
Passing by near these islands, strangers can see
something near the amount of stock they have on
hand, as it is heaped up in stacks for sale and exportation. A little way off these salt stacks and

their dwelling houses very much resemble the small houses on the prairies in the West, with their numerous wheat stacks dotted about them after harvest. Turk's Island salt is what is also called "rock salt." Here we moored our ship about a quarter of a mile from the shore, our anchor in forty fathoms or two hundred and forty feet of water, ready to ship our cables and put to sea at any moment of danger from change of wind or weather; and when the weather settled again, return and finish loading. In a few days we received from the natives, by their slaves, twelve thousand bushels of salt, which they handed us out of their boats by the half bushel in their salt sacks. The sea around this island abounds with small shells of all colors, many of which are obtained by expert swimmers diving for them in deep water. We returned to Alexandria, D. C., in the winter of 1820, where our voyage ended.

Before the cargo of the New Jersey was discharged, I was offered the command of the ship Talbot, of Salem, Mass., then loading in Alexandria for Liverpool. In a few weeks we were again out of the Chesapeake Bay, departing from Cape Henry across the Atlantic Ocean.

Soon after our leaving the land, a violent gale and storm overtook us in the Gulf Stream, attended with awful thunder and vivid streaks of lightning. The heavy, dark clouds seeming but just above our mast-heads, kept us enshrouded in almost impenetrable darkness, as the night closed around us. Our minds were only relieved by the repeated sheets of streaming fire that lit up our pathway, and showed us for an instant that there was no other ship directly ahead of us, and also the shape of the rushing seas before which we were scudding with what sail the ship could bear, crossing with all speed this dreaded, dismal, dark stream of warm water that stretches itself from the Gulf of Mexico to Nantucket shoals on our Atlantic coast. Whether the storm abated in the stream we crossed we could not say, but we found very different weather on the eastern side of it. I have heard mariners tell of experiencing days of very pleasant weather while sailing in this Gulf, but I have no knowledge of such in my experience.

After this we shaped our course so as to pass across the southern edge of what is called the Grand Banks of Newfoundland. According to our reckoning and signs of soundings, we were approaching this noted spot in the afternoon. The night set in with a drizzling rain, which soon began to freeze, so that by midnight our sails and rigging were so glazed and stiffened with ice that we were much troubled to trim them and steer the ship away from the bank again into the fathomless deep, where we are told that water never freezes. This was true in this instance, for the ice melted after a few hours' run to the south. We did not stop to sound, but supposed we were in about sixty fathoms of water on the bank, when we bore up at midnight. Here, about one-third of the three thousand miles across the ocean, and hundreds of miles from any land, and about three hundred and sixty feet above the bottom of the sea, we experienced severe frosts from which we were entirely relieved after a run south of about twenty miles. If we had been within twenty miles of land the occurrence would not have been so singular. We at first supposed that we were in the neighborhood of islands of ice, but concluded that could not be, as we were about a month too early for their appearance. This occurrence was in April.

In a few weeks from the above incident we arrived in Liverpool, the commercial city where ten years before I was unjustly and inhumanly seized by a government gang of ruffians, who took me and my shipmate from our quiet boarding house in the night, and lodged us in a press room or filthy jail until the morning. When brought before a naval officer for trial of my citizenship, it was declared by the officer of the ruffian gang that I was an Irishman, belonging to Belfast, in Ireland. Stripped of my right of citizenship, from thenceforth I was transferred to the naval service of King George III, without limitation of time. Then myself and Isaac Bailey of Nantucket, my fellow boarder, were seized by each arm by four stout men, and marched through the middle of their streets like condemned felons to the water side; from thence in a boat to what they called the Old Princess of the Royal navy.

During these ten years a great change had taken place with the potentates and subjects of civilized Europe. The dreadful convulsions of nations had in a great measure subsided. First by the peace between the United States and Great Britain, granting to the former "*Free trade, and sailors' rights;*" secured in a few months after the great decisive battle of Waterloo in 1815, followed by what had been unheard of before,—a conclave of the rulers of the great powers of Europe, united to keep the peace of the world. (Predicted in olden times by the great sovereign Ruler of the universe. Rev. vii, 1.)

The two great belligerent powers that had fo

about fifteen years convulsed the civilized world by their oppressive acts and mortal combats by land and sea, had closed their deadly strife. The first in power usurping the right to seize and impress into his service as many sailors as his war ships required, without distinction of color, if they spoke the English language. The second, with all his ambition to conquer and rule the world, was banished on what was once a desolate, barren rock, far away in the South Atlantic Ocean, now desolate and dying.

The people were now mourning the death of the first, namely, my old master, King George III. His crown was taken off, his course just finished, and he laid away in state to sleep with his fathers until the great decisive day. *Then* there was a female infant prattling in its mother's arms, destined to rule his vast kingdom with less despotic sway. During these ten years my circumstances also had materially changed. Press-gangs and war prisons with me were things in the past, so that I uninterruptedly enjoyed the freedom of the city of Liverpool in common with my countrymen.

As we were about loading with return cargo of Liverpool salt for Alexandria, a man dressed in blue jacket and trowsers, with a ratan whip in his hand, approached me with, " Please, your honor, do you wish to hire a ' lumper ' to shovel in your salt?" " No," I replied, " I do not want you." " Why, your honor, I am acquainted with the business, and take such jobs." I again refused to employ him, and said, " I know you." He asked where I had known him. Said I, "Did you belong to His Majesty's ship Rodney, of 74 guns, stationed in the Mediterranean in the years 1810–12?" He replied in the affirmative. " I knew you there," said I, "Do you remember me?" "No, your honor. Was you one of the lieutenants, or what office did you fill? or was you one of the officers of the American merchant ship we detained?" "Neither of these," I replied. But from the many questions I asked him, he was satisfied I knew him. We had lived and eaten at the same table for about eighteen months.

## Chapter Eleven.

*Who the Stranger was—Black List—Salt Shoveling— Peak of Pico—Voyage Ended—Visit my Family— Voyage to South America—Trade Winds—Sea Fish —Rio Janeiro—Desperate Situation—Monte Video —Returning North—Cutting in a Whale— Resolved Never to Drink Ardent Spirits—Arrival in Alexandria—Preparations for another Voyage—Visit my Family—Escape from a Stage—Sail for South America—Singular Fish—Arrival at Rio Janeiro —Sail for River La Plata—Dispose of my Cargo at Buenos Ayres—Catholic Host.*

THIS man was the ship's corporal or constable in the opposite watch from me, and was captain of those unfortunate ones called "black list men," subjected to perform the scavenger work of the ship, and also to scour the brass, copper, and iron, where and whenever it was called for. In this work he appeared delighted to honor the king. The ratan in his hand looked to me like the same one that he used to switch about some of those unfortunate men. I have before narrated, in part, how the first lieutenant (Campbell), threat-

ened me with an unmerciful whipping if I did not
move to suit him wherever I was stationed, because I had attempted to swim away from the St.
Salvadore del Mondo, a few days before I was introduced on board the Rodney, as I have before
shown. After watching me for more than a year
to execute his threat, he was one day told there
was a pair of trowsers between the mainmast
head and heel of the topmast. I acknowledged
they were mine, for which offense he kept me in
the "black list" for six months.

We had about two hours in a week to scrub and
wash clothes in salt water; sometimes a few quarts
of fresh water, if one could get it before the two
hours closed. And no clothes to be dried at any
other time, except our hammocks, when required
to scrub them. Every morning in the warm season we were required to muster with clean frocks
and trowsers: if reported not clean, the penalty
was the "black list." If I could have obtained
from the purser out of the slop chest the clothes I
absolutely needed, I should never have been put
to my wits' end, as I was, to avoid the "black
list." I had at different times stated to the officer of our division how destitute I was in compar-
ison with others, and begged of him to give me an
order for clothing to muster in. In this I failed,
and because my old clothes were too much worn
to be decent, I suffered as I did. I never knew
any other reason for thus requiring me, as it were,
to "make bricks without stubble or straw," than
my first offense to swim away from their service.
It was a government gain to serve clothes out to
us, for they were charged to us at their own price,
and deducted out of our scanty allowance of wages. I had an opportunity to know that it was

not because I lived in ignorance of my duty as many others did, for the same Mr. Campbell promoted me more than once to higher stations, and I was told that my wages were increased in proportion. This corporal never used his ratan on me, but the way he "*honored*" me *then,* was to turn me out of my hammock (if I was so fortunate as to get into it after doing duty on deck from the midnight hour), and set me at work with the "black list" gang, until it was time for me to take my station in my watch on deck again, and no more liberty for sleep until the night watch was set. In this way I sometimes got the privilege of about five hours for sleep below, and oftener but four hours out of the twenty-four! I was well satisfied he could have favored me in this matter if he pleased; but we obeyed, knowing well if he reported us slack or disobedient, our task would have been made still harder and more degrading. And all this for attempting to dry a pair of trowsers that my name might appear on the clean list!

Without gratifying his curiosity as to who I was, I learned from him the whereabouts of many of the officers and crew, a great many of whom I felt a strong attachment for. I employed two sturdy looking Irishmen to shovel our salt out of the salt scows into the "ballast port," a hole in the ship's side. While progressing in their work I saw them leaning over their salt shovels. Said I, "What is the matter?" "Matter enough, sir, your men do n't shovel it away as fast as we shovel it in!" Some seven or eight men were shoveling it away from them into the ship's hole. Said I, "What is the matter, men? are you not able to shovel the salt away as fast as these two men shovel it in?" They replied they were not. Said one of the Irishmen who was listening at the ballast port, "If we had as much meat to eat as you, then we would give you as much again salt." "Why," said one of my sailors, who seemed much troubled about this, "do n't you have any meat?" "No," said they, "we have not had any this fortnight." "What do you eat, then?" said the sailor. "Potatoes, sure," was the reply. My sailors were then living on all the varieties that good boarding houses afford in Liverpool. Many are of the opinion that meat imparts superior strength to the laboring class. Here, then, was one proof to the contrary.

On account of prevailing westerly winds on our homeward passage, we came into the neighborhood of the Western Islands. Here we saw the towering Peak of Pico mingling with the clouds. By our observations at noon we learned that we were eighty miles north of it. By running toward it sixty miles we should probably have discovered its base. We arrived safely in Alexandria, District of Columbia, in the fall of 1820. As no business offered for the ship, I returned to my family in New England, having been absent some sixteen months.

Early in the spring of 1821, I sailed again for Alexandria, and took charge of the Talbot again, to perform a voyage to South America. The bulk of our cargo was flour. My position was more responsible now than before, for the whole cargo as well as the ship was now confided to me for sales and returns. My compensation for services this voyage was more than doubled. My brother F. was my chief mate. We cleared for Rio Janeiro, in the Brazils. With a fair wind, a few hours' sail from Alexandria, we are passing ex-

President Washington's plantation at Mount Vernon. Sailors say that it was customary with some commanders to lower their topmast sails as a token of respect when they passed his silent tomb. About one hundred and fifty miles from Washington, the variegated and pleasant scenery of the Potomac is passed, by entering the Chesapeake Bay. We had an experienced and skillful pilot; but his thirst for strong drink requiring the steward to fix him gin toddy and brandy sling so frequently, awakened our fears for the safe navigation of the ship, so that we deemed it necessary to put him on an allowance of three glasses of grog per day, until he had piloted the ship outside of the capes of Virginia.

From the capes of Virginia we shaped our course east southerly for Cape de Verde Islands (as is usual), to meet the N. E. trade winds to carry us clear of the north-eastern promontory of the Brazils, or South America, down to the equator of the earth, where we meet the trade winds coming more southerly. In running down these N. E. trades, one is struck with the brilliant pathway the ship keeps rolling up in her onward course during the darkness of the night. The light is so brilliant, I have been tempted to read by it at the midnight hour, by holding my book open facing the shining track. But for the continual caving or tumbling of the sea to fill up the chasm under the stern of the ship, which blends the letters in the book, one could read common print by it in the darkest night. Some who have examined this strange phenomenon, tell us it is because the sea, particularly there, is filled with living animals, or little shining fish, called animalculæ. Undoubtedly these are food for larger fish. Further south we meet with another species of slender fish about a foot long, furnished with little wings. All of a sudden a large school of them rises out of the sea, wheel sometimes clear round, and then drop into their element again. The cause of this when seen sometimes, is a dolphin with all the colors of the rainbow, darting along like a streak of light, in pursuit of his prey that has eluded his grasp, by rising out of their element and taking an opposite course. In the night time they frequently fly on board the ship, affording the mariner a delicious breakfast.

On our arrival off the capacious harbor and city of Rio Janeiro we were struck with admiration, while viewing the antique, cloud-capped, ragged mountains, and especially the towering sugar loaf that makes one side of the entrance to the harbor. Here we disposed of a large portion of our cargo and sailed for Monte Video at the entrance to the river La Plata. A few days before our arrival we encountered a most terrific gale and storm, at the close of which we were drifting on to a rock-bound, uninhabited part of the coast. The wind died away to a dead calm, the sea and current setting us on to the rocks. Our only resort was to clinch our cables and drop our anchors. Fortunately for us they held the ship. With my spy-glass I ascended the mast head to survey the rocky shore. After a while I decided on the place, if we should break from our anchors and could get our ship headed for the shore, where we would plunge her, and if not overwhelmed with the surf escape to the shore. After thus deciding, we made every necessary preparation, in case the wind should come on again in the night, to cut our cables and make a desperate effort to clear the rocks under our lee.

After about thirty hours' anxious suspense, the wind began to rise again from the sea; we raised our anchors, and before midnight we considered ourselves out of danger from that quarter.

Soon after this event we arrived at Monte Video, and disposed of the balance of our cargo, and returned again to Rio Janeiro. I invested our funds in hides and coffee, and cleared and sailed for Bahia or St. Salvador. On the Abrolhos banks we fell in with the ship Balena, Capt. Gardiner, of New Bedford, trying out a sperm whale which they had harpooned the day before. Capt. G. was recently from New Bedford, on a whaling voyage in the Pacific ocean.

After getting these huge monsters of the deep along side of the ship, with sharp spades fitted on long poles, they chop off their heads, and with their long-handled "ladles" dip out the purest and best oil, called "head matter." Some of their heads yield twenty barrels of this rich product, which sells sometimes for fifty dollars per barrel. Then with their great iron "blubber hooks," hooked into a strip of their blubber, to which the huge winding tackles are fastened, with the fall at the end of the windlass, the sailors heave it round while the spade men are cutting the strip down to the flesh. As the strip of blubber rises, the whale's carcass rolls over until the blubber is all on board the ship. The carcass is then turned adrift, and soon devoured by sharks.

The blubber is minced up into small pieces, and thrown into large iron "try-pots," and tried out. When the scraps are browned they throw them under the try-pot for fuel. The hot oil is then put into casks, cooled, coopered, and stowed away for a market. While this work is progressing,

the cook and steward (if the captain thinks best)
are to work at the flour barrels, rolling out bushels of doughnuts, which are soon cooked in the
scalding oil as a general treat for all hands. Sailors call this having a good "*tuck out.*" The hot
oil is as sweet as new hog's lard.

Capt. Gardner furnished me with recent news
from home, and left letters with me for the States.
In a few days I arrived at Bahia, and from thence
sailed for Alexandria, D. C.

While on our passage home I was seriously convicted in regard to an egregious error which I had
committed, in allowing myself, as I had done for
more than a year, to drink ardent spirits, after I
had practiced entire abstinence, because I had become disgusted with its debasing and demoralizing effects, and was well satisfied that drinking
men were daily ruining themselves, and moving
with rapid strides to a drunkard's grave. Although I had taken measures to secure myself
from the drunkard's path, by not allowing myself
in any case whatever to drink but one glass of
ardent spirits per day, which I most strictly ad-
hered to, yet the strong desire for that one glass
when coming to the dinner hour (the usual time
for it), was stronger than my appetite for food,
and I became alarmed for myself. While reflecting about this matter, I solemnly resolved that I
would never drink another glass of ardent spirits
while I lived. It is now about forty-six years
since that important era in the history of my life,
and I have no knowledge of ever violating that
vow, only in using it for medicinal purposes.
This circumstance gave a new spring to my whole
being, and made me feel like a free man. Still it

was considered genteel to drink wine in genteel company.

We had a pleasant passage from Bahia to the capes of Virginia, and arrived in Alexandria about the last of November, 1821. A letter was awaiting me here from my wife, announcing the death of our only son. Mr. Gardner, the owner of the Talbot, was so well pleased with her profitable voyage that he purchased a fast-sailing brig, and an assorted cargo, in Baltimore, for me to proceed on a trading voyage to the Pacific Ocean, while the Talbot remained in Alexandria to undergo some necessary repairs. While preparations were being made for our contemplated voyage, I took passage in the mail stage from Baltimore to Massachusetts to visit my family. We left Baltimore on Wednesday, and arrived in Fairhaven, Mass., on first-day evening, after a tedious route of over four days, stopping nowhere only for a change of horses and a hasty meal until we reached Rhode Island. While passing through Connecticut, in the night, the horses took fright and sheered on the side of a bank, upsetting the stage. A very heavy man on the seat with me, held to the strap until it gave way, and fell upon me and crushed me through the side of the stage upon the frozen ground. If the driver had not leaped upon the bank as the stage was falling, and stopped his horses, we must have been killed. It was some weeks before I fully recovered. Still I rode on until I reached home.

After remaining with my family a few weeks, on my return to Baltimore, as we were entering Philadelphia about midnight in a close, winter coach, with one door, and seven men passengers, as we were passing over a deep gulley, the straps of the driver's seat gave way, and the two drivers fell under the wheels, unknown to us who were snugly wrapped up inside. I asked why the horses were going with such speed. "Let them go," said another, " I like to go fast." I was not so well satisfied, but threw off my cloak, got the door open, and hallooed to the driver; but receiving no answer, and perceiving that the horses were going at full speed down Third street, I reached around forward and found that the drivers were gone, and the lines trailing after the horses. I threw the step down, stepped out on it, perhaps a foot from the ground, and watched for an opportunity to jump on a snow bank, but the horses yet kept on the pavement where the snow was worn off. The passengers from behind were urging me to jump, as they wished to follow before the stage was dashed in pieces.

I finally sprang forward with the going of the stage with all my strength, and just saw the hind wheels clearing my body, when I pitched upon my head, and how many times I tumbled after that before I stopped I cannot tell. I found I had gashed the top of my head, from which the blood was fast flowing. I heard the stage rattling most furiously away down the street. By the aid of the moonlight I found my hat, and followed on after the stage. I soon came to Mr. G., my owner's son, who was in company with me from Boston. In his fright he had jumped square out of the stage, and was seriously injured. After getting him under a doctor's care, I started to learn the fate of the other five, and our baggage. I met the horses with a driver, returning with the stage broken down on the wheels. Four other passengers followed our example, and were not much injured.

The last man out was a very heavy one, and he jumped out after the carriage left the pavement, on the sand, uninjured.  The horses ran to the river and turned suddenly under a low shed, and crushed the stage upon the wheels, which would in all probability have killed every passenger that had dared to remain.  We learned in the morning that the drivers but just escaped with their lives, the stage wheels crushing the fingers of one and taking a hat from the other's head.  After a few days we were enabled to proceed, and arrived in Baltimore.

Soon after my return to Baltimore, I was placed in command of the brig Chatsworth, with an assorted cargo, suitable for our contemplated voyage, with unlimited power to continue trading as long as I could find business profitable.  Firearms and ammunition were also furnished to defend ourselves in cases of piracy and mutiny.  My brother F. was still my chief mate.  We cleared for South America and the Pacific Ocean, and sailed from Baltimore Jan. 22, 1822.  In a few weeks we were passing Cape de Verde Islands, bending our course for the Southern Ocean.

In the vicinity of the equator, in moderate weather and calms, we meet with a singular species of fish (more numerous than in higher latitudes), furnished with something analagous to oars and sails.  Naturalists sometimes call them " Nautilus." They are a kind of shell-fish.  With their great, long legs for oars to steady them, they rise and swell out above the water from four to six inches in length, and about the same in height, very much resembling a little ship under full, white sail.  They sail and sheer round about the ship, fall flat on the sea, as though they were upset by a squall of wind, rise erect again, and glide ahead with their accustomed speed, seemingly to show the mariner that they, too, are ships, and how they can outsail him. But as soon as the wind rises their courage fails them; they take in all sail and hide under water until another calm. Sailors call them "Portuguese men-of-war."

About the 20th of March we arrived and anchored in the harbor of Rio Janeiro. Finding no demand for the whole of our cargo, we sailed again for the River La Plata. As we approached the northern entrance of the river, in the stillness of the night, although some three miles from the shore, we could distinctly hear the sea-dogs (seals) growling and barking from the sand-beach, where they had come up out of the sea to regale themselves. The next day we anchored off Monte Video to inquire into the state of the markets, and soon learned that our cargo was much wanted up the river at Búenos Ayres. In navigating this, to us, new and narrow channel in the night, without a pilot, we got on to the bottom, and were obliged to lighten our vessel by throwing some of her cargo into the sea before she would float into the channel again. On our arrival at the city of Buenos Ayres, our cargo sold immediately at a great profit.

While lying at Buenos Ayres, at the head of ship navigation, a heavy "norther" blew all the water out of the river for many leagues. It was singular to see officers and crews of ships passing from one to another, and to the city, on hard, dry bottom, where but the day before their ships were floating and swinging to their anchors in fifteen feet of water. But it was dangerous to travel many miles off, for the dying away of the wind, or a change of wind at the mouth of the river, rushed the water back like the roaring of the cataract, and floated the ships in quick time again to swing to their anchors.

Until the suppression of the Inquisition in 1820, no other religion but Roman Catholic was tolerated in Buenos Ayres. It was singular to notice, as we had frequent opportunities so to do, with what superstitious awe the mass of the inhabitants regarded the ceremonies of their priests, especially the administering of the sacrament to the dying. The ringing of a small table-bell in the street announces the coming of the *Host*, generally in the following order : A little in advance of the priest may be seen a black boy making a " ding-dong " sound with this little bell, and sometimes two soldiers, one on each side of the priest, with their muskets shouldered, with fixed bayonets to enforce the church order for every knee to bow at the passing of the Host, or subject themselves to the point of the soldiers' bayonet. I was told that an Englishman, refusing to bend his knee when the Host was passing him, was stabbed with the soldier's bayonet. Persons on horseback dismount and kneel with men, women and children in the streets, and at the threshold of their dwelling-houses, groceries and grog-shops, while the Host, or the priest, is passing with the wafer and the wine. We foreigners could stand at the four corners and witness the coming of the Host, and pass another way before they reached us.

Some thirty miles below the city of Buenos Ayres is a good harbor for shipping, called Ensenado. To this place I repaired with the Chatsworth, and prepared her for a winter's voyage round Cape Horn.

# Chapter Twelve.

*Crossing the Pampas of Buenos Ayres—Preparation for the Pacific Ocean—Resolved never to Drink Wine—Aspect of the Starry Heavens—Alarming Position off Cape Horn—Double the Cape—Island of Juan Fernandez—Mountains of Peru—Arrival at Callao—Voyage to Pisco Scenery and Climate of Lima—Earthquakes—Destruction of Callao—Ship out of her Element—Cemetery and Disposal of the Dead.*

WHILE at Ensenado, our communications for business with Buenos Ayres required us to cross the pampas, or vast prairies lying on the south of that province. To do this, and also to protect ourselves from highway robbers, we united in bands, and armed ourselves for defense. Our way was first about twenty miles across the prairie, and then twenty miles further over the "loomas," or high lands, to the city. Once out on this vast prairie without a guide, is next to being on the vast ocean without a compass. Not a tree, nor a shrub, nor anything but reeds and tall, wild grass to be seen as far as the eye can extend. About the only things to attract attention and relieve the mind while passing through the deep and dangerous muddy reed-bogs, and still, miry marshes, fording creeks and running streams, were occasional flocks of sheep, herds of swine, horned cattle, and horses, all quietly feeding in their own organized order. On the two last mentioned might be seen large and small birds quietly perching on their backs, having no other resting place. Mounted on our hired, half-wild horses, stationing our well-paid postillion ahead, we thus passed over this twenty-mile prairie, rank and file, following in the cattle's miry mud-tracks, part of the time our arms around the horses' necks, fearing lest we should be thrown into a mud-hole among the reeds, or left to swim in the stream.

After some four hours' journeying, the "loom-as" would appear ahead, then a farm house, and then the half-way home, or tavern for dinner, and change of horses.   Soon a herd of one hundred or more horses were driven out from the prairies into a "carral," or yard, and set going with full speed around the yard, while the men with their lassos, or long hide ropes with a noose at the end, in a most dextrous manner, would throw their noose over their heads and bring them up to the post. Then, wild or not, they were held until the rider mounted, when they would start rank and file again after the postillion, and soon follow the leading horse without turning, as they had learned to go with the herds on the prairie.   The same order is observed on returning back to Ensanado.   During our stay here, the numerous arrivals from the United States overstocked the market and opened the way for me to purchase a cargo for the Pacific on reasonable terms.   The Chatsworth was now loaded and cleared for Lima, in Peru.

As I had resolved on my previous voyage never more to use ardent spirits only for medicinal purposes, so now, on leaving Buenos Ayres, I also resolved that I would never drink another glass of wine.   In this work of reform I found myself entirely alone, and exposed to the jeering remarks of those with whom I afterward became associated, especially when I declined drinking with them.

Yet after all their comments, that it was not improper or dangerous to drink moderately, &c., they were constrained to admit that my course was perfectly *safe !*

Passing from the northern into the southern hemisphere, one is struck with the remarkable change in the starry heavens. Before reaching the equator, the well-known north star is apparently setting in the northern horizon, and a great portion of the well-known stars in the nothern hemisphere are receding from the mariner's view. But this loss is supplied by the splendid, new and varied scenery in the southern heavens, as he sails onward toward the southern polar regions. Here, away in the south-western heavens, in the track of the milky way, every star-light night, can be seen two small, stationary white clouds, called by sailors the "Magellanic clouds." Ferguson says, "By the aid of the telescope they appear to be a mixture of small clouds and stars." But the most remarkable of all the *cloudy* stars, he says, "is that in the middle of Orion's sword, where seven stars (three of which are very close together) seem to shine through a cloud. It looks like a *gap in the sky*, through which one may see as it were a part of a much brighter region. Although most of these spaces are but a few minutes of a degree in breadth, yet since they are among the fixed stars they must be spaces larger than what is occupied by our solar system; *and in which there seems to be a perpetual, uninterrupted day among numberless worlds which no human art can ever discover.*"

This gap or place in the sky is undoubtedly the same that is spoken of in the Scriptures. See John i, 51; Rev. xix, 11. The center of this constellation (Orion) is midway between the poles of heaven,

and directly over the equator of the earth, and
comes to the meridian about the twenty-third of
January, at nine o'clock in the evening.    Inspiration testifies that "the worlds were framed by the
word of God."    Heb. xi, 3.    "He hangeth the
earth upon nothing."    "By his Spirit he hath
garnished the heavens."    Job xxvi, 7, 13.

On our passage from Buenos Ayres to Cape
Horn, we arrived in the vicinity of the Falkland
Islands, between three and four hundred miles
north-east of the cape.    Here we endeavored to
make a harbor during a storm, by beating up into
Falkland Sound, but the increasing gale obliged
us to bear up and continue our southern course.
On arriving off Cape Horn, about July and August,
the coldest and most stormy season of the year,
for about thirty days we were contending with prevailing westerly gales, and floating islands of ice,
from the polar regions, trying (as sailors say) to
double Cape Horn.    While lying to under a bal-
anced-reefed try-sail off the cape, in a heavy westerly gale, a heavy cross sea boarded us on our
larboard side, which stove in our bulwarks and
stanchions, and ripped up the plankshire, and
washed them up against the mast from near the
windlass to the cabin gangway.    In this exposed
and perilous condition, liable to be filled with
water and sunk immediately, we set the close-reefed
main-top-sail, and put the vessel before the wind;
and to keep her still more steady we packed on
also a reefed foresail, which increased her speed
so furiously that it prevented her from rolling the
open space under water only occasionally.    Fortunately we had a new main-hatch tarpaulin at
hand.    With strips of this all hands were now engaged, as opportunity offered, to get it over the

open spaces, and drive a nail to secure it, and rush back to our holding-on places until the ship rolled again to leeward. In about two hours we secured in this way, temporarily, the open space—took in our main-top-sail and foresail, and hove to again on the same tack under a balanced reefed try-sail. Then after pumping out the water and clearing away the wreck, we had time to reflect on our narrow escape from utter destruction, and how God in kindness had opened the way for us to save ourselves in this trying hour. After the gale had abated, next day, we repaired damages more thoroughly, and at the expiration of some thirty days' struggling off Cape Horn against westerly gales and driving snow-storms, we were enabled to double the cape and shape our course for the island of Juan Fernandez, some fourteen hundred miles north of us. The westerly winds were now in our favor, so that in a few days we changed our climate, and were passing along in sight of this far-famed island, once the whole world to Robinson Crusoe. After sailing north some twenty-six hundred miles from the stormy Cape, the towering mountains of Peru could be distinctly seen, though some eighty miles distant from the coast. Passing onward, we cast our anchor in the spacious bay of Callao, about six miles west of the celebrated city of Lima. North American produce was in good demand. Some of my first sales of flour were over seventy dollars per barrel. A few cargoes arriving soon after us, reduced the price to thirty dollars. Here I chartered the Chatsworth to a Spanish merchant for a voyage to Pisco, some one hundred miles further south, with the privilege of disposing of my cargo and returning with his.

Soon after our arrival here, the chief mate and two of the men went up to the village, about three miles from the harbor, to procure beef and vegetables for dinner. The men soon returned with the statement that the Patriot soldiers had descended from the mountains and besieged the village, and pillaged the stores where some of our cargo was exposed for sale, and had driven the mate out on one side of the village to shoot him, and also declared that they were coming down to take our vessel and dispose of me, because of the Spanish merchant we had brought there from Lima. The mate soon appeared on the beach. After the boat brought him on board, he said that the soldiers, on learning that he was the mate of the Chatsworth, drove him on one side of the village to shoot him. On arriving at the place, one of the soldiers persuaded the others not to kill him. They then concluded to let him go, but beat him most unmercifully with their swords. We made preparations to defend ourselves, but our enemies thought best not to expose themselves within reach of our cannon balls. Notwithstanding our opposing foes, who continued to threaten us, we disposed of all our cargo here at better prices than was offered at Callao, and returned to Callao with the Spanish merchant's cargo.

While at Callao, a whale made his appearance in the bay. A Nantucket whale-ship there at the time followed him with their boats and harpooned him. The whale rushed in among the shipping, with the boat in tow, like a streak through the foaming water, and dashed down directly under the bottom of a large English brig, giving her pursuers but a moment's warning to chop off their line and save their lives—something like leaving her compliments with her unknown foes, saying, "If you follow me here, you will never harpoon another poor whale." The whale rushed through the fleet of shipping to the head of the bay in shoal water. The boat followed, and fastened to her again, when she came streaming out of the bay, and in a little while we could but just discern the boat as the sun was setting, in the offing, with her waft flying, signifying that the whale was dead.

Lieutenant Conner, (now Commodore), who commanded the United States schooner Dolphin, got under way, and the next day arrived with the whale and boat in tow. By invitation, the day following, the citizens of Lima came down in numbers to witness how the North Americans cut in and stow away the big whales found in their waters.

The climate in this region is healthy, and the scenery most delightful. There are floating white clouds, beyond which may be seen the indigo-colored sky, apparently twice the distance from the earth that it is in North America. And then there is the sweet, salubrious air, and strong trade winds, and evergreen fields, and trees bending with delicious fruit, while the ground continually teems with vegetation for both man and beast. There are no storms of rain, and the people say it never rains there. Their city is walled and guarded on the east by towering mountains, easy of ascent, even above the white-capped clouds, which sail below the admiring beholder until they strike a higher ledge of the mountains, then rise and float away over the vast Pacific on the west. And still further in the distance, on the east, about ninety leagues, lie in huge piles the continually snow-capped Andes, all plain to the naked eye, which continually send forth gushing streams that water the plains below. This is also conveyed by means of walled ditches to the streets of the city.

Much more could be added to this interesting description to make a residence there very desirable. But one shock of an earthquake (and they are frequent there), perhaps in the dead of the night, when the inhabitants rush into the streets to save themselves from falling dwellings, crying, wailing and screaming aloud for mercy, is enough to make one perfectly willing and in a hurry to exchange his position for almost any region where the earth rests quietly on its own foundation.

It is stated in Mr. Haskell's Chronology of the World, that Lima was destroyed by an earthquake in October, 1746. This I think could not have been the *city* of Lima, but the sea-port of the city, called Callao. For the most celebrated and central part of the city of Lima is the Palace Square, on one side of which then stood a very ancient, long, one-story, wooden building, where the city officers transacted their business. I was frequently told that this building was the palace or dwelling-place of the Spanish adventurer, Pizarro, after his conquest of Peru. If this statement was correct, then it will be allowed that Pizarro occupied it long before the earthquake in 1746. Hence that part of the city could not have been destroyed. But her seaport, called Callao, was.

The city of Lima is situated about six miles in the interior from her seaport, Callao, and is about seven hundred feet above the level of the sea, on an inclined plane. While I was there in 1822–3, seventy-seven years after the earthquake, I frequently visited the place to view the massive piles of brick, from about eighteen inches under water to as far down as I could see, that composed the buildings and walls of the place at the time of the earthquake. I was told that a Spanish frigate was lying moored in the harbor at the time, and after its destruction by the earthquake she was found three miles inland, about half way from the port of Callao to the city of Lima, some three hundred and fifty feet above the level of the sea. Allowing this statement to be true, and I never heard any one attempt to disprove it, then it must have been the earthquake that caused the earth first to rise under the sea, causing the body of water between it and the land to rush on with such force that the frigate was carried up the inclined plane, and when the water receded she was left some three miles from the sea-shore.

From all appearances, Callao was overflowed by the sea, for its ruins lie nearly on a level with the sea, and are under a lake of water separated from the ocean by a sand-bar. I have heard, and also observed, that the sea does not rise and fall here, at stated periods, as it does in almost all other harbors and places. Hence it is clear that the body of water which covers the ruins of Callao, is not furnished from the sea.

Another singular curiosity in this place was the cemetery, about five miles out of the city, which was different from anything I had ever seen. At the entrance was the church with the cross. Part of the way round the cemetery was double-walled. The space or passway between these walls appeared to be about forty feet wide. The walls were about eight feet high and seven thick, with three rows of cells where they deposited the dead. These were rented to those who could afford to deposit their dead in this style, for six months or any length of time. Some of these cells were bricked up, and others had iron doors that were locked. The unoccupied ones were open for rent. In the center, between the walls, were deep vaults covered with iron gratings, in which we could see dead bodies all tumbled together without order. I learned that when the six months, or whatever time the cells were rented for, closed, the bodies were taken out and pitched into the vaults in the center. Thus they could accommodate others. In another department, the dead were buried underground in rows. Near by the church was a large circular vault, with a steeple-top covering, resting on pillars several feet above the vault. This was another burying-place. On looking over the railing placed around it to prevent the living from falling in, the sight was most revolting. Some stood erect, others with their heads downward, and in every imaginable position, just as they happened to fall from the hand-barrow, with their ragged, unclean clothing on in which they died. These of course were the abject poor, whose friends were unable to pay rent for a burying-place underground or in one of the white-washed cells in the walls. The dead soldiers were carried out of the forts and dumped in here with little ceremony. The air is so salubrious there that no offensive smell arises from these dead bodies. They literally waste away and dry up.

# Chapter Thirteen.

*Mint—Stamping Coin—Catholic Churches and Feasts
—How to Remember God—Spanish Inquisition—
Voyage to Truxillo—Sell the Chatsworth—Mode of
Smuggling—Spanish Horses—Indian Method of
Smuggling—Deliver up the Chatsworth—Passage to
Callao—Trouble with the Captain—Dinner Party.*

WE then visited the Peruvians' mint, to see them
make and stamp their coin. In the center of their
stamping-room was a pit about six feet deep, and
about five in diameter. In the centre of the bottom of this was the foundation in which was the
"lower pintle" of the standard on which the money
was laid or held to be stamped. The stamping
machine was fashioned at the top like a common
capstan, with holes pierced through to receive two
long levers, or bars, over twenty feet long, with a
man stationed at each end of the bar. From the
head of the capstan it tapered down to a point, on
which was fixed the stamp. One man in the pit
with a half bushel of silver pieces to be stamped
for half-dollars or quarters, as the case may be,
holds each piece between his thumb and fore-finger
on the bottom pintle. The stamp was on the bottom of the capstan, about one foot above his
fingers. The men would lay hold of the end of
the capstan bars and whirl the capstan half way
round, when it would stamp the silver with a crash,
and fly back with a spring to its place, where the
four men would seize the bars again and whirl it
back, and another piece was coined. In this way

they stamp several pieces in a minute. We were told that the stamp came down every time with about seven tons' weight. The stamp was now prepared to coin sixpences. I watched the man in the pit to see how he could hold these small pieces within as it were a hair's breadth of the stamp which came down with seven tons' weight several times a minute, or about as fast as he could place the uncoined pieces under the stamp. The man seemed to be perfectly at home in this business, and accomplished his work with as much ease as a seamstress would stitch a garment. "Because he was used to it," says one. But if he had lost his thumb and finger before he got used to it, how then? The wonder to me was how a man could get used to such a hazardous business without getting his fingers pinched.

These Peruvians were Roman Catholics, and had some sixty Catholic churches within the walls of their city, mostly built of stone and brick. Many of them were very costly, covering *acres of ground*, with beautiful gardens in the center plots, with so many apartments that it was necessary for strangers to employ a guide to prevent losing their way. Most splendid paintings and costly images of the saints could be seen in various apartments, with living beings kneeling before them, crossing themselves, and moving their lips as in the act of prayer. In many of their churches, particularly the place assigned for public worship, the supporting columns sustaining the heavy arched work were plated with silver. Their richly ornamented altars were studded with large golden horns. But the Patriots were stripping off the gold and silver, and coining it in their mint to pay off their armies.

Their feast days were numerous. They had

Saints' and All-Saints' days; but the most imposing feast that I witnessed, in the church, was the
imitation of Jesus and his disciples at the last
passover and supper. A large table near the center of the church might be seen loaded with silver
dishes, pitchers, silver plates, knives, forks, &c.
Then Jesus and the twelve apostles, as large as
life, were all seated in order around the table, gor-
geously dressed with silver steeple-top caps on
their heads. The people as they crowded in dropped upon their knees all around them, apparently
awe-struck with the imposing sight. While they
were worshiping in their accustomed attitude, the
officers were in pursuit of us Protestant strangers,
requesting us also to kneel. We were so anxious
to see how this feast was conducted that we kept
moving and changing our position, until so closely
pursued and required to kneel, that we passed out,
and visited other churches, which were also open
on this occasion.

Some of their churches are furnished with many
bells, and when occasion requires them all to be
rung at once, hardly anything else can be heard.
After my arrival in the city I was standing in the
street conversing with friends, when the bells began to strike a slow, funeral tone; all business
ceased in a moment. Carriages and all moving
vehicles stopped. Men, women and children, no
matter what were their engagements, or how interesting their conversation, ceased to speak. Men
on horseback dismount, and every man, with his
head uncovered, respectfully waits for one or two
minutes, when the solemn tone of the bells changes
to a joyous ringing, then business of all kinds was
resumed, and the people moved on again with their
heads covered as they were before the bells struck.

This was at the setting of the sun. I asked my Spanish friend (who appeared to be very devout during the ceremony) the meaning of this. "Why," said he, "that all the people may *remember God* at the close of the day." I thought, surely this was a most respectful ceremony, worthy of universal imitation. Yet after all, this people were living in continual violation of the second commandment of God. Their priests did not hesitate to visit gambling-rooms and play billiards on Sunday, as on other days.

When the Roman Catholics suppressed the Inquisition, there was a noted one in the city of Lima which occupied a large space of ground. The Peruvians not only suppressed this diabolical institution at that time, but they demolished the huge pile of buildings, and left it in a heap of ruins, except one of the court-rooms, where the implements of torture had been arranged for the cruel work of torturing heretics. We saw a number of places where the walls had been broken away in this room, and were told that these places were where the implements of torture had been removed. Some old-fashioned lead inkstands on the desks were left by the mob. We were also shown some of the dismal dungeons that were beneath the ruins under ground. In one corner we noticed a bed of earth stoned up a few feet above the wet ground for the prisoners' bed. We were pointed also to some recesses that were still standing. These were to torture heretics, and built just large enough for a person to stand upright with his hands down, and a door fastened against him—a position that a person could live in but a very short time. But we forbear to speak further at this time of these so-called Christian institutions of the Roman Catholic church, instituted and nourished for centuries by the Papacy, granting power to her bishops and priests to punish and put to death what they called heretics, by all kinds of torture that fiends in human shape could invent.

We took on board a number of passengers at Callao, to land in Truxillo, in latitude 8° south. Here we sold the Chatsworth for ten thousand dollars to a Spanish merchant. Seven thousand dollars were in lumps and pieces of Platapena, and virgin silver to be paid here. As this, and all gold and silver coin, was prohibited from exporta tion by the Peruvian government, various measures were invented by foreigners and their merchants to convey their specie on board their vessels. As my agreement was that the silver should be delivered to me outside of the breakers on board the C., when the time arrived for me to leave for Lima, I asked how this money was to be delivered. Said the merchant, "It will come off to you about midnight to-night." "But how?" said I. "We will send it to you by some Indians," (aborigines). I asked if the money was to be counted out to me before I left the shore, that I might identify the same, and the number of pieces as per invoice rendered, when brought off to me. The merchant replied that he had put the amount of silver specified in the invoice, into the hands of several Indians many weeks before, subject to his order. Said I, "What did they do with it?" "O, they buried it up in the ground somewhere." "Do you know where?" "No." "What security have you from them that they will keep it for you?" "None," said he. "How do you know that they will deliver it all to me to-night?" Said he, "I have employed them a great while, and put into their hands thousands of dollars in this way, and paid them well for their labor when they delivered what I entrusted them with, and there has never been any failure on their part, and I fear none. They are the most honest people in the world, particularly where they live separate by themselves."

The Chatsworth lay some two miles from shore. The breakers in-shore of us were too dangerous for ships' boats to pass. The government used a large boat manned with sixteen oars, by Indians trained for the business, and when occasion required her to pass out to the shipping, or return back through these dangerous breakings of the sea, another company of Indians standing on the shore, as soon as the boat approaches the breakers on her way out, and they discover the sea rising to break over her, would make a most hideous yell! The boatmen would instantly head their boat for the breakers, and take a position with their oars to obey the helsmman's orders to keep their boat headed directly to the sea, while she was being violently tossed by the breakers; and then they would pull for life to clear the sand-bar before another sea came. When the boat was returning, and they heard the watchmen's yell, the helmsman would steer the boat square before the rolling breakers, the oarsmen pulling with all their strength. After two or three struggles, the danger was passed. The watchmen on the shore would raise a mighty, joyous shout, joined by the boatmen, announcing to all around, "All's well!"

The people here, and in other places on the coast, have another kind of boats they call "caballos," or horses, on which they ride as people do on horseback. These horses are made of the common tall flags, or rushes, securely lashed together, about ten feet long, the large part about two feet in diameter, tapering to two inches at the small end. This end they turned up like the head of a boat to stand prominent out of the water which cuts through the sea. The large part is to ride on. None but those that were well trained could ride this kind of horses, or keep them right side up but a few moments at a time. The people, especially the Indians, would move through the water in a masterly manner, even much faster than a common boat, with a double paddle, or the paddle blade fitted at both ends, seated as on horseback. It was interesting to see them paddle alternately on each side for the breakers, and when about to pass them, lie down on their horse while the breakers washed over them, and then paddle clear before the next one came. I was told that this kind of horses was of great importance on some parts of the coast, where the breakers would not admit a ship's boat to approach. Communications and dispatches were there made through the medium of these caballos, or Spanish horses.

The Indians that were to convey the Platapena to us had to pass through this dangerous place in the dark night, while their watchmen on the shore were waiting in suspense and deep anxiety their safe return. When we set the watch at night, I requested my brother, the chief mate, to be on deck until midnight, and if he saw any one floating on the water, approaching us, to call me up. About midnight he called me, saying, "There are two men alongside, sitting in the water!" We lowered down empty water-buckets, and a lighted lantern, when the Indians unfastened the bags of silver that were securely hung with lines underneath their caballos, and placed them in the buckets for us to haul up on deck. When it was all safely aboard they seemed very much pleased at the accomplishment of the job. It appeared to me at that season of the night about an impossibility for them to pass through those dangerous breakers. We gave them some refreshment as they sat on their water-horses, for they dared not leave them, but soon moved away as fast as possible to relieve their waiting comrades on the shore, and to receive the compensation that their employer had promised them. As their employer had declared, every particle was delivered to me as per invoice.

I now delivered up the Chatsworth to the purchaser, took leave of my officers and crew, my brother succeeding me in the command of the C., the second officer succeeding him as chief mate, to remain in the employ of the new owners to trade in the Pacific Ocean. I then took passage to Lima on board a Peruvian schooner. I was aware that I was risking much in the hands of this stranger and his crew, who might think that the large amount of money placed in their hands was of more value to them than my life; but I had no other means of conveyance to Lima. I endeavored to manifest no fear, nor lack of confidence in him as a gentleman, but watched him very closely, and endeavored to keep the run of his vessel, and course steered. We anchored in Callao Bay after a passage of seven days. Here he refused to deliver me the seven thousand dollars in silver, which I had placed in his care until our arrival at Callao, alleging that the government of Peru did not allow him to deliver it to me. This he well

understood when I placed it in his care to deliver
it to me on our arrival at Callao. He also knew
that if he reported any specie on board belonging
to a foreigner, no matter how honestly he came by
it, the government would seize it for their own
use. As the matter stood he would neither let me
have it nor let the government know there was
any silver on board his vessel. He then immediately cleared for another country, weighed his anchor and proceeded to sea. I soon learned of his
dishonest and wicked intentions. I was at that time
on board of a New Bedford whale-ship, and saw
him under way. Capt. H. manned his whale-boat,
and we soon overtook him. He still refused to
deliver me the silver, until he saw that resistance
was vain. He then very reluctantly allowed me
to receive it, and continued on his voyage. We
transferred the silver to the United States ship
Franklin, 74, Commodore Stewart commanding, on
deposit until we were ready for sea, as other
Americans had to do for safe keeping.

Mr. Swinegar, our Peruvian merchant, gave a
large dinner-party to the captains and supercargoes of the American vessels, and a number of the
officers of the American Squadron, Feb. 22, in
honor of Gen. Washington's birth-day. As I was
the only person at the table that had decided not
to drink wine or strong drink because of its intoxicating qualities, Mr. S. stated to some of his
friends with him at the table that he would influence me to drink wine with him. He filled his
glass and challenged me to drink a glass of wine
with him. I responded by filling my glass with
water! He refused to drink unless I filled with
wine. I said, "Mr Swinegar, I cannot do so,
for I have fully decided never to drink wine."

By this time the company were all looking at us. Mr. S. still waited for me to fill my glass with wine. Several urged me to comply with his request. One of the lieutenants of the squadron, some distance down the table, said, "Bates, surely you will not object to take a glass of wine with Mr. Swinegar." I replied that I could not do it. I felt embarrassed and sorry that such a cheerful company should be so intent on my drinking a glass of wine as almost to forget the good dinner that was before them. Mr. S. seeing that I would not be prevailed on to drink wine, pressed me no further.

At that time my deep convictions with respect to smoking cigars enabled me to decide also that from and after that evening I would never smoke another cigar, or smoke tobacco in any way. This victory raised my feelings and elevated my mind above the fog of tobacco-smoke, which had to a considerable extent beclouded my mind, and freed me from an idol which I had learned to worship among sailors.

## Chapter Fourteen.

*Money Matters—Highway Robbers—Searching Ships for Specie—A Lieutenant Shot—Sail for Home— Tobacco—Serious Reflections—Pass Cape Horn— Equator—North Star—Violent Gale—A Sudden Change of Wind—Desperate Position—Joyous Sight of Land—Vineyard Sound—Arrival in Boston— At Home—Another Voyage—Off the Capes of Virginia—Outward Bound.*

As we received specie in payment for our cargoes of goods, and this as well as gold and silver was prohibited by the government from exportation, we were necessarily subjected to many inconveniences and losses in securing returns for our owners. Many of the captains trading in the Pacific were also supercargoes. Being obliged to transact our business at two custom-houses, Callao and Lima, six miles apart, it became necessary to have our own horses to pass between the two places. When returning to Callao, we generally loaded our persons with as much specie in dollars and doubloons as were deemed prudent to risk, in the bottoms of our boots and waist-belts, buckled around us under our dress. We did this because we were liable to be robbed on the way, and also because we were subjected to an examination by custom-house officers before embarking to our ships in the harbor. We generally distributed portions of it among our boat's crew until we got on board our vessels, and then deposited it for safe-keeping on board one of our war-ships, paying the commander one per cent. for deposit.

Our government officers in this way received and protected our property because it was ours. Two of my boat's crew were examined one day as I was about to embark, and ordered to the custom-house. I followed them. They had some two hundred dollars on their persons. The two officers who stopped the men, after counting the sum, wished to know how much I would give them if they would let the sailors pass without reporting the matter to the custom-house. "One doubloon," said I. "No," said they, "we will divide with you." I replied, "If you will not accept my offer, go and make your report and let the government take it all, if they will." They attempted to show me that my proceedings had been unlawful, and that I would have trouble. I gave them to understand that I should only have to lose my money, but they, something more, for offering to divide with me and appropriate the divided part to themselves. They concluded finally to return me all the money, except the doubloon I offered them. These men never troubled me when I was embarking after that. One day a small party of men were passing down with money, when a party of armed men on horseback rushed out upon them and demanded their money, and required them to strip off their clothing to be sure of getting all they had. After securing all, they fled to the mountains.

The ship Friendship, of Salem, Mass., was reported as having eleven thousand dollars on board, after having sold her cargo in Lima. The government sent a company of soldiers with officers of the custom-house to take possession of her. They made diligent search, but found none; still they kept charge of the ship for many days, and gave them much trouble. The money was there, stowed away so snugly between the "carlings" overhead in the cabin, where the ceiling was finished and painted, that one would not have suspected money could be there. After the government gave up the ship to the supercargo again, he took out the money and transported it to the United States ship Franklin, 74. Soon after this, a Boston ship was taken possession of in the harbor, in the night, and it was several months before the captain, who pursued them, recovered and brought her back.

In conversation one day with one of the Peruvian officers, who was boasting of the independence of Peru, and their freedom from the Spanish government, he was asked what his view of freedom was. "Why," said he, "if you have a good horse and I want him, if I am stronger than you, I'll take the horse!" It rather seemed that others, when they wanted our money and ships, were of the same opinion.

While we were here, a lieutenant in the Peruvian Patriot army absconded and joined their enemy. He was taken, tried, and condemned to be shot without the walls of the city of Lima. This was a manner of taking life which I had never witnessed. To gratify my curiosity I passed on with the vast multitude of citizens, and took my position on the top of the city wall, very near the place where the condemned man was seated, who was attended by a Catholic priest. A cap was soon drawn over his eyes. In front of him military officers were drilling and marshaling their troops, until about the appointed hour for him to be shot, when they were all arranged in columns, the front ranks about twenty yards from the condemned. At the word of command some six men advanced from the ranks within a few yards of the poor man, and leveled their muskets at his head. Again at the word of command they fired. His head dropped on his shoulder seemingly as quick as if it had been severed by a cleaver. He seemed to die without a struggle. The squadron army then wheeled away with the deafening sound of martial music. The dead man was carried away to his long home. The excitement of the morning was past. I soon found myself almost solitary amid the vast concourse of citizens, returning slowly to their places of abode, resolving in my mind that I never would voluntarily go again to see another man shot.

I had now been in the Pacific Ocean about fourteen months, and was closing my business and preparing to return to the United States. The ship Candace, Captain F. Burtody, was about to sail for Boston, Mass., in which ship I engaged my passage.

Captain B. and myself mutually agreed, when the Candace weighed her anchor, that we would from that hour cease chewing tobacco. About the last week of November, 1823, all hands were called to weigh anchor. None but those who experience these feelings can tell the thrill that fills every soul, from the captain to the cabin-boy, when the order is given to "Weigh anchor for home." New life, with energy and strength, seems to actuate all on board. The hardy sailors clinch their hand-spikes, the windlass begins to roll and bring the watery cable on deck. The gallant ship, seemingly participating with her joyous crew, advances step by step to her anchor, until the officer cries out, "Hold! the cable is a-peak!" The top-sails are now loosed, sheeted home, and hoisted to the mast-head, and the yards are braced to cant the ship's head out of the harbor. The windlass is now manned again. The ship is soon up with her anchor. A few more turns of the windlass, and the anchor breaks its hold, and the gallant ship is free. The anchor is up and swung to the cat-head, and the ship's sails fill with the freshening gale. The sailors cry, "We are homeward bound." The feelings of the sailors still left in the harbor are something like these: "That ship has weighed her anchor, and is standing out of the harbor, bound for home. Success to them. I wish we were going too." No matter how many seas there are to pass, or how many storms to meet, or how far from home, the joyous feeling still vibrates in every heart—

" Home, home, sweet home. Our anchor's weighed
for home !"

Our good ship now lay by with her main-top-
sail to the mast, until the boat came alongside from
the commodore with our specie and silver, which
Captain B. and myself had gained by trading.
When this was all safe on board, all sail was made
on the ship. It was now night, and we were passing our last landmark, (St. Lorenzo), and putting
out for a long voyage of eight thousand and five
hundred miles. The steward reported supper rea
dy. " Here goes my tobacco, Bates," said Captain B., taking it from his mouth and casting it
overboard. " And here goes mine, too," said I,
and that was the last that has ever polluted my
lips. But Captain B. failed to overcome, and labored hard with me to keep him company. I was
now free from all distilled spirits, wine and tobacco.
Step by step I had gained this victory—nature
never required either. I never used the articles,
except to keep company with my associates. How
many millions have been ruined by such debasing
and ruinous habits. How much more like a human
being I felt when I had gained the mastery in
these things and overcome them all. I was also
making great efforts to conquer myself of another
crying sin, which I had learned of wicked sailors.
That was the habit of using profane language. My
father had been a praying man from the time I
had any knowledge of him. My mother embraced
religion when I was about twelve years old. I
never dared, even after I was married, to speak
irreverently of God in the presence of my father.
As he had endeavored to train me in the way I
should go, I knew the way, but the checkered
scenes of the previous sixteen years of my life had

thrown me from the track which I was endeavoring now to regain. On our voyage from Cape Horn into the Pacific, I tried hard to break myself of the evil habit of swearing, and said to my brother that he must not swear, nor allow the sailors to, for I should not permit it. As I had plenty of leisure now, I read much of my time, and very often, especially on Sundays, many chapters in the Bible. By so doing I concluded that I was *making myself* a tolerably good Christian.

Our good ship continued to gain onward, and on reaching Cape Horn, we encountered a driving storm; but the wind was fair to go eastward, so that in forty-eight hours we were safely round the Horn in the south Atlantic Ocean, steering northward for home. As we approached the equator, some of the well-known stars in the northern hemisphere began to make their appearance—particularly the "Pointers," that always direct the wandering mariner to the north star. As our good Candace still continued to urge her way from the southern ocean to the equator, the "Pointers" indicated that the north star was at the northern horizon.

The night was clear, the watch on deck were all awaiting the appearance of the north star. At length it was seen just breaking from the mist of the northern horizon, apparently four or five feet aobve the surface of the ocean. The first sight of this well-known star to the mariners, ascending from the Southern Ocean, is often more cheering to their hearts than twenty-four hours of fair wind. If we had no way to ascertain our latitude by nautical instruments, we should know by the foregoing appearance of this star, that we were at least one hundred and twenty miles north of the equator. As our good Queen Candace advanced in her onward course into the Northern Ocean, staggering under the freshening gale from the N. E. trades, our hearts were cheered night after night on seeing the very same star rising still higher and higher in the northern heavens—an unmistakable sign that we were rapidly advancing northward, nearer, and still nearer home.

I have heard it stated of the Portugese sailors, that when their ships were returning on their homeward voyages from South America to Portugal, as soon as they saw the north star above the northern horizon, it was the time and place where they settled with, and paid off their ships' crews up to that date.

We had now passed to the windward of the West India Islands, away from the influence of the N. E. trade-winds, and were drawing into the dreaded Gulf Stream on the southern coast of North America, scudding onward before a rapidly increasing S. E. gale, appearing very much like the one of 1818, which I had experienced on board the ship Frances, before referred to. Captain B. and myself brought to remembrance our former experience in such trying times, and the dangerous position ships are placed in at meeting an instantaneous change of wind in such driving storms, often rendering them unmanageable, especially in and about this stream.

The Candace was in good ballast trim, and perhaps as well prepared to contend with such a storm as almost any other ship. She was now scudding before the terrific gale under a reefed foresail, and main-top-sail. As the dark night set in, the elements seemed in fearful commotion. The important work with officers and helmsmen now was to

keep the ship dead, or directly before the mountainous seas. As Captain B. had stationed himself on the quarter-deck, to give all necessary
orders respecting the management of the ship during the violence of the storm, and my confidence
being unshaken in his nautical skill, I concluded
to go below and rest if I could, and like other
passengers, be out of the way.

The rain was falling fast, and about midnight
I heard a fearful cry, "The ship's aback!" another cry to the helmsman, and another for all
hands on deck! I rushed to the cabin gangway,
where I saw that what we had most dreaded had
come, viz., the raging gale from the S. E. had
ceased all of a sudden, and was now raging from
the opposite quarter. As soon as I got on deck
I saw the storm-sails were pressing against the
mast, and the ship's head was paying round westward against the awful mountainous seas which
seemed almost to rush over us from the south, and
cause our immediate destruction. Captain B., with
all the ship's company that could be seen, were
hauling with all their strength on the starboard
main-braces. Seeing the imminent danger we
were in, without stopping to think that I was only a
passenger, I cried out at the top of my voice, "Let
go the starboard main-braces, and come over on
this side of the ship and haul in the larboard main-
braces!" Captain B. had supposed that the ship
would obey her helm, and pay her head off to the
eastward. When my shouting arrested his attention he saw that the ship's head was moving the
opposite way. They then let go the starboard
braces and crowded over and hauled in the larboard braces. The sails filled, and the ship was
once more under good headway, though in a most

dangerous position from the awful sea on her lee-beam. Before her sails filled she had lost her headway, and but just escaped being overwhelmed with a rushing sea, which gave her the appearance of going down stern foremost. How she escaped being engulfed with this sea was beyond our wisdom to discern. After order was restored, I apologized to the captain for assuming to take the command of his ship, and was cheerfully and freely forgiven.

With the passing of the gale we crossed the Gulf, and sounded in deep water on the coast. We now realized that it was mid-winter. At length the joyful cry was raised, "*Land Ho!*" It proved to be Block Island, R. I. Joyful sight indeed to see our own native land within forty miles of home, looming in the distance. Yes, to see any land after watching sky and water for three long months, was a great relief. But here comes a pilot-boat. "Where are you from?" "Pacific Ocean." "Where are you bound?" "To Boston." "Will you take a pilot through the Vineyard Sound? It's always the safest way in the winter season." "Yes, come alongside." In a few minutes more the pilot has full charge of the ship, bearing down for the Vineyard Sound. The pilot-boat then steers out to sea to meet another homeward-bound ship. The next thing is, "What's the news in the States, pilot?" "What's the news from Europe?" "What's the state of the world?" "Who's to be our next President?" &c., &c. Hardly waiting for an answer, "Have you any newspapers?" "Yes, but they are not the last." "No matter, they will be new to us; it's a long time since we have heard anything from the land of the living."

At night we cast our anchor in Holmes' Hole,

a spacious harbor in the Vineyard for ships wind-bound for Boston. A number of boats were soon alongside. From the many baskets of various kinds of pies, fried cakes, apples, &c., &c., that these people presented on our decks, we were led to suppose that the good people on shore divined that we were very hungry for their good things. Indeed, we feasted for a little while. Besides these, they were well stocked with large baskets of yarn stockings, mittens, &c. A supply of these, also, was very acceptable at this cold season. On leaving the ship in the evening, there was quite a stir among the boatmen to find their baskets. One man was looking round in the cabin passage, inquiring of his neighbor John if he had seen anything of his *knitting work?* What, thought I, do men knit stockings here? Do they carry their knitting work about with them? I soon learned that it was his basket of stockings which he called his "knitting work." The wind favored us, and we were soon passing around Cape Cod into Massachusetts Bay, and the next day anchored off the city of Boston, somewhere about the 20th of February, 1824, after a passage of three months from Callao Bay.

Our voyage was a very profitable one, but unfortunately one of the two owners failed during the voyage, which cost much time and expense before a settlement was accomplished.

Fifty-five miles by stage, and I was once more at home. A little blue-eyed girl of sixteen months, whom I had never seen, was here waiting with her mother to greet me, and welcome me once more to our comfortable and joyous fireside. As I had been absent from home over two years, I designed to enjoy the society of my family and friends for a little season. After a few months, however, I engaged myself to go another voyage to South America, or anywhere I could find business profitable. A new brig was now launched, rigged and fitted to our liking, named the Empress, of New Bedford. Part of an assorted cargo was received on board in New Bedford. From thence we sailed about the 15th of August, 1824, for Richmond, Va., to finish our lading with flour for Rio Janeiro and a market.

After finishing our lading in Richmond, we passed down James River and anchored in Hampton Roads, to procure our armament in Norfolk. Finding no cannon mounted, we proceeded on our voyage without. It is not as necessary now for merchantmen to carry guns as it was then, on account of piratical vessels. September 5th we discharged our pilot off Cape Henry Lighthouse, and shaped our course east southerly, to meet the N. E. trades.

From the time I resolved to drink no more wine (in 1822), I had occasionally drank beer and cider. But now on weighing anchor from Hampton Roads I decided from henceforth to drink neither ale, porter, beer, nor cider of any description.

My prospect for making a profitable and successful voyage was now more flattering than my last, for I now owned a part of the Empress and her cargo, and had the confidence of my partners to sell and purchase cargoes as often as it would prove to our advantage, and use my judgment about going to what part of the world I pleased. But with all these many advantages to get riches, I felt sad and homesick. I had provided myself with a number of what I called interesting books, to read in my leisure hours. My wife thought there were more novels and romances than was necessary. In packing my trunk of books, she placed a pocket New Testament, unknown to me, on the top of them. On opening this trunk to find some books to interest me, I took up the New Testament, and found in the opening page the following interesting piece of poetry, by Mrs. Hemans, placed there to arrest my attention:

Leaves have their time to fall,
  And flowers to wither at the north wind's breath,
And stars to set—but all,
  Thou hast *all* seasons for thine own, O Death!

Day is for mortal care,
  Eve for glad meetings round the joyous hearth,
Night, for the dreams of sleep, the voice of prayer,
  But all for thee, thou mightiest of the earth.

Youth and the opening rose
  May look like things too glorious for decay,
And smile at thee—but thou art not of those
  That wait the ripen'd bloom to seize their prey.

We know when moons shall wane,
  When summer birds from far shall cross the sea,
When autumn's hue shall tinge the golden grain,
  But who shall teach us when to look for thee?

Is it when spring's first gale
  Comes forth to whisper where the violets lie?
Is it when roses in our path grow pale?
  They have one season—*all* are ours to die!

Thou art where billows foam,
  Thou art where music melts upon the air;
Thou art around us in our peaceful home,
  And the world calls us forth—and thou art there.

# Chapter Fifteen.

*Conviction for Sin—Sickness and Death of a Sailor—
Funeral at Sea—Prayer—Covenant with God—A
Dream—Arrival at Pernambuco—Its Appearance—
Landing a North American Lady—Wine at a Din-
ner Party—Sell my Cargo—Another Voyage—Re-
ligious Views—Whaling—Brazilian Flour—Arrive
at St. Catherine's—Also Paraiba—Sell my Cargo—
Third Voyage.*

THE lines mentioned in the last chapter did arrest my attention. I read them again and again.
My interest for reading novels and romances
ceased from that hour. Among the many books,
I selected Doddridge's Rise and Progress of Religion in the Soul. This and the Bible now interested me more than all other books.

Christopher Christopherson, of Norway, one of
my crew, was taken down sick soon after our departure from Cape Henry. Nothing in our medicine chest availed to relieve him. His case appeared more and more doubtful. The first verse
of The Hour of Death, particularly the fourth
line, was almost continually in my mind :—

"Thou hast all seasons for thine own, O death!"

I longed to be a Christian ; but the pride of my
heart and the vain allurements of the wicked world,
still held me with a mighty grasp. I suffered intensely in my mind before I decided to pray. It
seemed as though I had delayed this work too
long. I was also afraid that my officers and men
would learn that I was under conviction. Fur-

thermore, I had no secret place to pray. When I looked back on some of the incidents in my past life, how God had interposed his arm to save me, when death was staring me in the face again and again, and how soon I had forgotten all his mercies, I felt that I must yield. Finally I decided to try the strength of prayer, and confess all my sins. I opened the "run scuttle" under the dining table, where I prepared a place so that I might be out of the sight of my officers, if they should have occasion to enter the cabin during my prayer season. The first time I bowed the knee here in prayer, it seemed to me that the hair on my head was *standing out straight*, for presuming to open my mouth in prayer to the great and holy God. But I determined to persevere until I found pardon and peace for my troubled mind. I had no Christian friend at hand to tell me how, or how long I must be convicted before conversion. But I remembered when I was a lad, during the great reformation of 1807, in New Bedford and Fairhaven, of hearing the converts, when relating their experience, say that they had been sorrowing for sin two and three weeks, when the Lord spake peace to their minds. It seemed to me that my case would be something similar.

A fortnight passed, and no light beamed on my mind. One week more, and still my mind was like the troubled sea. About this time I was walking the deck in the night, and was strongly tempted to jump overboard and put an end to myself. I thought this was a temptation of the Devil, and immediately left the deck, and did not allow myself to go out of my cabin again until the morning.

Christopher was very sick and failing. It occurred to me that if he should die, I should be doubly earnest about my salvation. I now removed him into the cabin, and placed him in a berth next my own, where I could give him more attention, and charged the officers as they waited upon him during their night watch, to call me if they saw any change in him. I awoke in the morning soon after daylight. My first thought was, How is Christopher? I reached over his berth and placed my hand on his forehead; it felt cold. He was dead. I called the officer of the morning watch, "Why, Mr. Haffards!" said I, "Christopher *is dead!* Why did you fail to call me?" Said Mr. H., "I was down to him about half an hour ago, and gave him his medicine, and saw no alteration then." Poor C. was now laid out on the quarter-deck, and finally sewed up in a hammock with a heavy bag of sand at his feet. After we had settled on the time to bury him, I was most seriously troubled in relation to my duty. I felt that I was a sinner in the sight of God, and dare not attempt to pray in public. And yet I could not consent to plunge the poor fellow into the ocean without some religious ceremony over him. While I was resolving in my mind what I should do, the steward asked me if I would not like to have a Church of England Prayer Book. "Yes," said I, "have you got one?" "Yes sir." "Bring it to me, will you?"

It was just the book I wanted, for when I was in the British service, I had heard the ship's clerk read prayers out of such a book when our sailors were buried. But this was the first burial at sea that ever occurred under my command.

I opened the book and found a suitable prayer for the occasion. A plank was prepared, with one end over the side of the vessel, on which his

body was laid, with his feet toward the sea, so that
by raising the other end of the plank, the body
would slide into the ocean feet foremost. All but the
helmsman stood around poor Christopher, to take
their final leave of him, and commit his body to the
deep as soon as the order should be given. The
idea of attempting to perform religious service
over the dead, while in an unconverted state,
troubled me much. I had requested the chief
mate to call me when he had made the preparation, and retired below. When the officer reported all ready, I came up trembling, with the book
open in my hand. The crew respectfully uncovered their heads. As I began to read, my voice
faltered, and I was so unmanned I found it difficult to read distinctly. I felt indeed that I was a
sinner before God. When I finished the last sen-
tence, I waved my hand to tip the plank, and
turned for the cabin. As I passed down the gangway, I heard poor Christopher plunge into the sea.
I passed down into my praying place and vented
my feelings in prayer for the forgiveness of all my
sins, and those of the poor fellow that was sinking
lower and lower beneath the rolling waves.

This was the 30th of September, twenty-six
days from the capes of Virginia. From thence I
felt a sinking into the will of God, resolving hence-
forward to renounce the unfruitful works of the
enemy, and seek carefully for eternal life. I believe now that all my sins were forgiven about that
time. Then I also made the following covenant
with God, which I found in Doddrige's Rise and
Progress of Religion in the Soul:

A SOLEMN COVENANT WITH GOD.

" Eternal and ever-blessed God : I desire to present myself before thee with the deepest humiliation and abasement of soul. Sensible how unworthy such a sinful worm is to appear before the Holy Majesty of Heaven, the King of kings and Lord of lords, . . . I come therefore acknowledging myself to have been a great offender. Smiting on my breast and saying with the humble publican, 'God be merciful to me a sinner,' . . . this day do I with the utmost solemnity surrender myself to thee. I renounce all former lords that have had dominion over me, and I consecrate to thee all that I am, and all that I have. . . . Use me, O Lord, I beseech thee, as an instrument of thy service, number me among thy peculiar people. Let me be washed in the blood of thy dear Son. To whom, with thee, O Father, be everlasting praises ascribed, by all the millions who are thus saved by thee. Amen."

Done on board the Brig Empress, of New Bedford, at sea, October 4, 1824, in Latitude 19° 50' north, and Longitude 34° 50' west, bound to the Brazils.

Jos. Bates, Jr.

I wish that I could always have the resignation to the will of God that I felt the morning that I signed this covenant. Yet I could not believe then, nor for many months after this, that I had any other feelings than a deep conviction for sin. I am satisfied that I have not always regarded this covenant in the solemn light in which I now understand it. But I am very glad I made it, and that God has still spared my life to allow me yet to do all that I therein covenanted to do.

After signing the afore-mentioned covenant, I had a remarkable dream respecting some commuications from the post-office. One appeared to be a written roll of paper, the other a long letter commencing with spaces as follows:

EXAMINE!     EXAMINE!     EXAMINE!

EXPERIENCE!     EXPERIENCE!     EXPERIENCE!

YOURSELF!     YOURSELF!     YOURSELF!

Then followed a long letter commencing with religious instruction, closely written, of which I read a few lines, when I awoke. I then wrote it on paper and filed it with other papers, but it is now missing. There was much more which I have forgotten, but I believe the dream, thus peculiarly set forth on paper, was to convince me that my sins were forgiven. But I failed to see it then, because I had conceived that God would manifest himself in such a manner that I should never doubt my conversion afterwards. I had not then learned the simplicity of God's gracious work on the sinner's heart.

It would have been a great relief to me if I could have been released from the heavy responsibilities of my trading voyage, considering how my mind was then exercised. But our voyage continued, and we arrived at Pernambuco, October 30th. There we found the state of commerce was very far from prosperous in relation to our voyage. But we were now at the best market for selling; we therefore disposed of our cargo. I was much disappointed also in not finding one professor of religion to converse with, among the many thousands of people here, but I was fully resolved to persevere for a full and free salvation.

Pernambuco, in Brazil, is situated on the border of the sea. On approaching it from the ocean, it has a commanding and beautiful appearance. But the shipping have to anchor in the open sea some distance from the land, and on account of the heavy surf on the shore, it is difficult getting safe to land.

Captain Barret, from Nantucket, Mass., arrived at this port soon after us. Concluding to sell here also, he sent his boat off to bring his wife on shore. As the boat with Mrs. B. was drawing in with the shore, quite a number of us assembled near the landing place with Captain B. to receive her. A number of black slaves were also waiting, whose business it was to wade out to the boats and shoulder freight and passengers, and if possible bear them safely through the breakers to the landing. The fare through the breakers for a passenger, without stumbling, was "one rial," or twelve and a half cents. It was soon decided who should have the honor of bringing the American lady through the breakers. Captain B. requested his wife to seat herself upon the shoulder of the black man that was now in waiting for her. This was a mode of traveling that Mrs. B. was entirely unacquainted with; besides, it was with her very doubtful whether the man could pass the breakers without being overwhelmed in the surf. Therefore she hesitated, and was silent. Captain B. and his friends urged, declaring there was no other mode of conveyance. Finally she seated herself upon his shoulder and grasped him by the head with both hands, when he steadily and manfully bore her in safety to the arms of her husband in our midst, while his comrades raised a joyous shout in commendation of the sturdy and manful manner in which he had performed the act of landing the American lady.

Here also, as in other places, I was assailed by my associates for refusing to drink wine or intoxicating drinks with them, especially wine at the dinner table, which was very common in South America. I will here give one instance. A large company of us were dining with the American consul, Mr. Bennet. His lady at the head of the table filled her glass, and said, " Captain B., shall I have the pleasure of a glass of wine with you ?" I responded, and filled my glass with water. Mrs. B. declined, unless I would fill my glass with wine. She was aware from our previous acquaintance that I did not drink wine, but she felt disposed to induce me to disregard my former resolutions. As our waiting position attracted the attention of the company, one of them said, " Why, Mr. Bates, do you refuse to drink Mrs. Bennet's health in a glass of wine ?" I replied that I did not drink wine on any occasion, and begged Mrs. B. to accept my offer. She readily condescended, and drank my health in the glass of wine, and I hers in a glass of water. The topic of conversation now turned on wine drinking, and my course in relation to it. Some concluded that a glass of wine would not injure any one. True, but the person who drank one glass would be likely to drink another, and another, until there was no hope of reform. Said one, " I wish I could do as Capt. Bates does; I should be much better off." Another supposed that I was a reformed drunkard. Surely there was no harm in drinking moderately. I endeavored to convince them that the better way to do up the business was *not to use it at all*. On another occasion one captain said to me, " You are like old Mr. ——, of Nantucket; he would n't drink sweetened water !"

After a stay of six weeks, having disposed of the greater part of our cargo in Pernambuco, we sailed on another voyage to St. Catherine's, in lat. 27° 30' south. Care, and a press of business, I perceived had in some measure deprived me of the spiritual enjoyment I possessed on my arrival at Pernambuco. I had more leisure just now to search the Scriptures, and read other books on the subject of religion. I here commenced a diary of my views and feelings, which was a great help to me. This I forwarded to my wife as often as I wrote to her. These sheets were bound up in a roll and laid by, and have not been read for about thirty-five years. I have supposed that this was one of the rolls of paper which I saw in the peculiar dream I had relative to my experience on my outward passage. I thought what a great privilege it would be to have just one professed Christian to compare my views and feelings with on this all-absorbing theme, or to be in a prayer-meeting for an hour or so that I might vent the feelings that were pent up within me.

We arrived at St. Catherine's about the first of January, 1825, where we purchased a cargo of provisions for the northern coast of Brazil. This island is separated from the main land by a narrow ship channel. St. Catherine's is the only commercial seaport for hundreds of miles on the coast. Its northern promontory is a high mountain, where watchmen, with their flag-staff planted, were watching for whales in the offing. When the signal was given that whales were in sight, the boats from the fishery, some ten or twelve miles distant, would row out for them, and if they were fortunate enough to harpoon and kill any, they would tow them to their try works, and manufacture them into oil. Fifty years ago this business was very flourishing there, but the whales visit them so seldom since that time, that their business has about ceased.

When I left Pernambuco, the province was in a state of revolution, and much in want of "farina." It was expected that the Brazilian government would allow foreign vessels to trade in this article on their coast, if the demand continued to increase as it had for a few months past. In anticipation of this, I proceeded to St. Catherine's and loaded for Pernambuco.

As many of my readers may be unacquainted with this article of food, I would state that it is first cultivated very much like the Carolina sweet potatoes, and resembles them, only being much longer. They mature in from nine to eighteen months, if not destroyed by frost, and are called "mandi-oker." The process of manufacturing it into flour in their sheds or shanties was as follows: A cow harnessed at the end of a shaft, traveling in a circle, moved a wheel banded with copper, having holes pierced through it like a grater. A man with his tub of scraped mandi-oker pressed it end foremost against the whirling grater, which ground it to pummace, piece after piece. This pummace was then placed in a machine like a cheese-press, and all the juice presed out. Then the pummace was thrown into large, shallow, iron pans over a heated furnace, where in about twenty minutes, two or three bushels were dried, and when taken out was put up for the market, and, I was told, would keep three years. This they call "farina," or Brazilian flour. The general way of preparing it for the table was merely to scald it with hot soup in plates, and pass it round for bread. The poorer classes and slaves gather it up with the ends of their fingers, and throw it into their mouths by the half ounce, and wash it down with water. At this time much of it is imported into the United States and retailed at the stores.

On my arrival at Pernambuco, farina was in good demand, but the government would not allow me to enter because it was unlawful for foreign vessels to trade coast-wise. In a few days a message came overland from a President of one of the northern provinces, inviting me to come to the port of Paraiba and dispose of my cargo. Here I sold my whole cargo at an advanced price, the government purchasing a large share of it for their troops. As the drought continued, and my vessel was a fast sailer, the President granted me permission to import another cargo forthwith, and gave me a letter of introduction to the President of St. Catherine's to help me onward. On my arrival at St. Catherine's the merchants learning about the demand for breadstuffs in the North, endeavored to prevent me from buying until they were ready to dispatch vessels of their own. After a few weeks' detention in this way, I employed an interpreter and proceeded in our boat some distance up the coast. Leaving our boat to return and come for us the next day, we went up into the mountains to purchase farina from the farmers. On some farms we found it by the room-full, bedroom, or sitting-room, just as they had places to stow it from the rain, for use and for sale. Some of their rooms were crowded and packed full with this article.

The merchants in St. Catherine's, hearing of our success in purchasing produce of the farmers, and towing it to our vessels in boats, tried hard to prejudice them against us. But our silver " patacks" of forty, eighty, and one hundred-and-twenty-cent pieces, with which we paid them for their farina at the highest market price, was far superior to their barter traffic, and proffered advice. The first night I spent on the mountain was a trying, sleepless one. I had two heavy bags of silver, and night had overtaken us at a house where we had made a purchase, to be delivered in the morning. I said to the man, through my interpreter, "Here are two bags of silver we have with us to buy farina; I want you to keep them safe for us until the morning." "Oh, yes!" he replied, and stowed them away in a case.

## Chapter Sixteen.

*Difficulty in Obtaining Cargo—Soul-Refreshing Seasons in the Forest—Effigy of Judas Iscariot—Sail from St. Catharine's—Arrive at Paraiba—Fourth Voyage—Arrive at the Bay of Spirits—Dangerous Position—St. Francisco—Rio Grande—Banks of Sand—A City in Ruins—Jerked Beef—Rio Grande to Paraiba—Kattamaran—Catholic Procession and Burial—Sail for New York—Arrival Home—Family Prayer—Religious Revival—Experience.*

AT bed time I was shown into a little, dark room by myself. I raised no objections, knowing that I should fare no better, after the confidence I had reposed in him in placing my money in his hands. After praying, I laid down, not to sleep, but to think of my unsafe position, and listen to the conversation of the stranger and my interpreter, which continued until a late hour, but a few words of which I could understand. My information respecting the treacherous character of this people proved to be without foundation, respecting this stranger at least, for when the morning came and we were prepared to pay him for his " farina," he manifested strong feelings of gratitude for the confidence we had placed in him. This opened our way to trade with his neighbors.

In my intercourse among this people, who were all Catholics, I found no one to converse with on the subject of religion. I often thought what a privilege it would be to meet with *one* Christian, and how delighted I should be to spend an hour in an assembly of praying Christians, or hear another's voice in prayer besides my own. I felt such a strong desire for some place of retirement, to free my soul and give utterance to my pent-up feelings, that it seemed to me if I could get into the dense forest I should, in a measure, be relieved. A way soon opened before me. With my Bible for my companion, I passed out of the city and followed the sea shore, until I found an opening into the thick forest, into which I entered. Here I enjoyed freedom in prayer beyond anything I had ever experienced before. It was indeed a heavenly place in Christ Jesus. When my business would permit, I used to spend the afternoon away somewhere in these forests; and sometimes, for fear of reptiles, used to ascend a large tree, and fix myself securely in the branches, where I enjoyed most precious seasons in reading the Scriptures, singing, praying, and praising the Lord. His precious truth seemed the joy of my soul, and yet, strange as it may seem, I did not *then* believe my sins were forgiven; but I rejoiced that I was still under conviction. When the time came that I could go again, I felt that I had made much dependence on being there, and I do not remember of ever returning without a special blessing. Oh! how dark it would seem, on returning back among the hum and crowd of the people, after such precious seasons.

The Catholics in Brazil observe their numerous feasts, and what they call "holy days." While lying in the harbor of St. Catherine's, at one of their annual holy days, it was our privilege to witness their indignation against their mortal enemy, Judas Iscariot, for betraying his Master. Early in the morning, the Catholic vessels "cock-billed their yards," pointing them end upwards to the heavens, and at a given signal at noon, their yards were all squared again, and at the outer end of the yard-arm of the commodore (for the day), Judas, the traitor, was hung in effigy. After waiting a suitable time for him to die, they let him fall from the yard-arm into the sea. Then they beat him awhile with clubs, and having swung him up to the yard-arm again by the neck, once more dropped him into the sea. Thus they continued hanging, drowning, and beating the traitor, until their indignant feelings were gratified. He was then towed on shore by the neck, not to be buried, but given into the hands of boys, who dragged him about the public square and streets, beating him with their clubs and stones until he was all used up.

We here cleared and sailed with another cargo, and on our arrival in Paraiba we learned that the famine still prevailed. The authorities, learning that we were handing out some of our provisions to feed the starving poor, opened their prison-doors to allow their prisoners to come also and beg from us. Being unauthorized by my owners to give away their property in this way, I felt reluctant to do it ; but I esteemed it a privilege on my own account, for a while to feed these poor, starving, and almost naked creatures, who lingered about our landing place, as though it was their only hope from starvation. I did not count them, but I think there were sometimes more than fifty receiving farina at a time. The way they ate it out of their calabashes, as they received it from our boat's crew, was evidence of their starving state.

A poor man from the interior came with a miserable, worn-out-looking horse, to buy a few bushels of farina for his family. He said he had come seventy leagues, more than two hundred miles. He represented the people and their cattle dying by starvation as he came along. I think he said there had been no rain for more than two years.

By the time we had disposed of our cargo, the President granted me liberty to import another, and gave me a letter of introduction, with a pressing request to the President of the province to allow us to purchase a cargo of provisions for Paraiba. About this time Captains J. & G. Broughton, of Marblehead, Massachusetts, arrived in Paraiba. These were the first professed Christians that I had known since leaving the United States. With Captain G. Broughton I enjoyed sweet intercourse during the few days of our acquaintance. It was truly a refreshing season. From the time I made a covenant with God, I had been in the habit of spending all my time before breakfast in prayer, reading the Bible, and meditation. This I have since learned to be the best way to commence the day.

August, 1825, we sailed from Paraiba on our fourth voyage. We cleared for " Espiritu Santo,"

or Bay of Spirits, in lat. 20° south.   On our arrival there we encountered some difficulty in finding our way to the anchoring place without a pilot.
I did not learn the reason why this place was
called the "Bay of Spirits," but I think it was
the most romantic, wild-looking place I had ever
seen.   The wind came whistling through the
crevices and dark-looking places in the ragged
mountains, in such sudden gusts, that I was fearful our anchor would break its hold before our
sails could be furled.   Afterward, in passing several miles in our boat to the town and residence of
the President, the same wild scenery presented
itself.   We presented our letter of introduction
and special request to the President, but he declined granting our request to purchase a cargo,
saying it was "contrary to law."   I was told that
*he* was shipping farina, and was very glad to learn
that Paraiba was the best market.

We sailed from thence south for Rio St. Francisco.   As we were running parallel with the land,
at sunset, we could but just discern the land from
the mast-head.   We then shaped our course so as
to be gaining an offing during the night.   About
eight P. M. we observed the water had become very
white ; at this time we were rushing onward rapidly under a heavy press of sail.   We cast our
deep sea lead from the bow, and to our astonishment, we had but five fathoms of water, or thirty
feet. We immediately hauled on a wind and steered
square off the land, with all the sail the brig could
bear, for about three hours, before we found deep
water.   During this time we were held in most
fearful suspense, fearing our vessel would strike
the bottom and dash in pieces when she settled
down between the short, rushing seas.   From our

calculations in the morning, we found that we were twenty miles from the land, in lat. 21° 30' south, when we first discovered white water at eight P. M. Our book of directions and chart were both silent respecting this dangerous place. We felt very thankful to the Lord for delivering us from this unlooked-for and dangerous position.

At Rio St. Francisco there were so many vessels loading we were unable to complete our cargo, but proceeded from thence to Rio Grande, some five hundred miles further south. Here, instead of the lofty, ragged mountains on the seaboard we left at the mouth, were nothing but low sand-hills, drifting about by every strong wind, like those on the coast of Barbary, or the snow-drifts in North America. The sea also drives it about under water in every direction. I was pointed to the light-house standing on a dry sand bank, and was told that that prominence now was where the ship channel formerly was. Instead of pilots going on board of vessels bound in, as I had always known, we saw a large open boat approaching, with pilots and men in her, one man bearing a flag staff, and others with long sounding poles, requiring us to keep a suitable distance behind them. As they pulled on, feeling for the deepest water, the waving of the flag staff to steer to the right and left, or to stop, was to be immediately obeyed, until they reached the light-house, where the pilots step on board the ship and direct them to their anchoring place.

The city of Rio Grande lies several miles up the river from the light-house. A few years previous to my being there, a violent gale drifted the sand into their city and literally filled their houses with it, some to the first, and others to the second-story windows, so that the inhabitants had to flee, and build again, some more than a mile distant, where they were then living. It was useless to shovel the sand out of their houses, unless they could remove it off some distance, the expense of which would more than build them new houses ; thus the old ones were left desolate. The sand was so fine that it found its way into their houses with all their doors and windows shut. This I witnessed more than once while I was there.

Subsequently I remember reading an account, given by an English traveler, who on reaching the tongue or shore of the Egyptian sea, penciled in his note book how easy it would be for God to fulfill the prophecy of Isa. xi, 15. I suppose he saw very clearly that a mighty wind toward the sea would soon drift the sand banks across it, something similar to the manner of drifting sand as above described in Rio Grande.

We made up our cargo at the city of Rio Grande with hides and jerked beef. After skinning their cattle, they strip the flesh from their bones in two pieces, and pickle them in vats some as tanners do their hides. After the salt brine saturates them, they hang them out and dry them on poles, and then roll them up in bundles for the market. In the same manner also they cure their pork, because meat will not keep if salted in barrels in their climate. Back from the sea shore, beyond the sand hills, the country formerly abounded with cattle.

After a passage of thirty days from Rio Grande, we arrived at Paraiba. Here, as usual, we took our pilot from a " Kattamaran," a kind of craft in these parts, used instead of boats. They simply consist of from four to eight twenty-feet logs lashed together, with a mast on which to hoist their sail. Sometimes we have seen them almost out of sight of land fishing in the ocean. At a short distance their appearance is like a man sitting on the water beside a long pole. These logs are of very porous, light wood, and soon fill with water and sink to the surface. When they return to the shore they are hauled up to drain and dry, before they use them again.

One of our seamen, whom we left here with the small pox, died soon after we sailed from Paraiba. I left him in care of the British Consul, who also kindly assisted me in the transaction of my business with the custom house. His chief clerk, a Brazilian, lost a little child about two years of age, which was to be buried the evening after I arrived. The consul was among the chief mourners in the procession. He invited me to walk next to him. As I had never witnessed a ceremony of this kind, I readily accepted his invitation. I now had the privilege of learning from him many things relative to the procession, &c., which I desired to know.

At about eight o'clock P. M., two lines of people were formed to march each side of the street. Wax candles, about three inches in circumference and four feet long, were now lighted, and given into the hands of each man in the procession. The corpse, which was richly dressed and adorned with fresh flowers, was placed in a little basket with four handles, four little boys carrying it. It looked like a sweet little child asleep. The procession, with the priest ahead of the child in the middle of the street, and two long lines of men with lighted candles on each side, was rather an imposing sight in the dark night. The walk was about one mile and a half, to an ancient-looking stone church in the upper town. As we passed into the church I saw one of the flagging stones of the floor raised up, and a small pile of bones and dirt beside it. The consul told me the little child was to be put in there. The child was set down by the altar. The priest occupied but a few moments in speaking, then took up a long handled cup or ball, perforated with holes like a grater, through which, as he uttered a few words, he sprinkled the child with what they call *holy water*, some of which, whether by accident or otherwise, fell on us who stood at the head of the procession. After this part of the ceremony, all but the child returned in order with the procession. Mr. Harden, the consul, on returning, told me how the child would be disposed of. Two black slaves left with it, would strip it of all its clothing, cover it with quick-lime to eat off its flesh, then pound it down in that hole with the other bones and dust, until the stone would lie in its place again, and they would have all its clothing for their labor. In this way they disposed of their dead in this dilapidated charnel-house, and place for divine worship. I was told it was one of the oldest towns in South America, being of nearly three hundred years' standing.

After disposing of our cargo in Paraiba, we invested our funds in hides and skins, and sailed for New York. After a pleasant and prosperous passage of some thirty days, with the exception of cold, freezing storms on our coast, we arrived at the quarantine ground several miles below the city of New York, about the last of March, 1826. As we had no sickness on board, I was allowed the privilege on Sunday to take my crew with me to hear service at the Dutch Reformed church.

This was the *first* religious assembly I had met with since I had covenanted to serve God, and I enjoyed it much. It seemed good to be there. In a few days we were relieved from quarantine, and I was made glad in meeting my companion and sister in New York. My brother F. took my place on board the Empress for another South American voyage, and I left for Fairhaven, to enjoy for a season the society of my family and friends, after an absence of some twenty months.

One of my old acquaintances came in to bid me welcome home again, and very kindly inquired how long it was since I entertained a hope, or *was converted*. I replied that I never had. She was a good Christian, and seemed very much disappointed at my reply. My wife had before this endeavored to encourage me to believe that God for Christ's sake *had* forgiven me. I begged her not to deceive me in such an important matter as this. She said that she did not wish to do so, but was satisfied from my letters and diary during my absence, that if she was ever converted I was. I replied that it seemed to me that I should be fully convinced of my conversion before I could rejoice in it.

I had fully resolved, on my return home, that I would erect the family altar. Satan tried hard to hold me back in various ways, but I resolved to commence as soon as we had breakfasted. At this point, one of my former associates, who was very much opposed to experimental religion, called in to see me. At first I felt some misgivings, but conscience and duty prevailed. I opened the Bible and read a chapter, and knelt with my family and commended ourselves and friend to the Lord. He looked very sober and soon withdrew. After this victory I do not remember of ever experiencing any such hindrance again. If I had yielded here, I am satisfied that I should have had more to overcome if I attempted to pray in like manner again.

I now had the privilege of religious meeting and Christian friends, and also a weekly prayer-meeting at my own house. Eld. H., a Congregational minister, and particular friend of my parents, invited me to attend an interesting revival of religion then in progress, in Taunton, some twenty miles distant. After I had related to him my past experience, and was drawing near to T., I requested Eld. H. not to call on me to speak in meeting, for I had no experience in that part of the work. In the evening I attended what was called an "inquiry meeting" of the converts, and those under conviction for sin. The pastor of the Congregational church, and Eld. H., commenced by inquiring into the state of their minds, and asking the converts to state what the Lord had done for them. As this was the first meeting of the kind in my experience, I listened with an unusual degree of interest and attention, to learn how all these persons had been converted in *so short* a time. The simple story of what the Lord had done for them when they felt convicted for sin, and were weighed down with a load of guilt and shame, and how they went to the Lord with all their burden and confessed their wrongs, and the various ways in which they found relief, some in secret prayer, some in the meeting, and others at home, how God spake peace to their troubled souls; also the various states of their feelings when their burdens left them, all seemed plain to me. There was such a similarity in this to my experience, that I said to myself, This is the operation of the Spirit of God on the heart through Jesus Christ.

After listening awhile to these simple testimonies, it appeared to me that I understood the same language, and I began to reason, and ask myself, Is this conversion from sin? Is this really it? Then I have experienced the same. "My heart was hot within me." Oh how I wished Eld. H. would then ask me to *speak*, that I might tell what the Lord had done for me.

For something like eighteen months I had been unwilling to believe that the Lord had forgiven me my sins, because I had been looking for some evidence, or manifestation of his power, (I did not know how or in what manner), which would convince me beyond a doubt. My limited views of conversion, and strong desire not to be deceived in this important matter, caused me to overlook the simple manner in which God graciously condescends to pardon the guilty, pleading sinner.

After meeting, my tongue was loosed to praise God for what he had done for me so many months before. From this time, all doubts and darkness respecting my conversion and acceptance with God, passed away like the morning dew, and peace like a river, for weeks and months occupied my heart and mind. I could now give a reason of the hope within me, and say with the apostle, "We know that we have passed from death unto life because we love the brethren." "Old things are passed away; behold all things are become new." 1 John iii, 14 ; 2 Cor. v, 17.

## Chapter Seventeen.

*Revival of Religion—Baptism—Join the Church—
Temperance Society—Cold-Water Army—Another
Voyage—Rules for the Voyage—Temperance Voy-
age—Altar of Prayer on Ship Board—Semi-weekly
Paper at Sea—Sunday Worship—Arrival in South
America—Paraíba—Bahia—Privateer—St. Cath-
erine's.*

DURING the spring of the year 1827 we were
blessed with a revival of religion in Fairhaven,
especially in the Christian church. At this season my own mind was more or less exercised in
regard to uniting with some denomination of Christians. My companion had been a member of the
Christian church several years previous to our
marriage. By attending with her, after our marriage, when I was at home, I had become acquainted somewhat with their views of the Bible. They
took the Scriptures for their only rule of faith and
practice, renouncing all creeds.

My parents were members of long standing in
the Congregational church, with all of their converted children thus far, and anxiously hoped that
we would also unite with them. But they embraced some points in their faith which I could
not understand. I will name two only: their
mode of baptism, and doctrine of the trinity. My
father, who had been a deacon of long standing
with them, labored to convince me that they were
right in points of doctrine. I informed him that
my mind was troubled in relation to baptism. Said
he, "I had you baptized when an infant." I an-

swered, that that might all be according to his faith; but the Bible taught that we must first believe and then be baptized (Mark xvi, 16; 1 Pet. iii, 21), but I was not capable of believing when I was an infant. Respecting the trinity, I concluded that it was an imposibility for me to believe that the Lord Jesus Christ, the Son of the Father, was also the Almighty God, the Father, one and the same being. I said to my father, "If you can convince me that we are one in this sense, that you are my father, and I your son; and also that I am your father, and you my son, then I can believe in the trinity."

Our trial in this matter led me to make my duty a special subject of prayer, particularly in relation to baptism; after which, on opening the Bible, my eye rested on the twenty-seventh Psalm. When I had finished the last verse, I said, "Lord, I will! If I wait on thee according to thy word, I must be immersed—buried with Christ in baptism." Col. ii, 12. God strengthened my heart and set me free from that moment, and my duty was perfectly clear. His promise was sweet and powerful. In a few days I was immersed and joined the Christian church.

The same day, while we were changing our clothes, I solicited Eld. M., who baptized me, to assist me in raising a Temperance Society. As my mind was now free with respect to this last duty, I was forcibly impressed with the importance of uniting my energies with others, to check, if possible, the increasing ravages of intemperance. Since I had ceased to use intoxicating drinks, I was constrained to look upon it as one of the most important steps that I had ever taken. Hence I ardently desired the same blessing for those around me. Eld. M. was the first person whom I asked to aid me in this enterprise; failing with him, I moved out alone, and presented my paper for subscribers. Eld. G., the Congregational minister, his two deacons, and a few of the principal men of the place, cheerfully and readily subscribed their names, twelve or thirteen in number, and forthwith a meeting was called, and the "Fairhaven Temperance Society" was organized.

The majority of our little number had been sea captains, and had seen much of the debasing influence ardent spirits exerts among its users, abroad and at home. They seemed the more ready, therefore, to give their names and influence to check this monster vice. Eld. G. exclaimed, "Why, Captain Bates, this is just what I have been wanting to see!" The meeting was organized by choosing Captain Stephen Merihew, President, and Mr. Charles Drew, Secretary. Pending the discussion in adopting the constitution, it was voted that we pledge ourselves to abstain from the use of ardent spirits as a beverage. Having no precedent before us, it was finally voted that rum, gin, brandy and whisky, were ardent spirits. Wine, beer and cider were so freely used as a beverage, that the majority of our members were then unwilling to have them in the list. Some doubts arose with the minority whether we should be able to sustain the spirit of our constitution without abstaining from all intoxicating beverages. One of our members who had always been noted for doing much for his visiting friends, said, "Mr. President, what shall I do when my friends come to visit me from Boston?" "Do as I do, Captain S.," said another. "I have not offered my friends any liquor to drink in my house these ten years."

"Oh, you are mistaken," said the President, "it is twenty!" This doubtless was said because the man had ceased to follow the fashion in treating his friends with liquor before others were ready to join with him.

Inquiry was then made whether there were any Temperance Societies then known. A statement was made that certain individuals in Boston had recently agreed together, that instead of purchasing their liquor in small quantities at the stores, they would get it by the keg, and drink it in their own houses. This association was called "The Keg Society." If any Temperance Societies had ever been organized previous to the one at Fairhaven, we were unacquainted with the fact. A short time after our organization, one of our number was reported to have violated his pledge. This he denied. "But, you were intoxicated," said we. He declared that he had not drank anything but cider, and that was allowed. (We were told that his wife said she had a great deal rather he would drink brandy, for when he got drunk on cider he was as ugly again.) During the trial of this member, he continued to declare that he had not violated the letter of the constitution. But it was evident to the Society that he had violated the intent and spirit of it, which he was unwilling to admit, or even promise to reform. He was therefore expelled.

The Society here saw the necessity of amending the constitution by striking out the words, "ardent spirits," and inserting in their place, "all intoxicating drinks," or something else that would sustain and aid the cause. From this a reform was introduced, which finally resulted in the disuse of all intoxicating drinks, except for medicinal purposes.    This reform gave us the name of "Tee-totalers."

Before this our Temperance Society had become exceedingly popular.    Our meeting-houses in their turn were crowded with all classes to hear lectures on the subject, and converts, both male and female, by scores cheerfully pledged themselves to the Temperance Constitution.    Many of the citizens of New Bedford who came to hear, also united with us.    From thence a society was organized in their town and other ones also.    Arrangements were soon made, and a Bristol County Temperance Society was organized, and soon followed the Massachusetts State Temperance Society.    Temperance papers, tracts and lecturers, multiplied throughout the land, and opposition began to rage like the rolling sea, causing the tide of Temperance to ebb awhile.    Then came "The Cold Water Army," of little children from four years and onward, commingling their simple little songs in praise of water—pure, cold water—no beverage like unmingled, cold water.    Their simple, stirring appeals, especially when assembled in their society meetings, seemed to give a new impetus to the cause, and re-arouse their parents to the work of total abstinence from all intoxicating drinks.    As I examined my papers the other day, I saw the book containing the names of nearly *three hundred children* which had belonged to our "Cold Water Army" at Fairhaven.

In the midst of our temperance labors, my brother F. arrived from South America in the Empress.    She was soon loaded again with an assorted cargo under my command, and cleared for South America.    We sailed from New Bedford on the morning of Aug. 9th, 1827.    I found it much more trying to part with my family and friends this time than ever before.

Our pilot now left us with a strong breeze wafting us out once more into the boisterous ocean for a long voyage. As usual, our anchors were now stowed away and everything secured in case we should be overtaken by a storm. As the night set in, on taking our departure from Gay Head Light, distant about fifteen miles, all hands were called aft on the quarter-deck. All but one were strangers to me, as they had come from Boston the day before. I read our names and agreement to perform this voyage, from the shipping papers, and requested their attention while I stated the rules and regulations which I wished to be observed during our voyage.

I spoke to them of the importance of cultivating kind feelings toward each other while we were alone on the ocean, during our contemplated voyage. I stated that I had frequently seen bitter feelings and continued hatred arise on shipboard by not calling the men by their proper names. Said I, " Here is the name of William Jones ; now let it be remembered while we are performing this voyage that we all call his name William. Here is John Robinson ; call him John. Here is James Stubbs ; call him James. We shall not allow any Bills, nor Jacks, nor Jims, to be called here." In like manner I read all their names, with that of the first and second mates, and requested them always to address each other in a respectful manner, and to call themselves by their proper names ; and if the officers addressed them otherwise, I wished it reported to me.

Another rule was, that I should allow no swearing during the voyage. Said William Dunn, " I have always had that privilege, sir." "Well," said I, "you cannot have it here," and quoted the third commandment, and was endeavoring to show how wicked it was to swear, when he said, "I can't help it, sir!" I replied, "Then I will help you to help it." He began to reason about it, and said, "When I am called up in the night to reef top-sails in bad weather, and things don't go right, I swear before I think of it." Said I to him, "If you do so here, I will tell you what I will do with you; I will call you down and send you below, and let your shipmates do your duty for you." Dunn saw that such a course would disgrace him, and he said, "I will try, sir."

Another rule was, that we should allow no washing nor mending clothes on Sundays. I said to the crew, "I have a good assortment of books and papers which you may have access to every Sunday. I shall also endeavor to instruct you, that we may keep that day holy unto the Lord. You shall have every Saturday afternoon to wash and mend your clothes, both at sea and in harbor, and I shall expect you to appear every Sunday morning with clean clothes. When we arrive in port you may have the same Saturday afternoon in your turn to go on shore and see the place, and get what you wish, if you return on board at night sober, for we shall observe the Sabbath on board in port, and not grant any liberty on shore Sunday.

At this Dunn remarked again, "That's the sailor's privilege, and I have always had the liberty of going on shore Sundays, and"— "I know that very well," said I, interrupting him, "but I cannot give you that liberty," and endeavored to show them how wrong it was to violate God's holy day, and how much better they would enjoy themselves in reading and improving their minds, than in joining all the wickedness that sailors were in the habit of in foreign ports on that day.

"Another thing I want to tell you is, that we have no liquor, or intoxicating drinks, on board." "I am glad of that!" said John R. Perhaps this was the first voyage he had ever sailed without it. Said I, "We have one junk bottle of brandy, and one also of gin, in the medicine chest; this I shall administer to you like the other medicine when I think you need it. This is all the liquor we have on board, and all that I intend shall be on board this vessel during our voyage; and I here strictly forbid any of you bringing anything of the kind on board when you have liberty to go on shore in foreign ports. And I would that I could persuade you never to drink it when on shore. When you are called to do duty during your watch below, we shall expect you to come up readily and cheerfully, and you shall retire again as soon as the work is performed, and also have your forenoon watch below. If you adhere to these rules, and behave yourselves like men, you shall be kindly treated, and our voyage will prove a pleasant one." I then knelt down and commended ourselves to the great God, whose tender mercies are over all the works of his hands, to protect and guide us on our way over the ocean to our destined port.

The next morning, all but the man at the helm were invited into the cabin to join with us in our morning prayer. We told them that this would be our practice morning and evening, and we should be pleased to have them all with us, that we might pray with and for them. Also, to further encourage the crew to read, and inform their minds, we proposed to issue a paper twice a week, namely, Tuesday and Friday mornings, during the voyage. Before sailing, I had prepared a stock of books, with the latest newspapers, also the last volume of an interesting religious weekly paper, published in Boston, called "Zion's Herald." We began our issue with the first number of the volume, requiring the return of the last number before issuing the next; this we placed under the volume, to be received again at the end of six months.

The novel idea of a semi-weekly paper at sea, interested the crew very much, and when the first number came forth again, and they began to re-read the volume, I heard nothing said with regard to their ever having seen it before. Their interest in the paper continued throughout the entire voyage. During their forenoon watch below, I used frequently to walk forward, unobserved, and listen to hear some one of them reading aloud from their morning paper, and their remarks thereon.

On Sundays, when the weather was suitable, we had religious worship on the quarter-deck, otherwise in the cabin, when we generally read some good, selected sermon, and from the Bible. When in port we could not have their whole attention on Sunday, as when at sea. It sometimes seemed hard for them to be deprived of the privilege of going ashore with other ship companies that were passing us for that purpose. But we enjoyed peace and quietness, while they were rioting in folly and drunkenness. After a few weeks it was truly gratifying to see them selecting their books from our little library on Sunday morning, and reading them, and also their Bibles, to inform their minds —it was so different from their former course on shipboard. They also appeared cheerful and willing to obey when called upon, and so continued.

After a passage of forty-seven days, we arrived in safety at Paraiba, on the east coast of South America. From thence we continued our voyage to Bahia, or St. Salvador, where we arrived the 5th of October. Finding no sale for our cargo, we cleared for St. Catherine's. The night before our arrival at Bahia, we were fired upon and detained by a Buenos Ayres privateer. The captain pretended to believe that I was loaded with muskets and powder for their enemy, the Brazilians. After satisfying themselves to the contrary, they released us.

---

## Chapter Eighteen.

*Overhauled by a Buenos-Ayres Privateer or Pirate— Seven hours' Detention—Plunder—Passengers made Prisoners—Search for Money—Doubloons Boiling with Salt Beef—Crew and Passengers Released— Season of Prayer—Arrival at Rio Janeiro—Bethel Meeting—Rio Grande—Dangers of the Coast—Concerning Fresh Water—Religious Views—Vessel Lost —Letter—Sail, and Arrive at St. Catherine's—Sail for New York—Singular Phenomenon.*

ON arriving at St. Catherine's, we landed, sold our cargo, and loaded again with rice and farina, and sailed for Rio Janeiro. Several days after we left St. Catherine's, a strange sail was discovered at a distance on our weather-quarter, bearing toward us, early in the morning. She soon began firing guns, but we paid little attention to her, and were standing on our course under a very light breeze. The Sugar Loaf, and other high mountains at the entrance of the harbor of Rio Janeiro were now looming in the distance, some eighty miles ahead of us. We saw the strange sail was gaining on us very fast, and by the aid of the spyglass discovered that she was sweeping with long oars and firing occasionally. We hoisted the stars and stripes, and soon discovered that she was a brig with the Buenos Ayres flag at her peak. We had eight gentlemen passengers on board, six of them Brazilian merchants, going to Rio Janeiro to increase their stock of goods. They were exceedingly agitated on learning that their enemy was approaching. I said to them, " If you think it best I will crowd on all sail, and if the breezes freshen up soon we can outsail them, but if not they will sweep down upon us, and in case they overtake us you will fare hard. I have no fear of them myself, while under the American flag. But if we heave to for them, they will cease their firing and treat you more kindly. I will do either of which you shall choose among yourselves." They soon decided that we had better heave to and let them come up with us. We did so, and calmly awaited the approach of the enemy.

In the course of an hour they rounded to, broadside to us, and cried out, " Brig ahoy ! Halloo ! Lower your boat down, sir, and come aboard here immediately !" " Yes, sir." They cried again, " Do you bear a hand about it, sir, and bring your papers with you !" " Yes, sir." I directed the second mate to take charge of the boat, to keep her from being stove while along side the privateer. On reaching the deck I was met by two ruffianly-looking men with their brace of pistols, and the captain standing in the cabin gangway who said,

"Why did n't you heave to, sir, when I fired at you? I have a good mind to blow your brains out here!" followed up with a volley of blasphemous imprecations. I replied, "I am in your hands, sir; you can do as you please," and then added, "I hove my vessel to as soon as I ascertained who you was;" and pointing to our flying colors I remarked, "That is the American flag, and I hope you will respect it." Then came another volley of oaths with a threat that he would sink my vessel, and he cried out, "Go away aft, there, sir, on the quarter-deck!" Here he took my papers. When I got aft I saw that my whole crew were with me. I said, "Mr. Bowne, why did you not stay in the boat?" "Why, sir, they ordered us all on deck after you, and put in a crew of their own; yonder they go on board the Empress." The privateer master then inquired, "Captain, what's your cargo?" "Rice and farina," was the reply. "You have got ammunition for the enemy under your farina." "No, sir; I have no such thing in my cargo. You have my invoice and bills of lading." He said he knew I was aiding the Brazilians, and that he would carry me down to Montevideo as a prize. Said I, "If you do, I shall find friends there." "Why," said he, "have you ever been there?" "Yes," I replied. Said he, "I will burn your vessel up, and sink her to the bottom;" and he hailed his officer and ordered him to take off the hatchways and sound her with rods to the bottom of the hold.

Their crew now came along side with our boat to discharge their plunder. Said I, "Captain, are you going to plunder my vessel?" "Yes," he answered, "I promised these men plunder if they would pull with the sweeps and overtake you." My remonstrating only made him curse and swear about what he would do to us. My papers and letters were then spread out on the quarter-deck. I asked him what he wanted with my private papers and letters. He answered that he wanted to find out my correspondence with his enemy, the Brazilians. Said I, "You have my wife's letters there from the United States." Said he, "You may have them, and your private property." The boat was unloading her plunder again, and I said, "Your men have just passed in my spy-glass; will you let me have it?" "No," said he, "I promised them plunder if they would overtake you, and I cannot stop them."

While examining the invoice he suddenly asked, "Where is your money?" I replied, "You have my papers with the invoice of my cargo; if you find any account of money, take it." He then ordered his officers to make thorough search for it on board. Not finding any, they told the steward they would hang him if he did not tell where the captain's money was. He declared that he had no knowledge of any. Our money was in silver coin; no one knew where it was but myself. I had stowed it away in bags where I had but little fear of pirates finding it. This captain was English, with a mixed, savage-looking crew, apparently ready for any kind of murderous work. Two or three times he had his vessel steered so near ours that I feared they would get foul of each other and be wrecked, or go down, and because I spoke by way of caution, he poured his abusive epithets on me unrestrained. After an hour or so his excitement began to subside, when he invited me to go down into the cabin with him and take a glass of grog. "Thank you, sir," said I, "I do n't drink any." Well, he did, and down he went for a few moments to swallow another deadly dram.

I said to the Brazilian merchants just before he came up with us, "Say nothing to me about your money; secure it the best way you can. I shall undoubtedly be questioned about it, and if I know nothing of it I can say so." They gave their gold watches to the sailors, who kept them upon their persons out of sight. I was afterward told that they threw a quantity of their gold doubloons into the cook's "coppers," where the beef and pork were boiling in salt water for our dinner. These merchants were well stocked with summer dresses and linen, which these greedy fellows laid hold of, stripping them all off except their shirts and pantaloons.

After a while the insatiate crew that were ransacking our vessel for money, feeling the gnawings of hunger, seized upon the beef and pork that were cooking in the boilers. It seemed that a merciful Providence checked them from discovering the golden treasure at the bottom of the coppers; for if they had discovered it, they would have suspected there was more of the same in other places, and most probably some of us would have been hung or shot before the search ended.

During this abusive detention of seven or eight hours, or from eleven in the fournoon until sundown, my boat's crew and self were crowded into a standing position away aft on the quarter-deck, with nothing to eat. Late in the afternoon the Brazilian merchants were brought on board the privateer as prisoners of war, and ordered to stand forward of the gangway on the lee-side, or, as sailors term it, "in the lee scuppers." Poor fellows, they looked most pitiful. Their prospects seemed most dark and dubious. I had heard of their saying, or talking among themselves soon after we sailed from St. Catherine's, because of our praying with them and our sailors morning and evening, that there would be no danger, but they would have a safe passage to Rio Janeiro. Their faith was now being tested. There they stood, with their eyes fastened on the captain of the privateer and our little company.

A little before sundown the captain ordered all his men on board from the Empress. As our boat returned with them, he said to me, "You may now take your papers and boat and go on board your vessel." "Thank you, sir," I replied. "Will you let the passengers go with me?" "No!" said he, "they are my prisoners." "I know that, sir; but I shall be greatly obliged to you if you will let me have them." He said he wished me to understand that he knew his own business. I was at liberty to go on board when I pleased, but I should not have his prisoners. My men had gone into the boat and were waiting for me.

These poor fellows did not understand English, but it was clearly manifest from their agonizing, agitated looks that they knew their fate was being settled. Everything to them seemed to hang on a few moments. I appealed to his English and humane feelings respecting their treatment of prisoners not found in arms against them, and said to him, "These men have behaved like gentlemen on board of my vessel; they paid me fifty dollars each for their passage before I left St. Catherine's; they were quietly prosecuting their individual business. In point of worldly interest I shall gain nothing, as I am already paid; but I want to fulfill my engagement with them, and land them safe in Rio Janeiro. They have never injured you, and they will be in your way here. Now, captain, why will you not let me have them?" "Take them," said he in a subdued tone. "Thank you, sir, for your kindness." The way these men passed over that vessel's side into our boat, when we pointed them to her, was pretty clear proof that they understood all we had been saying concerning them. The captain then endeavored to apologize some for his unkind treatment to me. I bade him good bye, and we were once more all on board the Empress at the setting of the sun.

Here we found things in great confusion; our long boat unstowed, hatches all thrown off, leaving the cargo exposed to the first sea that should come on our decks. Passengers and crew wrought diligently to put the Empress in sailing trim, and as night closed upon us we were out of reach of the privateer's guns, under a good wholesale breeze, and the passengers were congratulating each other at their safe deliverance from a cruel death. When order was restored, we assembled as usual in the cabin to thank the Lord for his daily mercies, and especially for his manifest interference in delivering us from the power of that reckless crew of pirates on the high seas. Thanks to his holy name! The sailors delivered the passengers their watches, and whatever else they had given them for safe keeping. Their doubloons were also safe in the coppers. The enemy got none of their money; but they entered their trunks, and left them in rather a sad plight to meet their friends in Rio. The afternoon of the next day we anchored in the harbor of Rio Janeiro. When the report of the matter reached the city, the Government despatched a frigate in pursuit of the privateer, but they did not find her.

On Sunday the Bethel flag was seen flying on board an English brig in the harbor. With my boat's crew, we joined them. There were not many present, and the dull, formal manner in which the meeting was managed seemed to strip it of all spiritual interest. After the meeting closed, the officers of the different ships in attendance were invited into the cabin, where a table was spread with various kinds of liquors, to which we were invited to help ourselves. I declined partaking in this part of the exercise, and returned to my vessel much disappointed at losing the blessing I had anticipated. Before leaving the harbor, however, some friends met with us on board the Empress, and we had an interesting prayer-meeting, with the blessing of Heaven.

As the custom-house authorities declined granting me liberty to sell my cargo in Rio Janeiro, we cleared and sailed again for St. Catherine's. On our arrival there, the President of the Province, having just received a communication from the Province of Rio Grande for two cargoes of farina for the troops in the South, granted me the first privilege, and gave me a letter to the authorities of Rio Grande. Thus prepared we sailed again, and arrived at the bar of Rio Grande on the last day of the year 1827. Mariners approaching this coast cannot be too cautious, as the sand banks, both above and under the sea, are constantly changing their position. As we were approaching the coast at the close of the day, the water "shoaled" so fast that we anchored in the open sea, and lay there until morning, when we ascertained that we were some thirty miles from the coast. The sand banks on the shore are from five to about twenty-five feet high, and make it extremely difficult sometimes to see the light-house before being in danger of striking the sand bars. The wrecks of vessels, as they were passing through the process of being buried in the sand by the surging of the heavy surf, lying strewed along the shore a few miles from the entrance of the harbor, is sufficient evidence to the observer that it requires the best attention and skill of navigators in approaching this place, to get in without damage.

It is singular how fresh water is obtained for the shipping in the harbor. The water casks are towed to the shore, and the sailors dig little holes in the sand, about twenty or thirty feet from the ocean's edge. In about two or three minutes these holes fill up with pure fresh water, which is easily scooped into the casks. The water thus obtained is often not more than two feet above the level of the salt sea-water. In pleasant weather, the women were frequently seen among the sand hills near the salt water, digging holes in the sand for fresh, soft water, sufficiently large to wash their fine, white clothes in. When spread on the sand, with a clear sunshine, they dry them in about an hour. When dry, with one shake the sand falls from them, and their clothes are not soiled, because the sand is free from dust.

While in this port we held meetings on board our vessel every Sunday; but none of our neighbors, who were anchored near by and around us, came to unite with us, but preferred to spend their leisure hours on shore. Their men returned in the evening, generally in a turbulent and riotous condition. Our temperance and religious principles on ship-board were new, and, of course, objectionable to all around us; but still they were constrained to admit that we enjoyed peace and quiet on board our vessel that they in general were strangers to, especially on Sunday nights. The supercargo of a Philadelphia brig, which was anchored near by us, used frequently to ridicule and swear about my religious views, in a violent manner, when I happened to meet him. He took occasion to do this especially in company where we transacted our business. Sometimes he would cool down and commend me for my forbearance, and promise that he would not swear when I was present. But his promises were always soon forgotten.

When his vessel was getting under way to leave for home, I wrote him a letter, entreating him to turn from his wicked course and serve the Lord, and spoke of the consequences that might follow if he still continued in the course he was pursuing, and gave it to him to read when he had more leisure. He proceeded on his voyage, and was approaching near his destined port, when one day while the officers and crew were down at dinner, suddenly and unexpectedly a squall struck his vessel and capsized her. The crew just escaped with their lives. They were picked up by another vessel, and the supercargo arrived in New York. He there fell in company with an old acquaintance of mine, to whom he related the circumstance of his becoming acquainted with me in Rio Grande, and referring to the religious instruction I gave him in the letter before referred to, he cursed and railed against me for being the cause of his misfortune and present suffering. This judgment, which God suffered to overtake him in such a sudden and irrevokable manner, made him feel, undoubtedly, that it was for the blasphemous course which he had pursued and was still indulging in. In seeking for some way to ease his troubled conscience and justify self, he doubtless found some relief in charging it all to me.

After some detention we sold our cargo to the government, and invested the most of our funds in dry hides, and cleared for St. Catherine's. After sailing some eight miles from our anchorage, to the lighthouse, at the entrance of the harbor, we were compelled to anchor for the night and wait for daylight and a fair wind to pass safely over the sand bars.

On receiving my account current from Mr. Carroll, the Brazilian merchant whom I employed to transact my foreign business, I ran it over without discovering any error. But still it seemed to me that I had received more cash in balance than was my due. But many other things then necessarily occupied my mind (as is usual on weighing anchor to proceed on a voyage), until we were obliged to anchor near the lighthouse. I discovered that the merchant had balanced the account wrong, in my favor. This, of course, was no fault of mine; but he had paid me over my due five hundred dollars in gold doubloons. Only one way was now open for me to communicate with him, and that was by sending my boat. Our unsafe situation near the sand bars and breakers seemed to demand that not only our boat, but also our crew, should be at hand, in case our anchors should fail to hold us during the night. But the money was not mine, and I felt that I should not be blessed of the Lord if I attempted to proceed on my voyage without an exertion on my part to pay it over. My vessel might never be heard from again, neither Mr. C.'s money; then, of course, the fault would be charged to me. I therefore dispatched my boat with the following letter :—

"MR. CARROLL, *Dear Sir:* Since I parted with you, I have been wondering how I came by so much money. Once I overhauled the accounts and concluded they were right. This evening, being more collected and free from care, and not satisfied, I have again spread them before me, and made a memorandum of sales and purchases, which led me to discover the error—five hundred dollars and thirty-four cents. I have been devising the best way to get this money safe to you ; as it is now late, and a prospect of a fair wind early in the morning, I have concluded to send my boat. To double the diligence of my men, I have promised them 960 "reis" each. I do not know of any other way that would be safe. JOSEPH BATES.
"*Brig Empress, at the bar off Rio Grande, March* 8, 1828."

By the blessing of God our boat returned in safety, with the thanks of the merchant, in time for us to put to sea early in the morning, with a fair wind. We were prospered with a safe voyage to St. Catherine's, where we finished our lading with hides and coffee, and cleared for New York. The Brazilian government was in such an unsettled state, owing to the war with Buenos Ayres, that their business was very much depressed.

Our passage home was pleasant and prosperous. We were cheered once more with the well-known north star, as we advanced a little way north of the equator, out from the Southern Ocean. After passing the north-eastern extremity of South America, as we steered away north-west, we soon came under the quickening influence of the north-east and east trade-winds, which wafted us onward toward our home and friends, sometimes at the rate of two hundred miles in twenty-four hours. Sailors reckon their days as astronomers do, from noon to noon. Every night, on the appearance of the north star, her ascension in the northern hemisphere was very perceptible, and also encouraging, proving our onward course northward.

As we were proceeding on our way toward the windward of the West India Islands, on coming on deck one morning, I observed the sails looked red. I hailed one of our seamen, who was aloft, and told him to rub his hand on the top-gallant sail, and tell me what was there. He answered, "It is sand!" I requested him to brush off some in his hand, and come down with it. He brought down what he could shut up in his hand, of fine red and grey sand. As soon as the sails became dry, by the shining of the sun, it all dropped off, and our sails were as white as they were the day before. On a thorough examination of my charts and book of directions, I ascertained that the nearest land eastward of us, from whence the wind was continually blowing, was the coast of Africa, some *fifteen hundred miles distant!* The northern and southern oceans were wide open before and behind us. Stretching along under our lee, many hundreds of miles west of us, lay the northern coast of South America. It was therefore clear that the quantity of sand on our sails, which was held there by reason of their being quite wet, came not from the west, the north, nor the south, but from the flying clouds passing over us from the deserts of Arabia, where we are told by travelers that the sands of those deserts have frequently been seen whirling upward in heavy columns to the clouds by whirlwinds. The same is referred to by Isaiah, the prophet, chapter xxi, 1.

According to the rate clouds are said to fly before a strong gale, these passed over us in about forty-eight hours after leaving the coast of Africa, and sifted out their loads of sand some fifteen hundred miles across the North Atlantic Ocean, and most likely also over the northern coast of South America into the Pacific.

---

# Chapter Nineteen.

*Revival at Sea—Arrive in New York—Bethel Ships and Meetings—Friendless Young Men—Arrival in New Bedford—Temperance Reform—Voyage Ended.*

DURING our homeward-bound passage, our crew seemed more thoughtful and attentive to the religious instruction we were endeavoring to impart to them. It was evident that the Spirit of the Lord was at work in our midst. One James S. gave good evidence of a thorough conversion to God, and was very happy during our voyage home. Religion seemed to be his whole theme. One night in his watch on deck, while relating to me his experience, said he, "Don't you remember the first night out on our voyage from home, when you had all hands called aft on the quarter-deck, and gave them rules for the voyage?" "Yes," I replied. "Well, sir, I was then at the helm, and when you finished, and knelt down on the quarter-deck and prayed with us, if at that time you had taken up a handspike and knocked me down at the helm, I should not have felt worse; for I had never seen such a thing before." Thomas B. also professed conversion at that time.

Our passage home was pleasant, with the exception of a heavy gale which troubled us some, but the good Lord delivered us from its overwhelming influence, and we soon after arrived safely in the harbor of New York city. The first news from home was, that my honored father had died some six weeks before my arrival. This was a trying providence for which I was not prepared. He had lived nearly seventy-nine years, and I had always found him in his place at the head of the family after my long voyages, and it seemed to me that I had not one serious thought but that I should see him there again if I lived to return home.

While in the city, I had the pleasure of attending an evening, Bethel prayer-meeting, on board a ship lying at the wharf. I enjoyed it very much. Such meetings were then in their infancy, but since that time it is common enough to see the Bethel flag on Sunday morning on board the ships for meeting, on both the east and north sides of the river, for the benefit of sailors and young men that are often wandering about the city without home or friends. Many, doubtless, have been saved from ruin by the efforts of those engaged in these benevolent institutions, while other homeless ones, who have not had such influences to restrain them, have been driven to deeds of desperation, or yielded to feelings of despair. The trying experience of my early days made me familiar with such scenes.

On one of my previous voyages, I had prevailed on a young man to accompany me to his home in Massachusetts. And while I was in the city this time, as I was passing through the park, among many others whom I saw was a young man seated in the shade, looking very melancholy, quite similar to the one just mentioned, and not far from the same place. I seated myself beside him, and asked him why he appeared so melancholy. At first he hesitated, but soon began to inform me that he was in a destitute state, nothing to do, and no-where to go. He said his brother had employed him in his apothecary store in the city, but he had recently failed and broken up, and left the city, and that he was now without home and friends. I asked him where his parents lived. He replied, in Massachusetts. "My father," said he, "is a Congregationalist preacher, near Boston." I invited him to go on board my vessel and be one of my crew, and I would land him within sixty miles of his home. He readily accepted my offer, and on our arrival in New Bedford, Mass., his father came for him, and expressed much gratitude to me for his safe return, and the privilege of again meeting with his son.

On our arrival in New York, my crew, with one exception, chose to remain on board and discharge the cargo, and not have their discharge as was customary on arriving from a foreign port. They preferred also to continue in their stations until we arrived in New Bedford, where the Empress was to proceed, to fit out for another voyage. After discharging our cargo, we sailed, and arrived in New Bedford about the 20th of June, 1828—twenty-one years from the time I sailed from thence on my first European voyage, in the capacity of a cabin boy.

Some of my men inquired when I was going on another voyage, and expressed a wish to wait for me, and also their satisfaction about the last as being their best voyage. It was some satisfaction to me to know that seamen were susceptible of moral reform on the ocean (as proved in this instance) as well as on the land; and I believe that such reforms can generally be accomplished where the officers are ready and willing to enter into it. It has been argued by too many that sailors continue to addict themselves to so many bad habits that it is about useless to attempt their reform. I think it will be safe to say that the habitual use of intoxicating drink is the most debasing and formidable of all their habits. But if governments, ship owners, and captains, had not always provided it for them on board their war and trading ships, as an article of beverage, tens of thousands of intelligent and most enterprising young men would have been saved, and been as great a blessing to their friends, their country, and the church, as farmers, doctors, lawyers, and other tradesmen and professional men have been.

Having had some knowledge of these things, I had resolved in the fear of God to attempt a reform, though temperance societies were then in their infancy, and temperance ships unknown. And when I made the announcement at the commencement of our last voyage that there was no intoxicating drink on board, only what pertained to the medicine chest, and one man shouted that he was "glad of it," this lone voice on the ocean in behalf of this work of reform, from a stranger, manifesting his joy because there was no liquor on board to tempt him, was cheering to me, and a strong evidence of the power of human influence. I believe that he was also deeply affected, and I cannot now recollect that he used it in any way while under my command, nor any of the others, except one Wm. Dunn, whom I had to reprove once or twice during the voyage for drinking while he was on duty on shore.

Then what had been considered so necessary an article to stimulate the sailor in the performance of his duty, proved not only unnecessary, but the withholding of it was shown to be a great blessing in our case.

Some time after this voyage, I was in company with a ship owner of New Bedford, who was personally interested in fitting out his own ships and storing them with provisions, liquors, and all the necessaries for long voyages. We had been agitating the importance of reform in strong drink, when he observed, "I understand, Captain Bates, that you performed your last voyage without the use of ardent spirits." "Yes, sir," I replied. Said he, "Yours is the first temperance vessel I have ever heard of."

My brother F. now took command of the Empress, and sailed again for South America, being fitted out to perform the voyage on the principles of temperance, as on her former voyage. During my last voyage I had reflected much on the enjoyments of social life with my family and friends, of which I had deprived myself for so many years; and I desired to be more exclusively engaged to better my condition, and those with whom I should be called to associate, on the subject of religion and moral reform.

---

# Chapter Twenty.

*At Home — Religion — Temperance — Farming — My Promise — Seaman's Friend Society — Missions — American Tract Society — American Colonization Society — Meeting-house — Religious Revival — Its Effects — Tea and Coffee — Change of Residence — Progress of the Temperance Cause — Progress of the Antislavery Cause — My own Position — Mob in Boston, Mass. — Falling Stars.*

CHAPTER nineteen closed with the account of my last voyage, leaving me in the enjoyment of the blessings of social life on the land, with my family and friends. My seafaring life was now finished. I once more esteemed it a great privilege to unite with my brethren in the Christian church. I also gladly re-engaged in the temperance reform with my former associates, who had been progressing in the work during my absence.

My father in his last will requested that I should

unite with my mother in the settlement of his estate. Before the year came round, my mother was also removed by death. I now turned my attention to farming, and commenced improving a small farm which my father had bequeathed me. Through the aid of an agricultural weekly, called the "New England Farmer," for a theory, and with some of my ready cash, I soon made some perceptible alterations on the farm, but with little or no income.

My companion had often said that she wished I had some way to sustain my family by living at home. I promised her that when I had gained a competency by following the sea, then I would relinquish the business and stay on shore. When asked what I considered a competency, I answered, Ten thousand dollars. After tasting the sweets of the Christian's hope, I found it much easier, with all the opening prospects before me, to say where I would stop in this business, if the Lord prospered me.

I now enjoyed the privilege of reading some of the periodicals of the times, especially those on religion and morals. The sailors' wants were now beginning to be agitated through a periodical called "The Sailor's Magazine." A few friends of the cause came together, and we organized the "Fairhaven Seaman's Friend Society." A little pamphlet called "The Missionary Herald," advocating the cause of foreign missions, also enlisted my feelings, and engaged my attention to some extent. My intercourse with what the Herald called the heathen, enabled me to see more clearly their moral and religious wants. I also became much interested in the work of the "American Tract Society," which was organized in Boston, Mass., in the year 1814, and was embracing all the evangelical denominations in the United States. I read with pleasure and helped to circulate many of their tracts on religious subjects and temperance reform;

but my interest began to wane when they manifested their unwillingness and determination not to publish any tracts in favor of the down-trodden and oppressed slave in their own land, when they were solicited by antislavery men so to do. It became manifest and clear that their professed unbounded benevolence embraced the whole human race, of all colors and complexions, except those who were suffering under their task-masters, and perishing for lack of religious knowledge within the sound of their voice, in their own churches, and by their firesides. Such inconsistency rests heavily on the managers of the Society.

About this time I began also to read "The African Repository," the organ of the American Colonization Society, organized in the city of Washington, D. C., in the year 1817. The character and tendency of this Society was after this fully set forth by Wm. Jay, of N. Y., in 1835. He says, "Of the seventeen vice-presidents, only five were selected from the free States, while the twelve managers were, it is believed, without one exception, slaveholders. The first two articles of the constitution are the only ones relating to the Society. They are as follows:"

"Art. I. This Society shall be called The American Society for colonizing the free people of color of the United States.

"Art. II. The object to which its attention is to be exclusively directed, is to promote and execute a plan for colonizing (with their consent) the free people of color residing in our country, in Africa, or such other place as Congress shall deem most expedient. And the Society shall act to effect this object in co-operation with the General Government, and such of the States as may adopt regulations on the subject."

The subject was new to me, having had but little knowledge of it while following the sea. For a while it appeared that the movers in this work were honest in their declarations respecting the free people of color, and the abolition of slavery from the Union. But when antislavery societies began, and were being organized, from 1831 to 1834, it became evident that they were the worst enemies of the free people of color, and clearly manifest that they labored to perpetuate slavery in the slave-holding States, and manifested the most bitter opposition to antislavery men and measures.

Up to 1832 the Christian church in Fairhaven, with which I had united, had occupied a rented hall, and now began to feel the need of having a house of worship of their own in a more convenient place. Four of the brethren united together and built one, which was called "The Washington-street Christian meeting-house." Soon after it was finished and dedicated, we commenced a series of religious meetings, in which the Lord graciously answered our prayers and poured out his Spirit upon us, and many souls were converted. The other churches became zealously affected, and the work of God spread throughout the village. For many weeks in succession the church-bells were ringing, morning, afternoon, and evening, for preaching, and social meetings. It was thought by those who spoke of it that the whole population of the unconverted were under the deep movings of God's Holy Spirit.

Our village had been blessed with several revivals before, but I was from home, except during two, the last of which I have just mentioned. The first one was in the year 1807, when the people were immersed in the love and pleasures of the world, and pride of life. The work was wonderful to them, and altogether unexpected. Although we had a stated ministry and regular preaching, it was ascertained that there were but two family altars in the place, viz., at Mr. J.'s, and my father's. I remember that I felt deeply interested in that work, and loved to attend their prayer-meetings, and have often thought that the Lord at that time forgave me my sins, but I, like too many other youth, neglected to tell my feelings to my parents, or any one, feeling that religion was for older ones than myself; and before the revival wholly sub-sided, my mind was occupied in preparing for my first European voyage.

From the year 1824, when I made my covenant with God, I had lived up to the principles of total abstinence from all intoxicating drinks, but had continued the use of tea and coffee, without much conviction about their poisonous and stimulating effects, for about seven years longer. With my small stock of knowledge on the subject, I was un-willing to be fairly convicted that these stimulants had any effect on me, until on a social visit with my wife at one of our neighbor's, where tea was served us somewhat stronger than our usual habit of drinking. It had such an effect on my whole system that I could not rest nor sleep until after midnight. I then became fully satisfied (and have never seen cause to change my belief since), that it was the tea I had drank which so affected me. From thence I became convicted of its intoxicating qualities and discarded the use of it. Soon after this, on the same principle, I discarded the use of coffee, so that now it is about thirty years since I have allowed myself knowingly to taste of either. If the reader should ask how much I have gained in this matter, I answer that my health is better, my mind is clearer, and my conscience in this re-spect is void of offense.

Sylvester Graham, in his Lectures on the Science of Human Life, says: "There is no truth in science more fully ascertained, than that both tea and coffee are among the most *powerful poisons* of the vegeta-ble kingdom."

Tea is spoken of in the Transylvania Journal of Medicine, as an anodyne, in some cases as truly so as opium. The Encyclopedia Americana says: "The effects of tea on the human system are those of a very mild narcotic, and, like those of any other narcotic, when taken in small quantities, exhilarating." Dr. Combe, in his valuable work on digestion and dietetics, observes that "when made very strong, or taken in large quantities, especially late in the evening, they [tea and coffee] not only ruin the stomach, but very seriously derange the health of the brain and nervous system."

I sold my place of residence in the year 1831, and was occupied much of my time in 1832 in locating my dwelling-house and outbuildings on my little farm, and was also associated with three of my Christian friends in building the Washington-street meeting-house. In 1831 it was stated that three thousand temperance societies were organized in the United States, with three hundred thousand members. (*See D. Haskell's Chronological View of the World,* p. 247.) Thus in four years—or from 1827—temperance societies had progressed from our small beginning in Fairhaven. Many ships were also adopting the temperance reform.

About the close of 1831, and commencement of 1832, Antislavery societies began to be organized again in the United States, advocating immediate emancipation. As the work progressed, antislavery advocates were maltreated and mobbed in many places where they attempted to organize or hold meetings to plead for the poor, oppressed slaves in our land. Colonization societies and their advocates were foremost in this shameful work, as any one may learn by reading William Jay's "Inquiry into their Character and Tendency." All their declarations of benevolence for the free people of color, and ardent desire to benefit the poor oppressed slaves, and finally save our country from the curse of slavery, vanished like the morning cloud and early dew, when reading of their disgraceful acts of violence in the city of New York and other places, to shut out the pleadings of humanity for the down-trodden and oppressed slave. The "New York Commercial Advertiser," and "Courier and Enquirer," were then among the best friends of colonization and slaveholding.

I then began to feel the importance of taking a decided stand on the side of the oppressed. My labor in the cause of temperance had caused a pretty thorough sifting of my friends, and I felt that I had no more that I wished to part with; but duty was clear that I could not be a consistent Christian if I stood on the side of the oppressor, for God was not there. Neither could I claim his promises if I stood on neutral ground. Hence my only alternative was to plead for the slave, and thus I decided.

In our religious meetings we talked and prayed, remembering "them that are in bonds, as bound with them." Heb. xiii. Some were offended, and some feared disunion. Notwithstanding the conflicting views and feelings in our midst, there were some in the churches that held to the principles of antislavery. And as the work advanced onward during the years of 1832 to 1835, in which there was much contention from all quarters of the Union about this matter, a call was made for a meeting, in which about forty citizens of Fairhaven came together and organized the Fairhaven Antislavery Society, auxiliary to the New England Antislavery Society. This drew down the wrath of a certain class of our neighbors, who also called opposition meetings, in which they passed resolutions denouncing us in very severe terms. Not for the principles which we had adopted in our constitution, for they were not contrary to the constitution of the United States, but because we had united together to plead for the abolition of American slavery, which they declared unconstitutional, and very unpopular. Threats were often made that our meetings would be broken up, &c., but fortunately we were left to go onward.

One of our members, on going to Charleston, South Carolina, was arraigned before the authorities of the city, charged with being a member of the Fairhaven Antislavery Society. To save himself from being dealt with in their way, he renounced his abolitionism, as he afterwards declared. But opposition was more clearly manifest in the North, where societies were continually organizing, than in the South.

William Lloyd Garrison, editor of an antislavery paper, called "The Liberator," published in Boston, Mass., was heralded in many of the periodicals of that time (1835), as a most notorious abolitionist. Rewards, some as high, I think, as fifty thousand dollars, were offered for his head! The citizens of Boston, in and about Washington street and vicinity, where the antislavery meetings were held, became most furiously excited, and assembled on a certain afternoon around the building which they learned he occupied, and pursued him to a carpenter's shop, where he had fled from them, and brought him forth to the assembled multitude in the street, and placed a rope around his neck, to put an end to his life. Some of his friends, who were watching their movements, seeing his imminent danger, rushed around him, assuming in the confusion to engage with them, by laying hold of the rope so as to keep it from tightening round his neck, while some of the mob held the other end of the rope, and all rushing furiously, with hallooing and shouting along the street, leaving the great body of the assembled multitude of "*gentlemen of property and standing,*" listening with breathless anxiety to learn what was being done with their victim. Meantime the mob and Mr. Garrison's friends had continued running on unrestrained, until they found themselves at the portals of Leverett-street jail. Once there, by some measures of his friends, the jail was opened, and Mr. Garrison, to the astonishment of his wicked persecutors, was placed out of their reach; nor would the jailor bring him forth without orders from the law-abiding officers. As soon as the storm abated, Mr. G. was honorably released, and resumed his position, again pleading for the abolition of American slavery. The proslavery papers of Boston, in attempting to remove the stain and disgrace of this uncivilized work from the capital of the pilgrims, and a portion of its citizens, labored hard to prevent its being recorded as the work of a mob, and they declared that the people assembled on that occasion were " gentlemen of property and standing."

Previous to the foregoing occurrence, and while the subjects of antislavery and proslavery were agitating the Union, a wonderful phenomenon occurred in the heavens, which caused consternation and dismay among the people, namely, *the stars falling from heaven!* Many watchmen in the cities, and sailors in their night-watches on the ocean, together with those that were up, and their friends whom they called up, to witness the exhibition of the falling stars, were now relating what they had witnessed, as were also the newspapers of the times.

I will here give a few extracts. First from the " New York Journal of Commerce," November 15, 1833 : Henry Dana Ward, in closing up his account of this thrilling scene (which has been so often republished), says :

"We asked the watchman how long this had been. He said, 'About four o'clock it was the thickest.' We gazed until the rising sun put out the lesser falling stars with the lesser fixed stars, and until the morning star stood alone in the east, to introduce the bright orb of day. And here take the remark of one of my friends in mercantile life, who is as well informed in polite learning as most intelligent merchants of our city, who have not made science their study. Sitting down to breakfast, we spoke of the scene, and he said, 'I kept my eyes fixed on the morning star. I thought while that stood firm we were safe ; but I feared every moment that it would go and all would go with it.' The reader will see that this remark proceeded from an almost irresistible impression of an intelligent eye-witness, that the firmament had given way, that the whole host of stars had broken up, yet hope clung to the morning star, which never shone more glorious."

### In a subsequent statement, he adds :

" The dawn was a full hour, that morning, earlier than usual, and the whole eastern sky was transparent like molten glass, so as I never witnessed before nor since. An open arch of brilliant light arose from the east, above which arch stood the morning star, inexpressibly glorious for its brilliance and firmness on the face of the dark, transparent, and bursting firmament."

### From the " Baltimore Patriot :"

"MR. MUNROE: Being up this morning (November 13, 1833), I witnessed one of the most grand and alarming spectacles which ever beamed upon the eye of man. The light in my room was so great, that I could see the hour of the morning by my watch which hung over my mantel, and supposing there was a fire near at hand, probably on my own premises, I sprung to the window, and behold, the stars or some other bodies presenting a fiery appearance, were descending in torrents as rapid and as numerous as I ever saw flakes of snow, or drops of rain, in the midst of a storm."

## From the "Christian Advocate and Journal," December 13, 1833:

"The meteoric phenomenon, which occurred on the morning of the 13th of November last, was of so extraordinary and interesting a character as to be entitled to more than a passing notice. The lively and graphic descriptions which have appeared in various public journals, do not exceed the reality. No language indeed can come up to the splendor of that magnificent display. I hesitate not to say, that no one who did not witness it can form an adequate conception of its glory. It seemed as if the whole starry heavens had congregated at one point, near the zenith, and were simultaneously shooting forth, with the velocity of lightning, to every part of the horizon; and yet they were not exhausted—thousands swiftly followed in the tracks of thousands, as if created for the occasion, and illuminated the firmament with lines of irradiating light."

## The "Commercial Observer," of Nov. 25, 1833, copied from the "Old Countryman," reads as follows:

"We pronounce the raining of fire, which we saw on Wednesday morning last, an awful type, a sure forerunner, a merciful sign, of that great day, which the inhabitants of the earth will witness when the sixth seal will be opened. The time is just at hand, described, not only in the New Testament, but in the Old. A more correct picture of a fig-tree casting its leaves (or green figs), when blown by a mighty wind, it is not possible to behold."

## Extracts from the "People's Magazine," Boston, Jan., 1834, on the falling stars of Nov. 13, 1833:

"The Rockingham [Va.] 'Register'" calls it a "rain of fire"—"thousands of stars being seen at once." Some said, "It began with a considerable noise."

## The Lancaster [Pa.] "Examiner" says:

"The air was filled with innumerable meteors or stars. . . . . Hundreds of thousands of brilliant bodies might be seen falling at every moment, . . . . sloping their descent toward the earth, at an angle of about forty-five degrees, resembling flashes of fire."

The Salem " Register " speaks of their being seen " in Moca, on the Red Sea."

The " Journal of Commerce " informs us that " three hundred miles this side of Liverpool, the phenomenon was as splendid as here," and that in St. Lawrence county, " there was a snow storm during the phenomenon, in which the falling stars appeared like lightning." . . . That in Germantown, Pa., " They seemed like showers of great hail."

A captain of a New Bedford whale-ship, one of my acquaintances, says that " while lying at anchor that night on the coast of California, in the Pacific Ocean, I saw the stars falling all around me."

Prof. Olmstead, of Yale College, says:

"The extent of the shower of 1833 was such as to cover no inconsiderable part of the earth's surface, from the middle of the Atlantic on the east to the Pacific on the west; and from the northern coast of South America to undefined regions among the British Possessions on the north, the exhibition was visible, and everywhere presented nearly the same appearance. Those who were so fortunate as to witness the exhibition of shooting stars on the morning of Nov. 13, 1833, probably saw the *greatest display of celestial fireworks that has ever been seen since the creation of the world.*"

---

# Chapter Twenty-One.

*Moral Reform—Raising Trees—Culture of Silk—Second Advent of Christ—William Miller's Theory—His Lectures in Boston—First Second-Advent Paper—Eld. D. Millard's Letter—Eld. L. D. Fleming's Letter—H. Hawley's Letter—From the Maine Wesleyan Journal.*

In connection with these portentous signs in the heavens, moral reform was working its way like leaven throughout the United States. To all appearance, some unseen agency was assisting those who were struggling in the up-hill work of opposing the masses, while they were soliciting and enlisting the energies and sympathies of men, women, and children, to help stay the tide of intemperance and slavery, which, to all human appearance, if not stayed, would demoralize and debase us below the moral standard of all the civilized nations of the earth, before the close of the then rising generation.

What appeared the most inexplicable in moving forward this work, was to see ministers, whose Christian characters were before unsullied in the community, pleading in favor of slavery, upholding rum-drinking and rum-selling, and keeping a large majority of their church and congregation under their influence. Others were mute, waiting to see how their friends decided. Some there were, however, who took a noble stand in the work of reform.

Moral-reform societies were multiplied in various places, as were also Peace societies, having for their object the abolition of war. They proposed to settle all disputes or difficulties of importance, by reference to a Congress of Nations.

After finishing my buildings on my farm, before referred to, I commenced the work of raising mulberry trees, to obtain their foliage to feed the silkworm, designing to enter into the culture of silk. I had erected a school-house on my place, in which I designed to have a manual-labor school for youth. I calculated to employ them a certain portion of the time to gather the mulberry foliage, and attend to the feeding of the silk-worms; and as the work advanced, other branches of the business also, such as reeling and preparing the silk for market. By an examination of able writers on the subject, I was satisfied that silk could be produced to advantage in New England as well as in Europe. While my trees were maturing, we raised and fed the silkworm two or three seasons on a small scale, which satisfied me that by attention and care the business could be made profitable. Many that commenced the business about the time I did, also entered into the speculation and excitement about raising the Chinese multicaulis tree for sale, which enriched some, disappointed many, and caused a failure, because silk-culture could not be made a money-making business in its infancy. I was endeavoring to raise my trees first, before entering upon the business, and had many trees which had begun to bear fruit, and my third orchard in a thriving condition, designing, if I lived, to attend to that business only.

In the fall of 1839, while engaged in my orchard, one Eld. R., an acquaintance of mine, and a preacher in the Christian connection, called upon me and inquired if I would like to go to New Bedford, about two miles distant, that evening, and hear him preach on the SECOND COMING OF CHRIST. I asked Eld. R. if he thought he could show or prove anything about the Saviour's coming. He answered that he thought he could. He stated that the North Christian meeting-house in New Bedford was offered him to give a course of five lectures on that subject. I promised to go with him, but I was very much surprised to learn that any one could show anything about the *time* of the Saviour's second coming.

A little previous to this, while spending an evening in a social company of friends, Eld. H. stated that he had heard that there was a Mr. Miller preaching in the State of New York that the Lord Jesus Christ was coming in about 1843. I believe this was the first time I had ever heard the subject mentioned. It appeared so impossible, that I attempted to raise an objection, but was told that he brought a great deal of Scripture to prove it. But when I heard Eld. R. present the Scripture testimony on the subject in his first lecture, I was deeply interested, as was also my companion. After meeting, we had ridden some distance toward home, absorbed in this important subject, when I broke the silence by saying, "*That is the truth!*" My companion replied, "Oh, you are so sanguine always!" I argued that Eld. R. had made it very clear to my mind, but we would hear further. The meeting continued with crowded congregations and increasing interest to the close, and I felt that my mind was much enlightened on this important subject.

I now obtained Wm. Miller's book of nineteen lectures, which I read with deep interest, especially his argument on the prophetic periods of Daniel's vision, which heretofore, when I read the Bible in course, appeared to me so intricate, and led me to wonder what importance there could be attached to those days connected with his pictorial prophecy of chapters vii and viii. But I now began to learn that those days were so many years, and those years were now to close in about 1843, at which period of time, according to Mr. Miller's view of the prophecies, Christ would personally appear the second time.

With my limited views of the subject of the second advent, I saw that if Mr. Miller was correct respecting the soon coming of the Saviour, then the most important point in his theory was to learn WHERE to commence Daniel's prophetic periods, and trace them to their termination. The first issue in pamphlet form by Mr. Miller is dated 1832. Some say his first lecture on the second coming of Christ was delivered in August, 1833. His first lectures in Boston, Mass., in the Chardon-street and Marlborough chapels, were in the winter of 1840. This opened the way for Eld. Joshua V. Himes, of Boston, to issue, as editor, the first periodical, or newspaper, published on the second advent of our Lord and Saviour Jesus Christ, called the "Signs of the Times," in Boston, Mass., March, 1840.

As Eld. J. V. Himes was as destitute of means as

any other minister who at that time boldly preached
and advocated the necessity of moral reform, and
was expressing an anxious desire to get up a paper
on the subject of the second advent, an aged sea-
captain from the State of Maine, being present,
handed him a silver dollar. "With this one dollar," said Eld. Himes, "we commenced to publish
the 'Signs of the Times.'"

To give some idea of the effect of Mr. Miller's
preaching on the second coming of Christ, in New
England, I will here give some extracts from letters
published in the "Signs of the Times," April 15,
1840. The first is from the pen of Eld. D. Millard,
Portsmouth, N. H. He writes:

"On the 23d of January, Bro. Miller came into town and
commenced a course of lectures in the chapel, on the second
coming of Christ. During the nine days he remained, crowds
flocked to hear him. Before he concluded his lectures a
large number of anxious souls came forward for prayers.
Our meetings continued every day and evening for a length
of time after he left. Such an intense state of feeling as now
pervaded our congregation we never witnessed before in any
place. Not unfrequently from sixty to eighty would come
forward for prayers in the evening. Such an awful spirit of
solemnity seemed to settle down on the place, that hard
must have been the sinner's heart that could withstand it.
All was order and solemnity. Generally, as soon as souls
were delivered they were ready to proclaim it, and exhort
their friends in the most moving language to come to the
fountain of life. Our meetings thus continued on evenings
for six weeks. For weeks together the ringing of bells for
daily meetings rendered our town like a continual Sabbath.
Indeed, such a season of revival was never before witnessed
in Portsmouth by the oldest inhabitants. It would be difficult at present to ascertain the number of conversions in
town. It is variously estimated at from 500 to 700. Never,
while I linger on the shores of mortality, do I expect to enjoy more of Heaven than we have in some of our late meetings, and on baptizing occasions. At the water-side thousands would gather to witness this solemn institution, and
many would return from the place weeping."

Another letter is from Eld. L. D. Fleming, of Portsmouth, N. H. He says:

"Things here are moving powerfully. Last evening about 200 came forward for prayers, and the interest seems constantly increasing. The whole city seems to be agitated. Bro. Miller's lectures have not the least effect to affright; they are far from it. The great alarm is among those that did not come near. But those who candidly heard are far from excitement and alarm. The interest awakened by the lectures is of the most deliberate kind, and though it is the greatest revival I ever saw, yet there is the least passionate excitement. It seems to take the greatest hold on the male part of the community. What produces the effect is this: Bro. Miller simply takes the sword of the Spirit, unsheathed and naked, and lays its sharp edge on the naked heart, and it cuts—that's all. Before the edge of this mighty weapon, infidelity falls and Universalism withers; false foundations vanish, and Babel's merchants wonder. It seems to me that this must be a little the nearest like apostolic revivals of anything modern times have witnessed."

April 6 he writes again:

"There has probably never been so much religious interest among the inhabitants of this place generally, as at present; and Mr. Miller must be regarded directly as the instrument, although no doubt many will deny it, as some are very unwilling to admit that a good work of God can follow his labors; and yet we have the most indubitable evidence that this is the work of the Lord. At some of our meetings since Bro. M. left, as many as 250, it has been estimated, have expressed a desire for religion by coming forward for prayers, and probably between one and two hundred have professed conversion at our meetings. And now the fire is being kindled through the whole city, and all the adjacent country. A number of rumsellers have turned their shops into meeting-rooms, and those places that were once devoted to intemperance and revelry, are now devoted to prayer and praise. Infidels, Deists, Universalists, and the most abandoned profligates, have been converted. Prayer-meetings have been established in every part of the city by the different denominations, or by individuals, and at almost every hour. I was conducted to a room over one of the banks, where I found from thirty to forty men of different denominations engaged with one accord in prayer at eleven o'clock in the daytime! In short, it would be almost impossible to give an adequate idea of the interest now felt in this city. One of the principal booksellers informed me that he had sold more Bibles in one month, since Bro. Miller came here, than he had in any four months previous."

## WHAT WAS SAID OF MR. MILLER AND HIS DOCTRINE BY OTHERS.

### H. Hawley, writing from Groton, Mass., to Eld. Himes, April 10, 1840, said:

"During an interview I had with you a few days since, you requested me to give a statement of the results, so far as I had witnessed them, of Mr. Miller's lectures in this vicinity. Before complying with your request, I beg leave to say, that I am not a believer in the theory of Mr. Miller. But I am decidedly in favor of the discussion of the subject. I believe that Mr. Miller's lectures are so fraught with gospel truth that, whatever may be his error in regard to the time of our Lord's appearing, he will do great good. I rejoice that there is a subject being discussed in the community so happily adapted to wake up the public mind to the great things of religion, and to check the growing worldliness and sensuality of the present age. Mr. Miller has lectured in this and other adjoining towns, with marked success, by precious revivals of religion in all of these places. I am bold to declare that I see nothing in the theory at all calculated to make men immoral; but I do believe it will have the opposite effect. Facts speak too plainly on this subject not to be credited."

### From the Maine "Wesleyan Journal" of May, 1840:

"Mr. Miller has been in Portland, lecturing to crowded houses in Casco-street church, on his favorite theme, the end of the world. As faithful chroniclers of passing events, it will be expected of us that we say something of the man and his peculiar views.

"Mr. Miller is about sixty years of age; a plain farmer, from Hampton, in the State of New York. He is a member of the Baptist church in that place, from which he brings satisfactory testimonials of good standing, and license to improve publicly. He has, we understand, numerous testimonials from clergymen of different denominations, favorable to his general character. We should think him a man of but common-school education; evidently possessing strong powers of mind, which, for about fourteen years, have been almost exclusively bent on the investigation of Scripture prophecy. The last eight years of his life have been devoted to lecturing on this favorite subject. Mr. Miller's theory is, that in 1843 Christ will make his personal appearance on earth. In a very ingenious manner he brings all the mystic numbers in the Scripture prophecy to bear upon the important epoch of 1843. First, he makes the 2300 days (or years) of Dan. viii, 14, to commence at the same time as the seventy weeks (or 490 years), which latter period terminated in the cutting off of the Messiah, A. D. 33. The former period, then, extends 1810 years longer, or till 1843, when the end will come.

"Mr. Miller is a great stickler for literal interpretation, never admitting the figurative unless absolutely required to make correct sense, or meet the event which is intended to be pointed out. He doubtless believes, most unwaveringly, all he teaches to others. His lectures are interspersed with powerful admonitions to the wicked, and he handles Universalism with gloves of steel."

---

# Chapter Twenty-Two.

*First Call for a Conference to Discuss the Subject of the Second Coming of our Lord Jesus Christ—Convened in Boston, Mass.—Conference Address sent forth to the World—Diving Bell—Gathering Stones from the Bottom of the Sea—First Second-Advent Conference—Wm. Miller's Lectures in Fairhaven, Mass.—Also in New Bedford—Address to Ministers —Ministers' Meeting—Antiochus Epiphanes—Thirty-two Square Rods for Every Person—Second Second-Advent Conference.*

THE "Signs of the Times," of Boston, Mass., Sept. 1 and 15, 1840, published a call for a General Conference on the coming of our Lord Jesus Christ, saying:

"The undersigned, believers in the second coming and kingdom of the Messiah at hand, cordially unite in the call for a General Conference of our brethren of the United States, and elsewhere, who are also looking for the advent near, to meet at Boston, Mass., Wednesday, October 14, 1840, at ten o'clock, A. M., to continue two days, or as long as may then be found best. The object of the Conference will not be to form a new organization in the faith of Christ, nor to assail others of our brethren who differ with us in regard to the period and manner of the advent, but to discuss the whole subject faithfully and fairly, in the exercise of that spirit of Christ, in which it will be safe to meet him immediately at the Judgment seat.

| | |
|---|---|
| WILLIAM MILLER, | DAVID MILLARD, |
| HENRY DANA WARD, | L. D. FLEMING, |
| HENRY JONES, | JOSEPH BATES, |
| HENRY PLUMER, | CHAS. F. STEVENS, |
| JOHN TRUAR, | P. R. RUSSELL, |
| JOSIAH LITCH, | ISAIAH SEAVY, |
| JOSHUA P. ATWOOD, | TIMOTHY COLE, |
| DANIEL MERRILL, | J. V. HIMES. |

"We have received other names, but too late for insertion. No person will be expected to take any active part in the Conference, except he confesses his faith in the near approach of our Lord in his kingdom; nor will any one be expected to take a part in the discussions until he has been introduced to the committee of arrangements, and has made known to them the part or point he is prepared to discuss."

In accordance with the call, the General Conference convened in Chardon-Street Chapel, Boston, Mass., October 14, 1840, and continued two days with increasing interest; at the close of which the communion of the Lord's supper was administered to about two hundred communicants of different denominations. Many of them were from remote distances. The meeting closed by singing the hymn beginning,

"When thou, my righteous Judge, shalt come."

The Spirit of the Lord had pervaded the meeting from its commencement, but now it seemed to vibrate and move the whole congregation. The singing of the hymn just mentioned, was "with the Spirit and with the understanding also." Thank the Lord now for that joyous occasion.

From this Conference, an address, in pamphlet form, of 150 pages, was circulated to thousands that were in (and those not in) the faith of Christ's second coming, in the United States and foreign lands. Eld. Joshua V. Himes entered into this work apparently with all the zeal of Joshua of old, in his preaching and editorial departments, in circulating all the light which could be elicited from every quarter on the subject of the second advent of the Saviour. Not because he believed that Christ was coming in 1843, for in conversation with him some time after he commenced the editorial department of the " Signs of the Times," he told me in confidence that he could not see it satisfactory to his mind, and therefore did not believe it. " Why," said I, "if this is your position," or words to that import, " why do you advocate it in this public manner ?" His answer was that he voluntarily took this position to bring out all the light that could be obtained on the subject, and that it was possible he should see it clear, and yet believe it—as he afterwards did, and admitted it.

I had known Eld. Himes from his youth, and for many years had been intimately acquainted and associated with him in the reforms of the day, and often cheered, strengthened and edified under his preaching. I knew him to be zealously affected in the cause of God, but not fanatical. And the instance here narrated was evidence of the strongest character to my mind, even to this time, that he was not moved out to take such a peculiar stand before the world altogether by human instrumentalities.

Previous to the Conference I had engaged myself as one of the proprietors of the New Bedford Bridge, to superintend its repairs, and at the same time keep it passable for carriages and footmen; hence there was some doubt about my getting to the meeting. At that time we were engaged with a vessel and diving-bell, in removing the stones that by some means had got into the channel of the draw-bridge, and were an obstruction to the heavy-laden ships passing through at low tides.

As some of my readers may wish to understand something respecting the operation of picking up rocks and stones from the bottom of the ocean, twenty-five or thirty feet under water, I will try to explain it.

A schooner, or two-masted vessel, is hauled up and secured by ropes close to the draw-bridge. There is a tackle between her mast-heads, the lower part of which is hooked into an iron eye-strap, which was fastened at the top of a diving-bell, standing on the schooner's deck.

The bell itself was in the form of a sugar-loaf, or cone, about nine feet high, and six feet in diameter at the bottom. It was provided with a seat inside for two persons, and when sunk to the bottom of the sea, the water would rise up about three feet in the open bottom. (Sink a teacup or bowl, bottom side up, in a pail of water, and you will have a very fair illustration of a diving-bell.) The space inside, above water, contained our allowance of air. For two persons it would last about an hour and a half; then it became necessary to be hoisted up to the surface for a supply of fresh air. To communicate with our companions on deck, three telegraphic lines (or cords) were in working order—the lower ends being hitched up inside of the bell. A few small glass blocks were set into the upper part of the bell, which lighted up our apartment while under water, about equal to the light above, at sunset.

I went down with the diver a few times, for the purpose of ascertaining more correctly how the work could be accomplished. The bell was provided with guys to change its position when at the bottom, and a kind of basket to put the stones in. It was then hoisted from the deck, and we crawled underneath and up into the seats about four feet from the bottom. When the bell reached the water, by lowering the tackle, and began to shut all the air out except what was contained where we were, it produced a shuddering sensation, and singular cracking noise in our heads, more especially on the ears, causing an involuntary working of the fingers there to let more air in, and relieve us of the painful sensation which continued to some extent while under water.

After the bell reached the bottom, we could telegraph to be moved any way within a small circle. When the diver loaded the basket with rocks and stones, by means of his iron instruments, it was made known to those on deck by pulling one of the cords, and then it was hoisted up and emptied. By means of a rope attached to the lower end of the basket, the diver would pull it back again, and thus he might continue his risky work until admonished for life to pull the telegraphic cord, and be hoisted up for a fresh supply of God's free air.

While at the bottom of the sea, we could learn very quickly when the tide turned to flow in, or ebb out, by its motion over the shells and stones, which we could see as plainly as in a little brook of water. No matter how deep the water, its ebbing and flowing moves the whole body alike from top to bottom. Where the tide ebbs and flows, the vast bodies of river and harbor waters are in constant rushing motion, from the top to the bottom. But this is only while the change of tide is taking place. And twice every twenty-four hours a new body of rushing waters are rolled into the harbors from the mother ocean, adding fresh sources of healthy action to the fish that swim, and the stationary shell-fish, and those buried beneath the sand at low water mark—all for the benefit of man, and especially the poor who live near the sea coast.

By persevering in our new business, in picking up rocks and stones from the bottom of the sea, the ship channel was cleared in time for me to leave, and with my companion, be present at the opening of the first Second-advent Conference in the world, much to our gratification and pleasure. Bro. Miller, in the wisdom of God, was suddenly taken ill about this time, and could not leave his home in Low Hampton, New York, to attend the Conference, which was a disappointment to many.

After the great Conference, mentioned in another part of this chapter, Second-advent preaching was called for in many places. In March, 1841, Bro. Miller commenced a course of lectures in the Washington-street meeting-house, in Fairhaven, Mass. I thought if he could be obtained to lecture on the second coming of Christ, to my friends and neighbors, I would willingly give my seat in the meeting-house to others, if the house should be crowded. I had been reading his lectures, and supposed I understood the most he would preach.

But after hearing his first lecture, I felt that I could not be denied the privilege of hearing the whole course, for his preaching was deeply interesting, and very far in advance of his written lectures.

The house was so crowded that a great portion could not be seated, and yet all was quiet and still as night. It seemed as though the people were hearing for *themselves*. I believe they did *then*. Passing round among them the day after the lecture, one would hear another inquiring of his neighbor, "Were you at the meeting last night?" "Yes." "Did you ever hear such preaching before?" "No." "What do you think of his doctrine?" &c., &c. Many called on Bro. Miller to converse with him relative to the doctrine he taught, and seemed highly pleased with his prompt and ready quotations of Scripture in reply. Elders Himes and Cole accompanied him to Fairhaven. His week's labor with us seemed to work a very apparent change among the people.

His next course of lectures commenced the next week, in the North Christian meeting-house, in the city of New Bedford, about two miles distant. It was supposed that here he had about fifteen hundred hearers, the number that the house would accommodate at one time. A large portion of the aristocracy and ministers were in attendance. No such religious excitement for the time was ever heard of there. The interest seemed deep and wide-spread. At the close of the last meeting, Bro. Miller affectionately addressed the ministers, and exhorted them to faithfulness in their responsible work, and said, "I have been preaching to your people on the soon-coming of our Lord Jesus Christ, as I understand it from the Scriptures," and added that, if they thought he was right, it was highly important that they should teach it to their respective congregations. But if he was wrong, he much desired to be set right, and expressed a strong desire to meet with them before he left the place, and examine the subject with them. The Baptist minister proposed the vestry of his church, in William street, at nine o'clock next morning.

I was not a minister then, but I had a strong desire to attend this meeting, to learn how the ministers received the Second-advent doctrine. By request, a number of lay members, with myself, were permitted to attend. When the meeting commenced in the morning, I counted twenty-two ministers present, belonging to the place and within a circle of a few miles around the city, and about forty lay members. After the meeting was organized, Bro. Miller proposed that they begin with the prophecy of Daniel, and requested the reader of the Scriptures to commence with the second chapter. Occasionally Bro. Miller would request the reader to pause, and then ask the ministers how they understood what had just been read. At first they looked upon each other in silence, seemingly unwilling to expose their ignorance in this matter, or to see who would reply. After some time, one of the learned ministers replied, " We believe it as you do, sir." " Well," said Bro. M., " if you are all agreed on this point, we will proceed." No other one replied. The reader proceeded until another question. All was silent again until the same learned minister answered, " We believe this as you do, sir." And thus they professed to believe with him to the end of the chapter. It was truly cheering to see how all these ministers of the various denominations were admitting and believing the doctrine of the second advent. They then commenced with chapter vii, and continued in harmony with Bro. M., until an objection was raised respecting the little horn of the fourth kingdom. The reader of the Scriptures, who raised the objection, said he wanted a little time for consideration here, and wished to know if the meeting could not be adjourned until the next day. A motion was made for an adjournment, and carried.

The next morning the adjourned meeting convened, when the reader of the Scriptures introduced his commentary, and attempted to prove therefrom that Antiochus Epiphanes, one of the kings which had ruled in the kingdom of Syria, was the little horn of the fourth kingdom. Bro. M.'s statement that it could not be so, but that the little horn was Rome, failed to satisfy them. Here the meeting closed without any further effort on their part. Since that time the subject of the little horn of Daniel vii and viii, has been thoroughly criticised, and settled that Rome *is* the power in question.

Says Eld. J. N. Andrews on this subject:

"Out of many reasons that might be added to the above, we name but one. This power was to stand up against the Prince of princes. Verse 25. The Prince of princes is Jesus Christ. Rev. i, 5; xvii, 14; xix, 16. But Antiochus died one hundred and sixty-four years *before* our Lord was born. It is settled therefore that another power is the subject of this prophecy. To avoid the application of this prophecy to the Roman power, Pagan and Papal, the Papists have shifted it from Rome to Antiochus Epiphanes, a Syrian king, who could not not resist the mandates of Rome. See notes of the Douay [Romish] Bible on Dan, vii, viii, ix. This application is made by Papists to save their church from any share in the fulfillment of the prophecy; and in this they have been followed by the mass of opposers to the Advent faith."

See also "Prophecy of Daniel and Twenty-three Hundred Days," pp. 30–33.

For further proof that Rome was the power, and that our Lord and Saviour was the Prince which that power stood up against, as noted in the prophecy, see Acts iii, 15; v, 31; iv, 26, 27.

Among the many questions with reference to the second advent of the Saviour, Bro. Miller was asked the following: "How can the whole human race stand upon the earth at *one time*, as mentioned in Rev. xx, at the last Judgment?"

ANS. "Allow 800,000,000 for every thirty years in six thousand years, and it will give 160,000,-000,000. Allow 50,000,000 square miles for the earth, and it would make five trillion one hundred and twenty thousand millions of square rods. This divided among 160,000,000,000 of inhabitants, would leave thirty-two square rods to every individual on the globe!"

The second Second-advent Conference was held in the city of Lowell, Mass., June 15–17, 1841. At this meeting was present Bro. Josiah Litch, of Boston, Mass. Bro. L., in the year 1838, sent out his exposition of the ninth chaper of Revelation, predicting the fall of the Ottoman empire, at the close of the prophetic period, "an *hour* and a *day* and a *month* and a *year*," which would expire August 11, 1840, when the sixth angel would cease to sound, and the second woe be past. Having obtained official accounts of the revolution that had then just closed in the Ottoman empire, he came to this meeting prepared to prove the accomplishment of his prediction, to which tens of thousands with intense anxiety had been looking. The mass of evidence in the official accounts connected with the prophecy of his interesting discourse, proved that the Ottoman supremacy *did cease* on the 11th day of August, 1840. " And the second woe was passed, and behold the third woe cometh quickly." This wonderfully aroused the people of God, and gave a mighty impulse to the Advent movement.

## Chapter Twenty-Three.

*Fall of the Ottoman Empire in August, 1840—Passing of the Second Woe—Quickly—Space of time to proclaim the First Angel's Message, Rev. xiv, 6, 7—Conferences—Trials on leaving the Church—Moral Reform Societies—Boston Conference in 1842—1843 Charts—First Camp-Meeting—Camp-Meetings in the Summer and Fall of 1842—In Littleton, Mass., in August—Taunton, Mass., in September—Salem, Mass., in October—Power and work of the First Angel's Message.*

CHAPTER twenty-two closed with the Conference in the city of Lowell, Mass. The history of the fall of the Ottoman Supremacy will be found in J. Litch's Prophetic Expositions, Vol. ii, pages 181–200. On pages 198 and 199 is the summing up of his conclusive argument, showing how clearly the prophecy in Rev, ix, 13–15 was fulfilled on the 11th of August, 1840. On pages 189 and 190 will be found the reliable testimony of an eye-witness, who states facts to prove the same point, seemingly without any knowledge of the prophecy, or Litch's exposition of it. Here it is:

"The following is from Rev. Mr. Goodell, missionary of the American Board at Constantinople, addressed to the Board, and by them published in the Missionary Herald, for April 1841, p. 160.

" 'The power of Islamism is broken forever; and there is no concealing the fact even from themselves. They exist now by mere sufferance. And though there is a mighty effort made by the Christian governments to sustain them, yet at every step they sink lower and lower with fearful velocity. And though there is a great endeavor made to graft the institutions of civilized and Christian countries upon the decayed trunk, yet the very root itself is fast wasting away by the venom of its own poison. How wonderful it is, that, when all christendom combined together to check the progress of Mohammedan power, it waxed exceedingly great in spite of every opposition; and now when all the mighty potentates of Christian Europe, who feel fully competent to settle all the quarrels, and arrange the affairs of the whole world, are leagued together for its protection and defence, down it comes, in spite of all their fostering care.' "

These astounding facts prove that the prophecy of the sounding of the sixth angel for three hundred and ninety-one years and fifteen days, ended on the 11th day of August, 1840, and at the same time the second woe passed, and behold the third woe cometh quickly.

Mark, this short space of time called "quickly," is the whole period of time from the passing of the second woe and sixth angel, to the commencing of the third woe, and sounding of the seventh angel. ☞ This space of time called *quickly*, defines the time to announce to every nation and kindred and tongue and people that Christ is coming, by the proclamation of the angel's message in Rev. xiv, 6, 7. This is in accordance with the testimony of the Saviour. Matt. xxiv, 3, 14.

No marvel, then, that those who had been looking with intense anxiety for the passing away of the Ottoman supremacy, saw with such clearness that the time had come for a body of people to proclaim the message in question from thence down to the ending of the prophetic periods of Daniel's vision. And that the time had then come for this message to go to every nation, was still further demonstrated by a call for a Second-advent Conference to be held in Boston about the time the Ottoman empire lost its supremacy, and many weeks before the news of its fall reached the United States. At the close of this Conference, which was convened a few weeks after the call, in October, 1840, an address of the Conference setting forth their views respecting the second advent of our Lord, was sent forth to the world, and from thence the work continued until the message ended in the autumn of 1844.

Opposition from various quarters was now being made manifest, nevertheless the cause was hourly increasing. In October, 1841, the third Conference was held in Portland, Maine, which gave a new impulse to the cause in that section of country. Conferences were held in other places during the winter, particularly in New York city, Connecticut, New Hampshire and Vermont. Early in the spring of this year Elders Himes and Fitch held a Conference in Providence, R. I. Here, for the first time, I became acquainted with Bro. Fitch. His clear exposition of the prophecies relative to the second coming of our Lord, were listened to with deep interest. In connection with Elder Himes, their preaching deeply affected the hearts of the people, and a great many professed strong faith in the near coming of the Lord.

It was truly wonderful to learn how fast professed Christians could believe the evidences of the near coming of the Lord from the teaching of the Bible and history, and then disbelieve on no better authority than a sneer, a laugh, or "how do you know? nobody knows anything about it," etc. Some of my brethren of the Washington-st. Christian church, also began to wane in their Advent faith, and would say to me sometimes at the close of our social meetings," "Bro. Bates, we wish you would not say so much about the second coming of Christ." "Why," said I, "don't you believe it is as true now as it was when Bro. Miller preached it here last year, and you believed it?" "Well, we believe Christ is coming, but no one knows when. Bro. Miller taught that it would be in about 1843. But we don't think so. We like to hear you exhort and pray, but we don't like to hear you say so much about the second coming of Christ, and the time."

About this time the church elected a pastor, which was a source of deep trial to those who were more deeply interested in the Advent movement. Several of these interested ones sought and obtained their dismission. I continued in deep trial on this point for several weeks, hoping for some change for the better. I besought the Lord for light in this matter, and that which was granted me was to quietly withdraw and be free. I did so, and notified the trustees of the meeting-house that I was ready to dispose of my interest to them which I held in the premises. They declined my offer, which left me at liberty to dispose of it publicly, which I did at quite a sacrifice. I was now relieved from about twelve years' responsibilities and care, in aiding to build up and sustain a free church, who took the Bible for their only rule of faith and practice.

Four of us, members of the church, had united and built the meeting-house at a cost of over nine thousand dollars, nearly three-quarters of which belonged to us at the time I withdrew. Some of my good friends that were engaged in the temperance and abolition cause, came to know why I could not attend their stated meetings as formerly, and argued that my belief in the coming of the Saviour should make me more ardent in endeavoring to suppress these growing evils. My reply was, that in embracing the doctrine of the second coming of the Saviour, I found enough to engage my whole time in getting ready for such an event, and aiding others to do the same, and that all who embraced this doctrine would and must necessarily be advocates of temperance and the abolition of slavery; and those who opposed the doctrine of the second advent could not be very effective laborers in moral reform. And further, I could not see duty in leaving such a great work to labor single-handed as we had done, when so much more could be accomplished in working at the fountainhead, and make us every way right as we should be for the coming of the Lord.

In May, 1842, a General Conference was convened in Boston, Mass. At the opening of this meeting, Brn. Charles Fitch and Apollos Hale, of Haverhill, presented the pictorial prophecies of Daniel and John, which they had painted on cloth, with the prophetic numbers, showing their fulfillment. Bro. Fitch in explaining from his chart before the Conference, said, while examining these prophecies, he had thought if he could get out something of the kind as here presented it would simplify the subject and make it much easier for him to present to an audience. Here was more light in our pathway. These brethren had been doing what the Lord had shown Habbakuk in his vision 2468 years before, saying, "Write the vision and make it plain upon tables, that he may run that readeth it. For the vision is yet for an appointed time." Hab. ii, 2.

After some discussion on the subject, it was voted unanimously to have three hundred similar to this one lithographed, which was soon accomplished. They were called "the '43 charts." This was a very important Conference. A camp-meeting was now appointed to convene the last week in June, at East Kingston, N. H., where an immense multitude assembled to hear the good news and glad tidings of the coming of our blessed Lord. I had not the pleasure of attending this meeting, but heard most stirring reports of what was accomplished there. Camp-meetings and conferences were now being multiplied throughout the Middle and Northern States, and Canada, and the messengers were proclaiming in the language of the message, " THE HOUR OF HIS JUDG-MENT IS COME !"

During the month of August, 1842, a Second-advent camp-meeting was held in Littleton, Mass. This was the first camp-meeting that I had ever attended. It was quite a novel thing to see such a variety of tents pitched around the ministers' stand, among the tall, shady trees. At the opening of the meeting, we learned that those who occupied them were families from the various towns in the vicinity of the camp, and the city of Lowell, who were interested in the Advent doctrine.

The subject of the prophecies, connected with the second coming of our blessed Lord and Saviour, was the theme of ministers and people. All, except a mob who came to break up the meeting, seemed deeply interested; and these, after becoming acquainted with the nature of the meeting, ceased to trouble us, and peace, harmony and love prevailed during the entire meeting.

In September following, another camp-meeting was held in the southern part of Massachusetts, in the town of Taunton, in a beautiful grove of tall pines, by the railroad, between Boston and New Bedford, Mass., and Providence, R. I. This meeting was one of deep interest to the Advent cause, and opened the way for tens of thousands to attend and hear the proclamation of a coming Saviour. The cars, passing to and from these cities twice a day, landed the people in crowds on the camp-ground. A large number of ministers were in attendance. Eld. Josiah Litch took the lead of this meeting, which continued for about a week. At one of our morning prayer-meetings, as the invitation was given for those to come forward who wished to be prayed for, among the mourners it was said there were about *thirty ministers* that prostrated themselves, some of them *on their faces* beseeching God for mercy, and a preparation to meet their coming Lord! The preaching was so clear, and accompanied with so much power of the Holy Spirit, that it seemed like sin to doubt.

During this meeting, Eld. Millard, on his way home from a tour in Palestine, stopped at the camp-ground. Eld. Litch asked him a number of questions before the congregation, in relation to his mission—what he had learned while abroad in that country relative to the doctrine of the second advent. He replied that it was known and spoken of there. This information was reliable and cheering. We had believed, but this was knowledge from another quarter, that the message of the flying angel was crossing land and sea to every nation, kindred, tongue and people. On Sunday, it was judged that there were ten thousand people in the camp. The clear, weighty and solemn preaching of the second coming of Christ, and the fervent prayers and animated singing of the new Second-advent hymns, accompanied by the Spirit of the living God, sent such thrills through the camp, that many were shouting aloud for joy.

While the committee were moving around in the congregation, receiving contributions to defray the expenses of the meeting, some of the sisters began to take out their ear rings and strip off their finger rings and other jewelry, which example was followed by many others; and all thrown into the contribution. From this a report was soon circulated abroad, that the Taunton camp-meeting had taken up in their collection about *three flour barrels full of jewelry!* The committee of arrangements anticipating some wrong report about this matter, dispatched one of their number on the first train to New Bedford, instructing him to sell all the jewelry for cash. He did so, and returned with *seven dollars!* We considered this about six times less than what it should have sold for, the whole of which would have filled a pint measure. This was in keeping with many other false reports from Second-advent meetings, and then retailed about the world for facts. This meeting was a very important one, and it opened the way for hundreds of Second-advent meetings in the various towns and villages in that region of country.

In about four weeks another camp-meeting commenced about three miles back of Salem city, Mass. This surpassed any meeting for interest and numbers that I had ever attended. Eld. Joshua V. Himes had the charge, and pitched his big tent there—said to hold about seven thousand people. On approaching this meeting from the city of Salem, the main streets, cross roads, lanes, and paths, seemed almost utterly jammed and crowded with teams and carriages loaded with people, beside the jam of foot passengers—all crowding through the thick, smothering dust, to the camp-ground. Here in the large stone-wall pasture ground, interspersed with high, ragged rocks, clumps of bushes and straggling trees, bounded by woods on two sides and water on another, the city of Salem in the distance in another direction, were pitched the numerous tents for the great meeting. The big tent loomed above them all like a light-house, pointing to the looked-for harbor of the mariner, inviting the pressing multitude to enter and listen to the messengers of God proclaiming with stentorian voices the second coming of our Lord Jesus Christ.

The preaching was on the great leading doctrines of the second advent. Ministers and people listened with profound attention, desiring to know if these things were so, and what to do to fit them for that day. The ministers present who preached were Elders Himes, Litch, Fitch, Hale, Plumer, Cole, and many others. So anxious were the people to hear on this great subject, that those who could not be accommodated in the big tent, could be seen in the distance congregated under trees and clumps of trees, listening to selected ministers, explaining from the '43 chart, fastened to the trees.

When the preaching meetings closed, prayer-meetings and praying circles for the unconverted commenced in the tents. The evenings were more especially devoted to this part of the work.

Anxious souls who became fully convinced by listening to the truth, sought and found relief in these praying circles. Sometimes after listening to the united, earnest prayers, the shout of victory would follow, and then the rush to the tents to learn who was converted, and to hear them tell what Jesus had done for them, and how they loved his appearing. And those who wished to see the onward progress of this work of God, could join with the groups of men and women with their selected ministers passing down to the water-bound side of the camp, and there, in accordance with their faith, and in obedience to Him who had set them free from sin, see them buried with him by baptism, and while returning on their way rejoicing, meet with others going to be buried in like manner.

Bro. Miller, with others, was attending conferences and camp-meetings in other States, and his engagements were such that he could not see it duty to be at either of these meetings in Massachusetts which I have mentioned. Eld. Cole, while speaking of his last meeting, on the preachers' stand, said, " Last evening I preached in the meeting-house in Merideth, N. H., to a crowded house, and the people were so absorbed in the subject of the coming of Christ, that they remained on their knees after I had closed the meeting, so that I had to pick out my way by stepping over their heads, to be out of the meeting in time to secure my passage to the Salem camp-meeting, and when I got out of the house the people in the yard were also on their knees, and thus I passed on, obliged to leave them."

At the time the train of cars was coming in from Newburyport, N. H., to Boston, Bro. Litch had reached a point in his discourse respecting the prophecy of Nahum, how that "in the day of His preparation the chariots shall rage in the streets, they shall seem like torches, they shall run like the lightnings," when he cried out, "*Don't you hear them?*" Yes, we did; for they were then dashing by us like a streak of light for the Salem station. The time and manner to prove to his audience the fulfillment of this prophecy, and make us feel that we had most clearly entered into the day of God's preparation, produced a thrilling sensation in the camp.

On Sunday, it was judged there were *fifteen thousand people* in the camp. Here Bro. Fitch took leave of his brethren and started for the West, to spread the glad tidings of a coming Saviour. Two brethren in the ministry also started about this time to preach the second advent of Christ in England. This meeting gave an impetus to the cause that was wide-spread and lasting. When the camp broke up, a multitude from thence repaired to the Salem depot to secure their passages for Boston and vicinity. Some accident occurring to the trains from Newburyport, detained us in the Salem station for some two hours. Here our company commenced singing Advent hymns, and became so animated and deeply engaged that the people in the city came out in crowds, and seemed to listen with breathless attention until the cars came and changed the scene. Elder S. Hawley, a Congregationalist preacher who confessed faith in the Advent doctrine about this time, was invited to preach on the subject in the city of Salem, on Sunday. On attending to his appointment a few weeks afterward, he reported that the excitement there on this subject was intense. It was judged that he had *seven thousand hearers.*

Second-advent publications were now multiplying, and through the daily journals it was astonishing to learn with what rapidity this glorious doctrine was being proclaimed throughout the length and breadth of the Union and the Canadas. The people in the various States, counties, towns, cities, and villages, were all being aroused to hear the glad tidings.

Elder E. R. Pinney, of New York, in his exposition of Matt. xxiv, says: "As early as 1842, Second-advent publications had been sent to every missionary station in Europe, Asia, Africa, America, and both sides of the Rocky Mountains."

As no work of God had ever aroused the nations of the earth in such a powerful and sudden manner since the first advent of the Saviour and day of Pentecost, the evidence was powerful and prevailing that this work was the fulfilling of the prophecy of the flying angel "in the midst of heaven, having the everlasting gospel to preach unto them that dwell on the earth, and to every nation, and kindred, and tongue, and people, saying with a loud voice, fear God and give glory to him, for the *hour of his judgment is come.*"

## Chapter Twenty-Four.

*Opposition to the Proclamation of the Second Advent
of the Saviour—Mr. Miller's Statement of Facts,
from his "Apology and Defense"—The singular
Manner in which he was Called out to Proclaim the
Advent Doctrine—Signs and Wonders in the Heavens.*

As Second-advent Conferences, prayer-meetings,
and social occasions were multiplying in various directions in the land, so in like manner opposition
arose.  Presidents and Professors of theological
seminaries, learned and unlearned, ministers and
laymen, religious and political newspapers, and
prejudiced individuals, labored hard, by fair means
and foul, to disprove what they called Miller's
doctrine.  Many of them assailed his character,
and denounced him in most violent terms.  That
they were unacquainted with his reputation, and
also the work in which he was engaged, will be
manifestly evident from the following extracts
from his Apology and Defense.

He dates his conversion from A. D. 1816, and
says :

"I was constrained to admit that the Scriptures must be
a revelation from God ; they became my delight, and in Jesus
I found a friend.  I then devoted myself to prayer and reading of the word. . . . I commenced with Genesis, and read
verse by verse, proceeding no faster than the meaning of the
several passages should be so unfolded as to leave me free
from embarrassment respecting any mysticism or contradic-
tions.  Whenever I found anything obscure, my practice was
to compare it with all collateral passages ; and by the help
of Cruden, I examined all the texts of Scripture in which
were found any of the prominent words contained in any ob-

scure portion. Then by letting every word have its proper bearing on the subject of the text, if my view of it harmonized with every collateral passage in the Bible, it ceased to be a difficulty. In this way I pursued the study of the Bible, in my first perusal of it, for about two years, and was fully satisfied that it is its own interpreter.

"I was thus brought in 1818, at the close of my two years' study of the Scriptures, to the solemn conclusion that in about twenty-five years from that time all the affairs of our present state would be wound up. . . . With the solemn conviction that such momentous events were predicted in the Scriptures to be fulfilled in so short a space of time, the question came home to me with mighty power, regarding my duty to the world in view of the evidence that had affected my own mind. If the end was so near, it was important that the world should know it. . . . Various difficulties and objections would arise in my mind from time to time. . . . In this way I was occupied for five years—from 1818 to 1823.

"I continued to study the Scriptures, and was more and more convinced that I had a personal duty to perform respecting the matter. When I was about my business, it was continually ringing in my ears, "Go and tell the world of their danger.' This text was constantly occurring to me: Eze. xxxiii, 8, 9.

"I did all I could to avoid the conviction that anything was required of me; and I thought that by freely speaking of it to all, I should perform my duty, and that God would raise up the necessary instrumentality for the accomplishment of the work. I prayed that some minister might see the truth, and devote himself to its promulgation; but still I was impressed, 'Go and tell it to the world; their blood will I require at thy hand.' . . . I tried to excuse myself to the Lord for not going out and proclaiming it to the world. I told the Lord that I was not used to public speaking, that I had not the necessary qualifications to gain the attention of an audience, that I was very diffident, and feared to go before the world, that they would not believe me, nor hearken to my voice, that I was slow of speech, and of a slow tongue. But I could get no relief. In this way I struggled on for nine years longer, pursuing the study of the Bible. . . . I was then fifty years old, and it seemed impossible for me to surmount the obstacles which lay in my path to successfully present it in a public manner.

"One Saturday, after breakfast, in the summer of 1833, I sat down at my desk to examine some point, and as I arose to go out to work, it came home to me with more force than ever, 'Go and tell it to the world.' The impression was so sudden, and it came with such force, that I settled down into my chair, saying, 'I can't go, Lord.'  'Why not,' seemed to be the response; and then all my excuses came up, my want of ability, &c. ; but my distress became so great, I entered into solemn covenant with God that if he would open the way I would go and perform my duty to the world.  'What do you mean by opening the way?' seemed to come to me. 'Why,'' said I, 'if I should have an invitation to speak publicly in any place, I will go and tell them what I find in the Bible about the Lord's coming.' Instantly all my burden was gone, and I rejoiced that I should not probably be thus called upon; for I had never had such an invitation: my trials were not known, and I had but little expectation of being invited to any field of labor.

"In about half an hour from this time, before I had left the room, a son of Mr. Guilford, of Dresden, about sixteen miles from my residence, came in and said that his father had sent for me, and wished me to come home with him. Supposing that he wished to see me on some business, I asked him what he wanted?  He replied that there was to be no preaching in their church the next day, and his father wished to have me come and talk to the people on the subject of the Lord's coming.  I was immediately angry with myself for having made the covenant I had; I rebelled at once against the Lord, and determined not to go.  I left the boy without giving him any answer, and retired in great distress to a grove near by.  There I struggled with the Lord for about an hour, endeavoring to release myself from the covenant I had made with him; but I could get no relief. It was impressed upon my conscience, 'Will you make a covenant with God, and break it so soon?' and the exceeding sinfulness of thus doing overwhelmed me.  I finally submitted, and promised the Lord that if he would sustain me I would go, trusting in him to give me grace and ability to perform all he should require of me.  I returned to the house and found the boy still waiting; he remained until after dinner, and I returned with him to Dresden.

"The next day, which, as nearly as I can remember, was about the first Sunday in August, 1833, I delivered my first public lecture on the second advent.  The house was well filled with an attentive audience.  As soon as I commenced speaking, all my diffidence and embarrassment were gone, and I felt impressed only with the greatness of the subject, which, by the providence of God, I was enabled to present. At the close of the services I was requested to remain and lecture during the week, with which I complied.  They flocked in from the neighboring towns, a revival commenced, and it was said that in thirteen families all but two persons were hopefully converted. On Monday following I returned home, and found a letter from Eld. Fuller, of Poultney, Vermont, requesting me to go and lecture there on the same subject.

"The most pressing invitations from the ministry and the leading members of the churches, poured in continually from that time during the whole period of my public labors, and with more than one-half of which I was unable to comply. I received so many urgent calls for information, and to visit places, with which I could not comply, that in 1834, I concluded to publish my views in pamphlet form, which I did in a little tract of sixty-four pages. The first assistance I received from any source to defray my expenses, was two half dollars, which I received in Canada, in 1835. The next assistance I received, was the payment of my stage-fare to Lansingburgh, in 1837. Since then I have never received enough to pay my traveling expenses. I should not have alluded to this, were it not for the extravagant stories which have been circulated to my injury.

"From the commencement of that publication ('Signs of the Times,' in 1840) I was overwhelmed with invitations to labor in various places, with which I complied as far as my health and time would allow. I labored extensively in all the New England and Middle States, in Ohio, Michigan, Maryland, the District of Columbia, and in Canada East and West, giving about four thousand lectures in something like five hundred different towns.

"I should think that about two hundred ministers embraced my views, in all the different parts of the United States and Canada, and that there have been about five hundred public lecturers. In nearly a thousand places Advent congregations have been raised up, numbering, as near as I can estimate, some fifty thousand believers. On recalling to mind the several places of my labors, I can reckon up about six thousand instances of conversion from nature's darkness to God's marvelous light, the result of my personal labors alone; and I should judge the number to be much greater. Of this number, I can call to mind about seven hundred who were, previous to attending my lectures, infidels; and their number may have been twice as great. Great results have also followed from the labors of my brethren, many of whom I would like to mention here, if my limits would permit."

From the foregoing statement of facts we learn, first, how deeply Mr. Miller's mind was impressed

with the importance and necessity of proclaiming
the doctrine of the second advent of Christ, after
his first two years' study of the Bible; second,
how that he continued to make the Bible his study
fourteen years longer, under the same conviction
that he must proclaim it to the world; third, the
peculiar and clear manner in which he was finally
moved out to proclaim it; and then the final results of his labors, all go to prove that he was
moved upon in a most extraordinary manner to
discharge his duty, by leading out in the proclamation of this important doctrine, and that, too,
as we have before shown, in the right time.

The year 1843 was remarkable for signs and
wonders in the heavens; so much so that people
said those Adventists were the most fortunate
people in the world, for they had signs in the
heavens to help prove their doctrine. I will here
name one that was seen by millions of witnesses,
which I believe was supernatural. It was a brilliant stream of light which suddenly made its appearance in the path of the setting sun, a short
distance above the horizon, soon after dark, and
was very visible every clear night for three weeks
in the month of March. While attending an evening meeting in Rhode Island during this time, the
awfully grand and sublime appearance of this light
was the cause of much excitement.

During the time of this phenomenon, many
sought to quiet their feelings by saying it was a
comet; but without proof. I will here give a few
statements from different authors, selected from a
small pamphlet entitled, "Modern Phenomena of
the Heavens," by Henry Jones.

From the "New York Herald:"

"THE STRANGE SIGN IN THE HEAVENS.—The mystery which continues to hang over this strange and unknown visitor to our usually quiet solar system, has very greatly increased the excitement in relation to it."

## From the Hydrographical office, Washington, D. C.:

"THE STRANGE LIGHT.—Soon after we had retired, the officer of the watch announced the appearance of the comet in the west. The phenomenon was sublime and beautiful. The needle was greatly agitated, and a strongly-marked pencil of light was streaming up from the path of the sun, in an oblique direction, to the southward and eastward; its edges were parallel. It was about 1° 30′ (ninety miles) broad, and 30° (eighteen hundred miles) long."—*M. F. Maury, Lieut. U. S. N.*

Henry Jones makes the following statement concerning the appearance of this phenomenon in Connecticut:

"MESSRS. EDITORS: On the evening of the 5th, 6th, 7th, and 9th, instant, or commencing with Sunday evening last, the inhabitants of this town witnessed such a phenomenon as they had never before seen or heard of, being seen for about the space of an hour on each occasion, and mostly between seven and eight o'clock. Just about in the west on each of these evenings, the heavens being clear, there appeared a white streak of light, similar in color to the more common light in the north. It seemed about twice the width of the sun when in the same direction, and arose from the place of the setting sun."—*East Hampton, Ct., March* 10, 1843.

### He further says:

"Bro. Geo. Storrs, late of this city, and having recently called here on his way from the South, informs us that at Norfolk, Va., the late streak of light in the west, or the great comet, so called, appeared of a blood red color, that it caused great excitement among the inhabitants."

### In closing his statement, he adds:

"With regard to further notices of the comet, I have before me a host of them in print which need not now be copied concerning it, all combining to establish the important facts that the same phenomenon was seen during about the same period, or three weeks of time, through the length and breadth of the Union and eastern continent; that it was something *strange*.

"In regard to the natural cause of this wonder of the world I would be the last man to attempt to assign any other than that Jehovah himself is the sole cause of it, that he has done it by his own omnipotence to fulfill his word of promise concerning it, and to apprise his oppressed, cast down, and suffering saints, that he is now very soon coming for their deliverance."

Should the reader desire any further facts about this strange light of 1843, or other signs equally startling, he can be gratified by reading the pamphlet referred to in this article.

## Chapter Twenty-Five.

*The Stated Year for the Coming of the Lord—Sell my Place of Residence—Go with the Message to the Slave States—Meetings on Kent Island—Meetings in Centerville, Eastern Shore of Maryland—Judge Hopper—Advent Meetings on the Eastern Shore of Maryland—Meetings in Centerville—In Chester—Threatened Imprisonment—Feeling among the Slaves—Power of the Lord in the Meeting—Conviction of the People.*

As Mr. Miller had always stated the time for the coming of the Lord to be *about* 1843, he was now pressed to state the point of time more definitely. He said the Lord would come "some time between the 21st of March, 1843, and March 21, 1844." Before the close of this memorable year, Conferences were appointed to be held by Brn. Miller, Himes, and others, in the cities of New

York, Philadelphia, Baltimore, and Washington, to re-arouse and give the last warning, and if possible wake up and warn the household of Cæsar. It was a season of thrilling interest to all who truly loved the Second-advent doctrine.

About this time I sold my place of residence, including the greater portion of my real estate, paid up all my debts, so that I could say once more that I owed "no man anything." For some time I had been looking and waiting for an open way to go down South into the slaveholding States with the message. I was aware that slaveholders in the South were rejecting the doctrine of the second advent, and but a few months before had ordered Brn. Storrs and Brown from the city of Norfolk, Virginia, and I was told that if I went South the slaveholders would kill me for being an abolitionist. I saw there was some danger, but imperative duty and a desire to benefit them and unburden my own soul, overbalanced all such obstacles.

Bro. H. S. Gurney, now living in Memphis, Mich., said he would accompany me as far as Philadelphia. The steamer on which we took passage from Massachusetts, had much difficulty in getting through the floating sheet-ice on the last end of her passage, through Long Island Sound and Hurl Gate, to the city of New York. In Philadelphia we attended some of the crowded meetings of Bro. Miller and others. It was truly wonderful to see the multitudes of people gathered to hear him preach the coming of the Lord. Bro. G. now concluded to accompany me South. We reached the city of Annapolis, Maryland, by the way of Washington, and crossed the Chesapeake Bay through the ice to the central part of Kent Island, on which I had been cast away some twenty-seven winters before. At the tavern we found the people assembled for town meeting. The trustees of two meeting-houses who were present, were unwilling to open their doors for us, and intimated the danger of preaching the doctrine of Christ's coming among the slaves. We applied to the tavern-keeper for his house; he replied that we could have it as soon as the town meeting closed.

We then made an appointment before them, that preaching on the second advent would commence in the tavern the next afternoon at a given hour. Said the keeper of the tavern, "Is your name Joseph Bates?" I answered, "Yes." He said that he remembered my visiting his father's house when he was a small boy, and informed me that his mother and family were in another room and would be glad to see me. His mother said she thought she knew me when I first came to the house.

The notice of our meeting soon spread over the island, and the people came to hear, and soon became deeply interested about the coming of the Lord. Our meetings continued here, I think, for five successive afternoons. The mud was so deep, on account of a sudden thaw, that we held no evening meetings. The tavern was a temperance house, and accommodated us much better than any other place we could have found in the vicinity.

At the commencement of our last afternoon meeting, a brother who had become deeply interested in the cause, called Bro. G. and myself aside to inform us that there was a company about two miles off at a rum store, preparing to come and take us. We assured him that we were not much troubled about it, and urged him to go into the meeting with us and leave the matter in their hands. The people seemed so earnest to hear that my anxiety increased to make the subject as clear as I could for them, so that the idea of being taken from the meeting had entirely passed from me. But before I had time to sit down, a man who was at the meeting for the first time, whom I knew to be a Methodist class-leader, and one of the trustees that refused us the use of their meeting-house, arose and commenced denouncing the doctrine of the Advent in a violent manner, saying, that he could destroy or put down the whole of it in ten minutes. I remained standing, and replied, "We will hear you." In a few moments he seemed to be lost in his arguments, and began to talk about *riding us on a rail.* I said, "We are all ready for that, sir. If you will put a saddle on it, we would rather ride than walk." This caused such a sensation in the meeting that the man seemed to be at a loss to know which way to look for his friends.

I then said to him, "You must not think that we have come six hundred miles through the ice and snow, at our own expense, to give you the Midnight Cry, without first sitting down and counting the cost. And now, if the Lord has no more for us to do, we had as lief lie at the bottom of the Chesapeake Bay as anywhere else until the Lord comes. But if he has any more work for us to do, you can't touch us!"

One Dr. Harper arose and said, "Kent, you know better! This man has been giving us the truth, and reading it out of the Bible, and I believe it!" In a few minutes more Mr. Kent shook me heartily by the hand and said, "Bates, come and see us!" I thanked him, and said my work was so pressing I did not think I should have time; but I would come if I could. But we had no time to visit only those who had become deeply interested, and wished us to meet with them in their praying circles. At the close of our meeting we stated that we had the means, and were prepared to defray all the expenses of the meeting cheerfully, unless some of them wished to share with us. They decided that they would defray the expenses of the meeting, and not allow us to pay one cent.

On leaving Kent Island we passed along on the east side of the Chesapeake Bay, called the Eastern Shore of Maryland, to the county town of Centerville, about thirty miles distant, where we had sent an appointment to hold meetings. We chose to walk, that we might have a better opportunity to converse with the slaves and others, and furnish them with tracts which we had with us. On reaching Centerville we inquired for a Mr. Harper. On arriving at his store we presented our introductory letter, and were introduced to Judge Hopper, who was engaged in writing. A number of men and boys came crowding into the store, apparently full of expectation, when one of them began to question us respecting our views, and soon came to the point that Christ could not come now, because the gospel had not been preached to all the world. I replied that it had been preached to every creature. When he showed his unwillingness to believe, I inquired for a Bible, and read the following: "If ye continue in the faith, grounded and settled, and be not moved away from the hope of the gospel, which ye have heard, and which was preached to *every creature* which is under heaven," &c. Col. i, 23.

Said the man, "Where are you going to preach?"

Judge Hopper said, in their " new meeting-house."
" Well," said he, " I will come and hear you."
Mr. Harper invited us and the Judge to tea, and
to spend the evening. The Judge had a great
many questions to ask us respecting our faith, and
at about ten o'clock insisted on our going home
with him to spend the night. Before reaching his
house, which was about a mile out of town, said
he, " Mr. Bates, I understand that you are an abolitionist, and have come here to get away our
slaves." Said I, " Yes, Judge, I am an abolitionist, and have come to get your slaves, and *you too !*
As to getting your slaves *from* you, we have no
such intention ; for if you should give us all you
have (and I was informed he owned quite a number), we should not know what to do with them.
We teach that Christ is coming, and we want you
all saved."

He appeared satisfied and pleased with our reply, and in a few moments more we were introduced to his family. The Judge and Mr. Harper
were the principal owners in a new meeting-house
(as I understood), just erected for a new sect called
" The New-Sides," which had seceded from the
Methodist Episcopal Church, called " The Old-
Sides." These two friends stated that their new
meeting-house was free for us to occupy. We commenced there the next forenoon with a large congregation. Judge Hopper invited us to make his
house our home during our series of meetings.

Our meetings in Centerville, Maryland, continued about three days with much interest ; many
became deeply interested to hear for the first time
about the coming of the Lord. Judge Hopper
was very attentive, and admitted that he was almost persuaded of the correctness of our position.

We were told that one of his slaves was deeply convicted, and professed to have been converted during our meetings.

The second day of our labors the Judge arrived at his house before us, and was engaged reading his paper, by the last mail. It was the "Baltimore Patriot." When we came in said he, "Do you know who these were?" and commenced reading in substance as follows: "Two men who came up in a vessel from Kent Island, were in at our office, and related a circumstance respecting two Millerites that were recently there, preaching about Christ's second coming and the end of the world. When threatened with riding on a rail, they replied that they were all ready, and if they would put a saddle on the rail, it would be better to ride than to walk!" The editor added that, "The crush of matter and the wreck of worlds would be nothing to such men." We replied that such an occurrence did take place when we were on the island a short time previous, and that probably we were the individuals alluded to. He laughed heartily and pressed us to relate the circumstance while his family were gathering to the dinner table.

He then inquired which way we were going; we stated that we should like to go to the next county seat north-east. He gave us a letter of introduction to a friend of his, a lawyer, who had charge of the court-house in his absence, telling him to open the house for us to hold meetings in while we stayed. We arranged our appointments for five meetings, and sent them to the lawyer to publish, who was also editor of their village paper.

The name of this town was Chester, I believe, distant about twenty-five miles. One of our interested hearers sent his private carriage to convey us on our way. We were walking just before we came to the village, and met a man on foot seemingly in great haste, who stopped and inquired if we were the two Millerites who were going to preach in that place! We answered in the affirmative. "Well," said he, "I have traveled thirteen miles this morning to see you?" As he stood gazing on us, I said, "How do we look?" Said he, "You look like other men." His curiosity being gratified, we passed on and saw him no more. On arriving at the tavern for dinner, the tavern-keeper slipped the village paper into the hand of Bro. Gurney, for him to read the notice of the Miller meeting—supposing that we were the strangers expected. The notice closed by hoping that "the old women would not be frightened at these men's preaching about the end of the world."

After dinner we called to see the lawyer at his office, where we were entertained for hours listening to his skeptical views about the second advent, and answering his numerous questions. He was very punctual at all our meetings, and became so deeply convicted of the truth that he was as much, if not more alarmed about his preparation for the coming of the Lord, than the old women he was so troubled about. The people came out to hear, and listened attentively, particularly the slaves, who had to stand on the back side of the white congregation and wait until they had all passed out. This gave us a good opportunity to speak with them. So we asked them if they heard what was said. "Yes, massa, ebery word." "Do you believe?" "Yes, massa, believe it all." "Don't you want some tracts?" "Yes, massa." "Can you read?" "No, massa; but young missus, or massa's son will read for us."

In this way we distributed a good number of tracts, with which we had furnished ourselves from Elder Himes in Philadelphia. They seemed delighted with the Advent hymns. They heard Bro. Gurney sing the hymn, "I'm a pilgrim and I'm a stranger." One of the colored men came to our lodgings to beg one of the printed copies. Bro. G. had but one. Said he, "I'll give you a quarter of a dollar for it;" probably it was all the money the poor fellow had. He lingered as though he could not be denied. Bro. G. then copied it for him, which pleased him very much.

There were three denominational meeting-houses in the village where the people met to worship. Out of respect to them we gave notice that we should hold but one meeting on Sunday, and that would commence at candlelight. The next morning, while mailing a letter, the postmaster said that the ministers of the place were so enraged about the people's going to our meeting, that they were talking about having us imprisoned before night. I said to him, "Please give them our compliments, and tell them we are all ready; the jail is so nearly connected with our place of meetings that they will have but little trouble to get us there!" We heard nothing more from them. Our fears were not so much about going to jail, as that these ministers would influence the people to shut us out from giving them the Advent message. But the Lord in answer to prayer suffered them not to close the open door before us, for our meetings continued without interruption.

The last meeting was deeply interesting. The Lord helped us wonderfully. Our subject was the woe trumpets of Rev. ix, proving in accordance with Mr. Litch's calculation that the sixth angel ceased to sound, and the second woe passed in August, 1840, with the fall of the Turkish empire, and that the third woe was coming "quickly," when great voices would be heard in Heaven saying, "The kingdoms of this world are become the kingdoms of our Lord and of his Christ." When we closed the meeting, the white people remained fixed and silent. The poor slaves stood behind gazing and waiting for their superiors to move first. There sat the lawyer who had so faithfully warned the old women not to be scared about the preaching of the end of the world. He, and one or two others, had been taking notes of our subject. We sang an Advent hymn and exhorted them to get ready for the coming of the Lord, and dismissed them again. They remained silent and immovable. Bro. G. exhorted them faithfully, but they still remained silent, and appeared as though they had not the least desire to leave the place. We felt fully satisfied that God was operating by his Holy Spirit. We then sang another hymn, and dismissed them, and they began slowly and silently to retire.

We waited to have some conversation with the colored people. They said they understood, and seemed much affected. When we came out of the court-house the people stood in groups almost silent. We passed along by them, bidding them good-bye. The lawyer and the principal of the academy were watching for us, and walked with us to the hotel. Both of them were powerfully convicted, and apparently subdued. The teacher had argued with us several times to prove that this movement was all delusion; but now he began to confess. The lawyer seemed now to ask questions for himself, and was so intent on the subject that he detained us in conversation at the side of the hotel, until we were compelled by the cold to go in to the fire. We exhorted him to confess all his sins, and give his heart to the Lord. The principal of the academy said, "Now, brethren, I want you to go with me to my room, where we will have a good fire. I want to talk more about this work." He there confessed how skeptical he had been, and the opposition he had manifested, and how he had attended the meetings and taken notes on purpose to refute the doctrine. "But," said he, "I believe it all now. I believe, with you, that Christ is coming." We labored and prayed with him until after midnight. We were told next morning that some of the inhabitants were so powerfully convicted that they had not been in bed during the night. Two men who stopped at the hotel, said they had come thirty miles on horseback to attend the meetings. While here the way opened for a series of meetings some thirteen miles northward, at a place called The Three Corners. We were told that we had better not go, for the tavern keeper was a rank Universalist, and would oppose us.

# Chapter Twenty-Six.

*The Three Corners— Crowded Meeting— Singing—*
*Universalism— Places for Meeting— Opposition—*
*Dream—Extensive Front Yard—Slaves Ordered to*
*go to the Advent Meeting— Convicted of the Truth—*
*Return Home from Maryland— Visit to some of the*
*Islands of the Sea—First Disappointment in the*
*Second Advent Movement— Waiting for the Vision.*
*—Tarrying Time.*

ON our arrival at the place called "The Three
Corners," we feared from its appearance we should
have but few hearers.   An academy, a tavern, and
a Methodist meeting-house in the distance, with a
few scattered dwellings, were about all there was
to be seen.   Our appointment was to commence
the meeting that evening.   The Methodist trustees
refused us the use of their house.   We finally obtained the academy for our evening meeting, and
put up at the "Universalist tavern," kept by a
Mr. Dunbar.   A Methodist preacher on this circuit said to us, "I held a meeting in the academy
last first-day, and had but eighteen hearers; I
suppose your doctrine will call out a *few more.*"
Imagine our surprise at the hour of meeting to
find the house crowded, so that a great portion of
the congregation were perched on top of the seats,
looking over each other's heads.   We found a
place finally to hang up the "'43 chart."   Bro.
Gurney began to sing one of the favorite Advent
hymns, which stilled them into silence, and the
meeting continued with deep interest to the close.
We then stated our wish to hold four meetings

more, and commence the next afternoon, but we had no place open for us.   After waiting a moment, our landlord said: "Gentlemen, appoint your meeting at my house."   I hesitated, doubting whether it would be proper to appoint an Advent meeting where liquor was vended and drank without restraint.   As no other person spoke, I made the appointment at *Mr. Dunbar's tavern*, the next afternoon!   I believe it was two o'clock. After getting to the tavern, Mr. D. came in, followed by a number of ladies, saying: "Gentlemen, these ladies have come to hear you sing more of your new hymns; they are delighted with the singing, and interested about your doctrine."

After breakfast next morning, our host began in a very gentlemanly manner to show the inconsistent views of professed Christians, and the beauties of the doctrine of Universalism.   In order to relieve us both from long arguments, we told him we had nothing to do with the Universalist doctrine.   We had come there to preach the coming of Christ, and we wanted him and his neighbors to get ready.   Our conversation closed here, and he went out.   After a while he came home, saying, "Well, gentlemen, the Methodist meeting-house is open for you to lecture in.   The trustees have had some feeling about refusing you the use of their house.   It is now ready for your meeting this afternoon.   I did not believe they would let you hold your meetings in *my* house."

Soon after our meeting commenced in the afternoon, a well-dressed, intelligent-looking man entered and seated himself near the center of the house, and while I was explaining a passage of scripture from the book of Revelation, he looked at me earnestly and shook his head.   I said to the audience, "Here is a gentleman shaking his head. *He do n't believe.*" Before I had finished my discourse, and was quoting another passage from the same source, he repeated the operation. I said, "This gentleman is *shaking his head again.* He does not believe." His countenance changed, and he appeared confused. As Bro. Gurney and myself came down from the pulpit after closing the meeting he pressed his way through the crowd and took my hand, saying, "I want you to go home with me to-night." I thanked him and said, "I would with pleasure, but I have a friend here." Said he, "I want him to go, too, and I want you should bring that chart (pointing to it) with you." Another man pressed us to ride home with him, some two miles, to supper. Said this gentleman, "I'll go, too." He did so.

In the evening our congregation was larger, and very attentive. After meeting, our new friend took us into his coach with his wife. Soon after we left, he asked his wife if she remembered the dream that he told her. She said, "Yes." "Well," said he, "these are the two angels that I saw." Here he began to relate his dream. The following, in substance, is about all I now remember:

Just previous to our coming to the place, he dreamed of being in company with two angels that were declaring good news, and he remembered particularly how they looked. "Then," said he, "when you spoke about my shaking my head the second time, I looked again. I thought I had seen you. Here my dream came to me, and I knew by your sallow countenances that you were the two persons, and more especially you, because of that *mole* on your right cheek, which I saw there in my dream."

He stepped out and opened his gate, and I thought surely we shall be at the house soon. After a while we learned from him that it was *three miles from his front gate to his house!* His plantation was large, with a great number of slaves. He was a man of leisure, and had learned from some author peculiar notions about the book of Revelation. This was why he shook his head at my application, because of the opposite views. He and his wife entertained us a good part of the night, and until time for meeting the next afternoon, asking questions about the doctrine of the advent, the chart, &c. When Mr. Hurt's carriage was ready, he apologized for his remissness in not asking us to address his servants (slaves). I felt relieved at this, as I had rather. speak to them in the mixed congregation. But as we were getting into the coach, he said to his hostler, who was holding the reins, " Sam "—Harry, or some such name—" do you tell all hands to come to meeting this evening." " Yes, massa." " Don't you forget—ALL OF THEM." " No, massa." This was cheering to us—we wanted them to hear with their master.

The preceptor of the academy, and Mr. Dunbar, the landlord, were the two great leading Universalists in that section of the country. Both of them had now become interested in this new doctrine. The preceptor closed his school to attend the last afternoon meeting, and came in with three great books under his arm, expecting, I suppose, to confound us in some of our expositions of the prophecies by quotations from the dead languages. He appealed to his books but once, and, failing to prove his point, said no more. From their appearance, I was satisfied that he and Mr. D. were deeply convicted of the truth. As he was lugging home his books after meeting, I said in passing him, "What do you think of the subject now?" Said he, "I will give up."

In the evening the gallery was crowded with colored people; unquestionably the majority of them were Mr. Hurt's slaves. They listened with marked attention. Any thing that would work deliverance from perpetual bondage was good news to them. The congregation appeared remarkably willing to hear. At the close of the meeting we stated that our appointment had gone forward to Elktown, twenty-five miles north, for us to meet with the people the next evening, and we wished to engage one of their teams to carry us. Mr. Hurt courteously offered to see us there in his private carriage, and engaged us to tarry with him for the night. While waiting for the carriage after meeting, Mr. Dunbar came to us privately to ask if this doctrine was preached at the North, and also in England, and if this was the way Mr. Miller presented it. We answered that it was, only that Mr. Miller set it forth in a superior manner, and in far clearer light than we had ability to do. He walked about seemingly in deep distress.

Mr. Hurt now rode up, and we passed on with him. He seemed much troubled while he related the experience of himself and wife, and how he had refused to be a class-leader among the Methodists, and regretted that they could not be baptized. On our way in the morning we stopped at the tavern, and when we came out of our room with our baggage to settle our fare, Mr. Dunbar and the preceptor sat in the bar-roon, with their

Bibles open, listening to Mr. Hurt's dream concerning us, and his faith in the advent doctrine. Mr. Dunbar and the preceptor said they saw the truth as never before, and importuned us to stay and continue our meetings. "Besides," said they, "you are invited to lecture in a town some twelve miles east from this." We replied that our previous appointment at Elktown required us to be there that evening. They then pressed us to return, but as our arrangements were still farther north, we could not comply with their request.

From this place Mr. Hurt took us in his carriage to Elktown, some twenty-five miles distant, introducing us and the message to his friends on the way. In Elktown also he exerted himself to open the way for our meetings. When parting with us, after praying with him, he said, "I would give all I possess here, if I could feel as I believe you do in this work." We heard no more from him.

We held five meetings in the court house in Elktown. Some professed to believe, and were anxious to hear further, if we could have staid with them longer. From Elktown we took the cars to Philadelphia, and thence to New York city. Here we met with Mr. Miller, who had just returned from Washington, D. C., where he had been to give a course of lectures. At New York we took passage for the east, on board a Long Island steamer, for Fall River, Mass. In the evening, after passing Hurl Gate, we hung up the chart in the center of the passengers' cabin; by the time we had sung an advent hymn, a large company had collected, who began to inquire about the pictures on the chart. We replied, if they would be quietly seated, we would endeavor to explain. After a while they declared themselves

ready to hear, and listened attentively for some
time, until we were interrupted by an increasing
heavy gale from the east, which caused us to bear
up for a harbor. In consequence of the violence
of the gale, the route of the boat was changed,
and the passengers landed on the Connecticut
shore, who proceeded in the cars to Boston. The
subject of the advent of the Saviour was resumed
on board the cars, and continued to be agitated
until we separated at the passenger station at
Boston.

Before the passing of the time, we visited some
of the islands in the sea, belonging to Massachusetts and Rhode Island, namely, Nantucket, Mar-
tha's Vineyard, and Block Island. Of the ten or
twelve thousand inhabitants on these islands, many
professed to believe, and united in the advent
movement.

As we came down to the spring of 1844, and
approached the long-looked-for time published by
Mr. Miller and others, for the closing up of the
prophetic periods of Daniel's vision, and coming
of our Lord and Saviour, the work became more
and more exciting. Probably nothing since the
flood, in the days of Noah, has ever equaled it.

The most difficult point then to settle, was,
*where* in the history of the world the 2300 days
commenced. It was finally settled that 457 years
before Christ was the only reliable time. Thus
the sum of 457 years before Christ, and 1843 full
years after Christ, made just 2300 full and complete years.

Scripture testimony was also clear that every
year commenced with the new moon in the spring,
just fourteen days before the yearly passover. See
Ex. xii, 1–6; xiii, 3–4. It was therefore settled

that the 17th day of April, 1844, Roman time, was the close of the year 1843, Bible time.

The passing of this time was the first disappointment in the advent movement. Those who felt the burden of the message were left in deep trial and anguish of spirit. They were surrounded by those who were exulting with joy because of the failure of their calculation. In this trying time the Scriptures were searched most diligently, to ascertain, if possible, the cause of their disappointment. In the prophecy of Habakkuk were found a few points relative to the vision, which had never been particularly examined before. It reads thus: "For the vision is yet for an appointed time, but at the end it shall speak and not lie: though it *tarry*, *wait* for it; because it will surely come, it will not tarry." Hab. ii, 2, 3.

At this period it was said that there were some fifty thousand believers in this movement in the United States and the Canadas, who never, until the passing of the time, had realized or understood that there was a tarry or waiting time in the vision. This, and other scriptures of like import, encouraged the tried ones to hold on with unyielding faith. They were often attacked by their opponents with, "What are you going to do now, your time is past? You know you set the time for Christ to come at the termination of the 2300 days of Daniel's vision. Your time is now past, and he has not come; now why don't you confess your mistake, and give it all up?" Ans. "Because the Lord said, 'Wait for it.'" "Wait for what?" Ans. "*The vision.*" "How long?" Ans. "He did not say; but *he did say*, "WAIT FOR IT; BECAUSE IT WILL SURELY COME.' Give it up, did you say? We dare not!" "Why?" "Because the command of the Lord to his confiding and disappointed people, at this particular point of the Second-advent movement, was to WAIT."

## Chapter Twenty-Seven.

*Midnight Cry—First Angel's Message—The Ten Virgins—Second Disappointment—Three Angel's Messages—The Sabbath—Progress of the Work—Conclusion.*

THE first work of the Advent body in their disappointment was to re-examine the 2300 days of Daniel's vision. But they were unable to discover any error in their calculation. It was still evident and clear that it required every day of 457 years before Christ, and also every day of 1843 years after Christ to complete the 2300 years of the vision, on which the Advent movement started from 1840. It was also clear that the year must correspond and terminate with the Jewish sacred year.

At this important crisis, the "Advent Shield," was published, reviewing all the past movement, especially the prophetic periods, showing that we had followed them down correctly. We quote from Vol. i, No. 1, p. 87.

" We look upon the proclamation which has been made, as being the cry of the angel who proclaimed, ' The hour of his judgment is come.' (Rev. xiv, 6, 7.) It is the sound which is to reach all nations ; it is the proclamation of the everlasting gospel. In one shape or other this cry has gone abroad through the earth, wherever human beings are found, and we have had opportunity to hear of the fact."

"Joseph Wolfe, D. D., according to his journals, between the years 1821 and 1845, proclaimed the Lord's speedy advent, in Palestine, Egypt, Mesopotamia, Persia, Georgia, throughout the Ottoman empire, in Greece, Arabia, Turkistan, Hindostan, in Holland, Scotland and Ireland, at Constantinople, Jerusalem, St. Helena, and in New York city to all denominations," &c., &c.— *Voice of the Church, pp.* 343, 344.

From the foregoing historical facts, the unbiased reader will not fail to see with what wonderful speed the glorious doctrine of the second advent. of our Lord and Saviour spread throughout the whole habitable globe, and then ceased as suddenly, with those who were proclaiming it, as daylight with the setting sun. Those who were engaged in this most solemn work were some of the honest and faithful from all the churches. Said the "Advent Shield," p. 92:

"No cause of a moral or religious character, probably ever made such rapid advances as the cause of Adventism. Its votaries have been the most humble, pious, devoted members of the different churches. . . . Never have a set of men labored more faithfully and zealously in the cause of God, or with purer motives. Their record is on high."

While in this tarrying, waiting position, searching and praying for light on the track of prophecy, it was further seen that our Lord had given the parable of the ten virgins to illustrate the Advent movement. In answer to the question, "What shall be a sign of thy coming and of the end of the world?" (Matt. xxiv, 3,) our Lord pointed out some of the most important events with which the Christian church was to be connected from the time of his first to his second advent, such as the destruction of Jerusalem in A. D. 70, following which was the great tribulation of the Christian church for more than sixteen hundred years, under Pagan and Papal Rome. Then the darkening of the sun in 1780, and the falling stars in 1833. From thence the proclamation of his second coming in his kingdom, closing with a description of two classes of Adventists. And "then shall the kingdom of Heaven be likened unto ten virgins," (Matt. xxv, 1–13,) "which took their lamps and went forth to meet the bridegroom," &c. The words "kingdom of Heaven" undoubtedly refer to the same portion of the living church which he was pointing out in chapter xxiv, 45–51, who continue in their history with the same proclamation of his second coming. And all the way to verse 13, in every important move they make, their history is likened, or compared to the history of the ten virgins in the parable, namely, "tarry of the vision," "tarry of the bridegroom," midnight cry, "Behold the bridegroom cometh," &c.

Soon after the tarry of the vision of 2300 days, the second angel's message began to be proclaimed. See Rev. xiv, 8. While moving on in this message into the summer of 1844, the definite time for the close of the vision began to be taught. But the leading ministers opposed. A camp-meeting was appointed to convene in Exeter, N. H., on the 12th of August. On my way there in the cars, something like the following was several times very forcibly presented to my mind: "You are going to have new light here! something that will give a new impetus to the work." On my arrival there, I passed around among the many tents to learn if there was any new light. I was asked if I was going to the Exeter tent, and was told that they had new light there. I was soon seated among them, listening to what they called "the midnight cry." This was new light, sure enough. It was the very next move in Advent history, (if we moved at all,) wherein Advent history could be fitly compared to that of the ten virgins in the parable. Verse 6. It worked like leaven throughout the whole camp. And when that meeting closed, the granite hills of New Hampshire were ringing with the mighty cry, "Behold the bridegroom cometh; go ye out to meet him." As the loaded wagons, stages, and railroad cars, rolled away through the different States, cities and villages of New England, the cry was still resounding, "Behold the bridegroom cometh!" Christ, our blessed Lord, is coming on the tenth day of the seventh month! Get ready! get ready!!

After an absence of five days, I returned home to Fairhaven in season for an evening meeting. My brethren were slow to believe our report respecting the new light. They believed they were right thus far, but the midnight cry was a strange doctrine to connect with Advent history. Sunday morning I attended the Advent meeting in New Bedford, some two miles distant. Bro. Hutchinson, from Canada, was preaching. He appeared much confused, and sat down, saying, "I ca n't preach." Eld. E. Macomber, who had returned with me from the camp-meeting, was in the desk with him. He arose, apparently much excited, saying, "Oh! I wish I could tell you what I have seen and heard, but I cannot," and down he sat also. I then arose from my seat in the congregation, saying, "I can!" and never do I remember of having such freedom and flow of words, in all my religious experience. Words came like flowing water. As I sat down, a sister came to me across the hall, saying, "Bro. Bates, I want you to preach that same discourse to us this afternoon." Bro. Hutchinson was now relieved from all his stammering, and said, " If what Bro. Bates has said is true, I do n't wonder he thought my preaching was like carpenter's chips," &c. When the meeting closed the next evening, stammering tongues were loosed and the cry was sounding, " Behold the bridegroom cometh ; go ye out to meet him !" Arrangements were quickly made for meetings, to spread the glad tidings all around.

On the 22d of August, S. S. Snow issued a paper called the " Midnight Cry," setting forth all the points in the types, with the calculations showing that the definite time for the ending of the vision of 2300 days would be on the tenth day of the seventh month, 1844. Following this, at a camp-meeting in Pawtucket, R. I., Elder J. V. Himes, and several of the leading Advent ministers, pressed their objections respecting the genuineness of the midnight cry. But before the meeting closed they were returning to their stations, and a few days after, the " Advent Herald" was heralding their confessions, and how all their objections were removed, and their faith in the cry steadfast and unwavering.

We have not space here to present the arguments by which the midnight cry was sustained, but so convincing and powerful were they that all opposition was swept before them, and with amazing rapidity the sound was heralded throughout the land, and the poor, discouraged souls who had "slumbered and slept" "while the Bridegroom tarried," were awakened from their apathy and discouragement, and "arose and trimmed their lamps " to go forth and "meet the Bridegroom."

All hearts were united in the work, and all seemed in earnest to make a thorough preparation for the coming of Christ, which they believed to be so near. Thousands were running to and fro, giving the cry, and scattering books and papers containing the message.

But another sad disappointment awaited the watching ones. Shortly before the definite day the traveling brethren returned to their homes, the papers were suspended, and all were waiting in ardent expectation for the coming of their Lord and Saviour. The day passed, and another twenty-four hours followed, but deliverance did not come. Hope sunk and courage died within them, for so confident had they been in the correctness of the calculations that they could find no encouragement in a re-examination of the time, for nothing could be brought to extend the days beyond the tenth day of the seventh month, 1844, nor has there been to this day, notwithstanding the many efforts of those who are continually fixing upon some definite time for the coming of Christ.

The effect of this disappointment can be realized only by those who experienced it. Advent believers were then thoroughly tested, with various results. Some turned away and gave it up, while a large majority continued to teach and urge that the days were not ended. Still others believed that the days had ended, and that duty would soon be made plain. All, excepting this latter class, virtually rejected their former experience, and in consequence were left in darkness relative to the true work for the Advent people now to engage in.

Those who believed that the time was right, and had really passed, now turned their attention to the examination of their position. It soon became apparent that the mistake was not in the time, but in the event to take place at the end of the period. The prophecy declared, " Unto two thousand and three hundred days, then shall the sanctuary be cleansed." We had been teaching that the sanctuary was the earth, and that its cleansing was its purification by fire at the second advent of Christ. In this was our mistake, for, upon a careful examination, we were unable to discover anything in the Bible to sustain such a position. Light begun to shine upon the word of God as never before, and by its aid a clear and well-defined position was obtained on the subject of the sanctuary and its cleansing, by means of which we were enabled to satisfactorily explain the passing of the time, and the disappointment following, to the great encouragement of those who held fast to the message as being of God. The nature of this work forbids an examination of that position in these pages, but we refer the reader to a work entitled, " Sanctuary and Twenty-three Hundred Days," published at the Review Office, Battle Creek, Mich.

We were also greatly cheered and strengthened by the light which we received on the subject of the three angels' messages of Rev. xiv, 6–12. We fully believed that we had been giving the first of these—" Fear God and give glory to him ; for the hour of his judgment is come ;"—that the proclamation of definite time, that mighty movement which roused the world, and created such a general and wide-spread interest in the advent doctrine, was a complete and perfect fulfillment of that message. After the passing of the time, our eyes were opened to the fact that two other messages followed, before the coming of Christ: the second angel announcing the fall of Babylon, and the third giving a most solemn warning against false worship, and presenting the commandments of God and the faith of Jesus.

In close connection with the giving of the first message, we became convinced that the fall of Babylon indicated the moral fall from the favor of God of the nominal churches which rejected the light from Heaven, and shut out from their places of worship and from their hearts the doctrine of the advent, because they had no love for it, and did not desire it to be true.

The first and second messages being given, attention was now turned to the third, and an examination as to its nature and claims was instituted. As before remarked, it contains a most solemn warning against the worship of the beast and his image, and presents to notice the commandments of God and the faith of Jesus. By the expression, "commandments of God," we understand the moral law of ten commandments, which has been recognized by the church in all ages as binding upon mankind, and containing those moral precepts which regulate our duty to God and to our fellow-men. This being made the burden of a special message just before the coming of Christ, coupled with such a solemn warning, renders it apparent that the church must be remiss in the matter, and that some gross error in regard to the commandments of God must lie at their door.

A careful examination of the practice of the church reveals the fact that the fourth commandment is not observed—as it enjoins the seventh day of the week as the Sabbath, while almost all the world have been keeping the first day. Hence, the necessity of a reform in this matter. Before Christ comes his people must observe all of God's

commandments, and thus be prepared for transla
tion.

An investigation of the claims of the Sabbath
brings to view the following facts:

1. God in the beginning sanctified the seventh
day, and no other, as the holy Sabbath, because
that in it he had rested.

2. Having sanctified it, he commanded man to
remember it and keep it holy.

3. We find no record of his ever having removed
the sanctity from that day, or that he ever transferred his blessing from the seventh to the first
day of the week.

4. We find no intimation in the Bible that man
was ever released from the obligation to sacredly
observe the day on which God rested.

5. Our Saviour, in his example and teachings,
recognized the claims of the Sabbath, and declared
that it " was made for man."

6. The disciples and apostles observed the day,
by holding meetings and preaching upon it, calling
it " the Sabbath," and recognizing it as the day
for Christian worship.

7. The New Testament uniformly speaks of the
seventh day as " the Sabbath," while the first day
is never once honored by that title.

8. The term, " first day of the week," occurs
eight times in the New Testament, and never in
connection with any intimation that it is to be kept
holy, or observed as a rest day.

9. Leaving the Scriptures, we find by reliable
history that the early church observed the seventh
day as the Sabbath, until, corrupted by the apos-
tasy, the first day of the week began to be observed, in compliance with the customs of the

heathen world, who observed *Sunday* in honor of their chief god, the sun.

10. The first definite commandment ever given by a law-making power for the observance of Sunday, was the edict of Constantine, a pagan ruler, who professed conversion to Christianity, and issued his famous Sunday law, A. D. 321.

11. The Roman Catholic Church adopted the Sunday institution, and enforced it upon her followers by pretended authority from Heaven, until its observance became almost universal; and Protestants, in renouncing the errors of the Romish church, have not entirely rid themselves of her unscriptural dogmas, as evinced by the general observance of Sunday.

In the light of the above facts, the message of the third angel assumes an importance entitling it to the serious and candid attention of all Bible believers, and especially of those who profess to be making a preparation to meet the Lord at his coming. And as they were presented to the attention of those who had been giving the two former messages, those who were moving in the counsel of God, and recognized his hand in the work thus far, and in the disappointment being of itself a fulfillment of prophecy, gladly embraced the truth, and commenced keeping the Sabbath of the Lord. Although at first the light on this subject was not one-tenth part as clear as it is at the present time, the humble children of God were ready to receive and walk in it.

From that time, the progress of the work has been steadily onward. Rising in comparative obscurity, rejected by many who gladly embraced the first and second messages, presented at first by but few preachers, struggling along in want and poverty, contending with the opposition of many and the prejudices of all, it has gradually and steadily worked its way upward, under the blessing of God, until it now stands on a firm foundation, presenting a connected chain of argument and a bold front of truth, which commend it to the consideration of the candid and thoughtful wherever the message is preached.

It is now twenty-three years since we commenced keeping the Sabbath of the Lord, since which time we have endeavored to teach it to others, both in private and by public labors, by the fireside and from the sacred desk. We have presented this and kindred truths in New England, many of the Western States, and the Canadas, and our labors have been blessed by seeing scores and hundreds turn from the traditions of men to the observance of all of God's commandments.

By the untiring efforts of our esteemed brother, Eld. James White, and his companion, who were pioneers in this work, there is now established in the city of Battle Creek, Mich., a well-furnished Office of Publication, owned and controlled by the "Seventh-day Adventist Publishing Association," a corporate body engaged in the publication of this message. The Association employs two power presses in carrying on its business, and issues "The Advent Review and Sabbath Herald," weekly, "The Youth's Instructor," monthly, "The Health Reformer," monthly, and a large assortment of books and tracts on various Bible subjects.

In closing this work, I desire to express my gratitude to God that I am permitted to bear a humble part in this great work; and while my past life has been a checkered and eventful one, it is my earnest desire to spend the remainder of my days in the service of God, and for the advancement of his truth, that I may have a place in his soon-coming kingdom. And that reader and writer may meet in that happy abode, is my most earnest prayer.

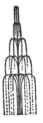

# CATALOGUE OF WORKS

ISSUED AND FOR SALE BY THE

## SEVENTH-DAY ADVENTIST

# Publishing Association.

———————◆———————

THIS Association was incorporated in Battle Creek, Mich., May 3, 1861. Its object is to issue "periodicals, books, tracts, documents, and other publications, calculated to impart instruction on Bible truth, especially the fulfillment of prophecy, the commandments of God, and the teachings of Jesus Christ." Its capital stock is raised by shares at $10 each; and every shareholder is entitled to one vote in all the deliberations of the Association, for every share that he or she may hold. The Association has now a large and well-furnished Office of publication, established in Battle Creek, Mich., and employs two steam power presses in carrying on its business. A meeting of the stockholders is held each year, at which a board of trustees is elected to manage its business, and editors chosen to conduct its periodicals, till the ensuing meeting. All persons employed in the publishing department, are engaged at stipulated wages, and all profits accruing from the business, are strictly applied by the Association to the carrying out of the object of its formation, and to its charitable uses and purposes. All lovers of truth, who "keep the commandments of God and the faith of Jesus," are still invited to take shares in the Association, and have a voice in all its deliberations.

## The Advent Review and Sabbath Herald

Is a large sixteen-page religious family paper, issued weekly by the S. D. A. Pub. Association, and devoted to an earnest investigation of all Bible questions. It is designed to be an exponent of momentous and solemn truths pertaining to the present time, some of which are set forth by no other periodical in the land. The fulfillment of prophecy, the second personal advent of the Saviour as an event now near at hand, immortality through Christ alone, a change of heart through the operation of the Holy Spirit, the observance of the Sabbath of the fourth commandment, the divinty and mediatorial work of Christ, and the development of a holy character by obedience to the perfect and holy law of God, as embodied in the decalogue, are among its special themes. And while it will endeavor to present impartially both sides of all important questions, it has a definite theory to teach, and hence will not devote its space to an indiscriminate and aimless mass of conflicting sentiments and views.

Regular price, $3.00 per year, or $1.50 for a volume of 26 numbers. On trial for six months $1.00. No subscriptions taken for less than six months. To the *worthy* poor—free, by their reporting themselves and requesting its continuance, once in six months. The friends of the Review are invited to earnest and unceasing efforts to extend its circulation.

## The Youth's Instructor

Is a monthly sheet, published as above, and designed to be to the youth and children what the Review and Herald is to those of riper years. You who wish to see your children instructed in the great truths which so interest you, will here find a sheet in which these things are set forth in a plain and interesting manner, free from the popular fables and errors of the age. It should not only visit regularly every youth and child who pro-

fesses to be a follower of Jesus, but should be taken and
read in every Sabbath-keeping family. Do n't forget
the children. See that they have the Instructor. Terms,
50 cts. per year in advance.

### The Health Reformer.

This is the title of a monthly health journal, "devoted to an exposition of the laws of our being, and the
application of those laws in the preservation of health
and the treatment of disease." It is an earnest advocate of the true philosophy of life, the only rational
method of treating disease, and the best means of preserving health. Practical instructions will be given
from month to month relative to water, air, light, food,
sleep, rest, recreation, &c. Health, its recovery and
preservation, is a subject of world-wide interest, whatever may be a person's tenets in other respects; and to
this the Reformer will be exclusively devoted. Edited
by H. S. Lay, M. D., Managing Physician of the Health-
Reform Institute. Terms $1.00 in advance for a vol-
ume of twelve numbers. Address Dr. H. S. Lay,
Battle Creek, Mich.

### The Sabbath Question

Is becoming a theme of wide-spread and absorbing interest. To those who wish to give the subject a thorough investigation, we recommend the History of the
Sabbath. As a work setting forth a connected Bible
view of the Sabbath question, its history since the
Christian era, and the different steps by which the human institution of the first day of the week has usurped
the place of the Bible institution of the seventh day, it
is unsurpassed by any publication extant. Between two
and three hundred quotations from history are given, to
each of which is appended a full reference to the authority from which it is taken. It is replete with facts
and arguments which challenge denial or refutation.
Other works on this subject, from the penny tract to

the largest size pamphlet, will be found noticed in our book list. There is no other Bible subject upon which a more extensive misunderstanding exists, than upon the Sabbath question. Circulate the books, and spread abroad the light on this subject.

## The Second Advent.

The works upon this important subject to which we would call especial attention, are, The Prophecy of Daniel, The Sanctuary and 2300 Days, and The Three Messages of Rev. xiv. The first gives an exposition of the plain and thrilling prophecies of Daniel ii, vii, and viii, showing from the course of empire that the God of Heaven is about to set up his kingdom. The Sanctuary question is the great central subject of the plan of salvation, and yet there are but few, comparatively, who have any acquaintance with it. It gives a new interest to a great part of the Bible, leads to an intelligent view of the position and work of Christ as our great High Priest in Heaven, completely explains the past Advent movement, and shows clearly our position in prophecy and the world's history. The three messages bring to view present duty, and future peril. All should read these books, and ponder well their teaching.

## Immortality through Christ Alone.

We call the special attention of the reader to the subjects of the nature of man, his condition in death, and the destiny of the wicked. More than ordinary importance attaches to these subjects, at the present time. We would confidently recommend to all a thorough reading of the work by H. H. Dobney entitled, Future Punishment, as advertised in our book list. The reader will find it a work exhaustive in its investigations, and remarkable for its candor, and the strength and clearness of its reasoning. Which? Mortal or Immortal? is a lower-priced and more condensed work on the same subjects. While "The End of the Wicked," and the one, two and three cent tracts may be found sufficient to awaken interest with those who would not commence with larger works.

## Packages of Tracts.

For the convenience of those who may wish to purchase books for general circulation, we have put up assorted packages of tracts in two sizes, which we will send post-paid at 50c., and $1.00 respectively

The 50c. package contains Sabbath Tracts Nos. 1, 2, and 3, End of the Wicked, Mark of the Beast, Sin of Witchcraft, Objections to Second Advent Answered, Death and Burial, Positive Institutions, Much in Little, Truth, Preach the Word, Law, by Wesley, and Miscellany.

The $1.00 package contains The Three Messages, Which? Mortal or Immortal? Prophecy of Daniel, Saints' Inheritance, Signs of the Times, Seven Trumpets, Celestial R. R., Perpetuity of Spiritual Gifts, Scripture References, Wicked Dead, Sabbath by Elihu, Infidelity and Spiritualism, War and Sealing, Who Changed the Sabbath, Seven Reasons for Sunday-keeping Examined, Institution of the Sabbath, Thoughts for the Candid, Appeal to Men of Reason, Personality of God, Seven Seals, and Time Lost.

Those who order these packages, save their postage. We cannot too strongly urge upon all the circulation of our publications, books and papers. Many, now rejoicing in the truth, can attribute their first interest in these things to these silent preachers; while in some instances they have opened the way for the formation of well-established and flourishing churches.

## Our Book List.

THOUGHTS ON THE REVELATION, by Uriah Smith; a volume of 328 pages, containing the entire text of the book of Revelation, with Thoughts Critical and Practical on the same. A new and harmonious interpretation of the Prophcy. Cloth, $1.00, weight, 12 oz. *

THE HISTORY OF THE SABBATH AND FIRST DAY OF THE WEEK, by Eld. J. N. Andrews, showing the Bible record of the Sabbath, and the manner in which it has been supplanted by the Heathen Festival of the Sun; pp. 342. Cloth, 80c., weight, 12 oz.

LIFE INCIDENTS, by Eld. James White; a work of over 300 pages, filled with graphic Sketches of Interesting Incidents, which have occurred in a life spent in advocating the doctrine of the Soon Coming of the Lord, and furnishing a panoramic view of the Advent Movement from its commencement to the present time. Price, $1.00, weight, 12 oz.

LIFE OF ELD. JOSEPH BATES; being an Interesting Narrative, written by himself, embracing a long life on the Ocean, and including his Experience in the Advent Cause; pp. 320. Muslin, $1.00, weight, 12 oz.

FUTURE PUNISHMENT, by H. H. Dobney, a Baptist Minister of England; an elaborate argument on the Destiny of the Wicked; with an Appendix, containing "The State of the Dead," by John Milton. Cloth, 75c.; weight, 16 oz.

SPIRITUAL GIFTS, Vol. I; or, the Great Controversy between the forces of Christ and Satan, as shown in Vision; pp. 219. Cloth, 50c., 8 oz.

SPIRITUAL GIFTS, Vol. II; or, the Experience and Views of E. G. White, with Incidents that have occurred in connection with the Third Angel's Message; pp. 300. Cloth, 60c., 8 oz. Vols. I and II bound in one book, $1.00, 12 oz.

SPIRITUAL GIFTS, Vol. III; or, Facts of Faith, in connection with the history of Holy Men of Old, as shown in Vision; pp. 304. Cloth, 60c., 8 oz.

---

* See page 318, under the head of "POSTAGE," which shows how much to send to prepay postage on bound books and pamphlets.

SPIRITUAL GIFTS, Vol. IV; or, Facts of Faith continued, and Testimonies for the Church; pp. 220. Cloth, 60c., 8 oz.

SABBATH READINGS; or, Moral and Religious Stories for the Young, from which the popular errors of the age are carefully excluded; pp. 400. In one volume, cloth, 60c., 8 oz. In five pamplets, 50c., 8 oz. In twenty-five tracts, 40c., 8 oz.

HOW TO LIVE; Treating on Disease and its Causes, and all subjects connected with healthful living. An important work; pp. 400. Cloth, $1.00, 12 oz. In pamphlet form, 75c., 10 oz.

APPEAL TO THE YOUTH: The Sickness and Death of H. N. White; with his Mother's Letters. Excellent instruction for both Youth and Parents. Cloth, 40c., 8 oz. Paper, 20c., 2 oz. Without likeness, 10c., 2 oz.

THE BIBLE FROM HEAVEN; or, a Dissertation on the Evidences of Christianity. 30c., 5 oz.

BOTH SIDES; a Series of Articles from T. M. Preble, on the Sabbath and Law, Reviewed. 20c., 4 oz.

THE MINISTRATION OF ANGELS, and the Origin, History, and Destiny of Satan. This is a new and interesting work; being a clear and forcible argument, and showing all that the title imports. 20c., 4 oz.

THE ATONEMENT, by Eld. J. H. Waggoner; a critical Examination of the Subject in the light of Reason and Revelation; pp. 172. 20c., 4 oz.

MODERN SPIRITUALISM: Its Nature and Tendency. The Heresy condemned from the mouths of its own advocates. Third edition, revised and enlarged. 20c., 5 oz.

SANCTIFICATION; or, Living Holiness. Many common mistakes on this important subject corrected. One of the best works ever published on this Subject. 15c., 4 oz.

THE THREE MESSAGES OF REV. XIV, especially the Third Angel's Message, and Two-horned Beast. 15c., 4 oz.

THE HOPE OF THE GOSPEL; or, Immortality the Gift of God, and the State of Man in Death. 15c., 4 oz.

WHICH? MORTAL, OR IMMORTAL? or, an Inquiry into the Present Constitution and Future Condition of Man. Third edition. 15c., 4 oz.

THE KINGDOM OF GOD: The Time and Manner of its Establishment. A Refutation of the doctrine called Age to Come. 15c., 4 oz.

MIRACULOUS POWERS: The Scripture Testimony on the Perpetuity of Spiritual Gifts, illustrated by Narratives of Incidents that have transpired all through the Gospel Dispensation. 15c., 4 oz.

APPEAL TO MOTHERS, on the Great Cause of the Physical, Mental, and Moral Ruin of many of the Children of Our Time. 10c., 2 oz.

REVIEW OF SEYMOUR: His "Fifty Unanswerable Questions" on the Sabbath Question Answered. 10c., 3 oz.

THE PROPHECY OF DANIEL: An Exposition of the Prophecy of the Four Kingdoms, the Sanctuary, and the 2300 Days, Dan. ii, vii, and viii. 10c., 3 oz.

THE SAINTS' INHERITANCE Shown to be the Kingdom under the whole Heaven, in the Earth made New. 10c., 3 oz.

SIGNS OF THE TIMES, in the Moral, Physical, and Political Worlds, showing that the Coming of Christ is at the Door. 10c., 3 oz.

THE LAW OF GOD: Its Observance from Creation, its Immutability and Perpetuity, proved from the testimony of the Old and New Testaments. 10c., 3 oz.

VINDICATION OF THE TRUE SABBATH, by J. W. Morton, late Missionary of the Reformed Presbyterian Church at Hayti; with a Narrative of the Author's Personal Experience, of thrilling interest. 10c., 3 oz.

REVIEW OF SPRINGER on the Sabbath and Law. 10c., 3 oz.

BAPTISM: Its Nature, Subjects, and Design. 10c., 3 oz.

THE COMMANDMENT to Restore and Build Jerusasalem. A conclusive argument that it is to be dated from the 7th year of Artaxerxes, B. C. 457. Just the book for these days of wild conjecture on the prophetic periods. 10c., 2 oz.

THE SEVEN TRUMPETS: An Exposition of Revelation viii and ix. A New Edition, thoroughly revised and enlarged. 10c., 2 oz.

KEY TO THE CHART: An explanation of all the Symbols illustrated upon the Prophetic Chart. 10c., 2 oz.

THE SANCTUARY, and 2300 Days of Daniel viii, 14; its cleansing, and the Time of its Accomplishment. 10c., 2 oz.

THE CELESTIAL RAILROAD: A most happy Exposure of the Inconsistencies of Popular Religion. A New Edition, revised and adapted to the present time. 4c., 1 oz.

THE SABBATH OF THE LORD: A Discourse by J. M. Aldrich. 5c., 2 oz.

THE END OF THE WICKED. 5c., 1 oz.

MATTHEW XXIV: A Brief Exposition of the Chapter, showing that Christ is at the Door. 5c. 2 oz.

MARK OF THE BEAST, and Seal of the Living God; showing how we may avoid the one, and secure the other. 5c., 1 oz.

THE SABBATIC INSTITUTION, and Two Laws; showing when the Sabbath was Instituted, and the plain distinction between the Moral and Ceremonial Laws. 5c., 1 oz.

BIBLE STUDENT'S ASSISTANT: A Compend of Scripture References on Important Subjects. 5c., 1 oz.

AN APPEAL FOR THE RESTORATION OF THE SABBATH: An Address from the Seventh-day to the First-day Baptists. 5c., 1 oz.

REVIEW OF FILLIO on the Sabbath Question. 5c., 1 oz.

MILTON ON THE STATE OF THE DEAD. 5c., 1 oz.

EXPERIENCE OF F. G. BROWN on Second Advent. 5c., 1 oz.

SYSTEMATIC BENEVOLENCE: An Address, &c. 5c., 1 oz.

THE SECOND ADVENT: Sixteen Short Answers to Sixteen Common Objections. 4c., 1 oz.

SAMUEL AND THE WITCH OF ENDOR: An Exposition of this remarkable portion of Scripture, showing the State of the Dead, and the Sin of Witchcraft. 4c., 1 oz.

## Tracts in Other Languages.

LIV OG DÖD: "Life and Death;" a work in Danish, on the Nature of Man, the Saints' Inheritance, and the Destiny of the Wicked; pp. 280. Paper cover, 40c., 12 oz.

THE BIBLE STUDENT'S ASSISTANT, in Danish: A Work on the plan of the Assistant in English, containing Scripture References on a variety of subjects, adapted to the Danish Bible. 5c., 1 oz.

FORTY QUESTIONS ON IMMORTALITY, in Danish. 2c., 1 oz.

THE SABBATH: Its Nature and Obligation, in German. 10c., 2 oz. The Sabbath, in Holland. 5c., 1 oz. In French. 5c., 1 oz. In Danish. 10c., 1 oz.

AN EXPOSITION of Dan. ii and vii in French. 5c., 1 oz.

## Half-Cent Tracts.

GOD'S ANSWERS to Man's Excuses for not Keeping his Sabbath.

SOME FEATURES OF OUR TIMES.

THE HEAVENLY MEETING: A Thrilling Rhapsody on the joy of the Saint as he first meets his Saviour and the Heavenly Host.

## One-Cent Tracts.

THE SEVEN SEALS: An Exposition of Rev. vi.

THE TWO LAWS: The distinction shown between them.

PERSONALITY OF GOD: A Popular Error disproved.

THE LAW OF GOD, THE TEN COMMANDMENTS, by John Wesley.

APPEAL TO MEN OF REASON, on Immortality.

THOUGHTS FOR THE CANDID, on the Nature of Man.

STATE OF THE DEAD: Brief Thoughts. Author unknown.

TIME LOST: or, Old and New Style Explained.

WHAT IS TRUTH? A Series of Questions and Answers relative to the Subject of Immortality.

THE DRESS REFORM: An Appeal to the People in its Behalf.

### Two-Cent Tracts.

GEOLOGY AND THE BIBLE: or, a Pre-Adamic Age of Our World Doubtful; showing that no true claims of Geology are against Bible facts.

SUNDAY-KEEPING: The Reasons for it Examined and Refuted.

THE SABBATH: The Time of its Institution.

THE SABBATH: A Stirring Argument by Elihu.

INFIDELITY AND SPIRITUALISM shown to be of like character.

WAR AND SEALING: An Exposition of Rev. vii.

WHO CHANGED THE SABBATH? Roman Catholic Testimony.

PREACH THE WORD: An Argument for the Sabbath.

DEATH AND BURIAL: or, Scriptural Baptism.

TRUTH: Showing the Unity of the True Church.

POSITIVE INSTITUTIONS, Their Nature and Claims.

### Three-Cent Tracts.

MUCH IN LITTLE: A Collection of Choice Extracts on Eternal Misery.

THE RESURRECTION OF THE BODY: Popular Objections to this Scriptural Doctrine briefly considered. This thorough little Treatise removes in a masterly manner the difficulties supposed to lie in the way of the resurrection of the identical matter that goes into the grave.

THE STATE OF THE CHURCHES: Showing the fallen state of the Popular Churches; being extracts from Orthodox speakers and writers.

THE LAW OF GOD, by H. H. Dobney, England.

JUDSON'S LETTER ON DRESS: An Appeal to the Female Members of the Christian Churches of the United States.

SCRIPTURE REFERENCES.  Same as Bible Student's Assistant without cover.

MARK OF THE BEAST, and Seal of the Living God.

SPIRITUAL GIFTS: An Argument to show that the Gifts set in the Church (1 Cor. xii; Eph. iv, &c.) were to continue to the end of time.

THE WICKED DEAD: A thorough and Scriptural Exposition of the Parable of the Rich Man and Lazarus.

## Charts.

THE LAW OF GOD on a Chart of a size to be used by Preachers, varnished and mounted, $2.00.

THE PROPHECIES OF DANIEL AND JOHN, illustrated upon a Chart, to be used by Preachers, varnished and mounted, $2.00.  The two Charts with Key, $4.00.  The two printed on cloth, with Key, $3.00.  The two on cloth, without rollers, by mail, postpaid, $2.75.

SMALL CHART: A Pictorial Illustration of the Visions of Daniel and John, on paper, 20x25 inches.  Price, 15c. by mail, postpaid.

## Postage.

The law requires the prepayment of postage on books, as follows: Bound books, four cents for each four ounces, or fractional part thereof; Pamphlets and Tracts, two cents for each four ounces, or fractional part thereof.  In the foregoing list, the weight of each book is given in connection with the price; and all who order books can estimate the amount of postage required, which should invariably be sent with the order, in addition to the price of the books.  Thus, two 2 oz. books can be sent for the same postage as one; or, four 1 oz books for the same postage as one, two, or three of the same kind, and so on.

## Address.

All communications in reference to the Publishing Association, the Review, Instructor, and any of the foregoing books, should be addressed to "J. M. ALDRICH, Battle Creek, Mich."  All business pertaining to the Health Reform Institute, or Health Reformer, should be addressed to "DR. H. S. LAY, Battle Creek, Mich."

# Appendix A

The "Editor's Preface," "Introduction," and "Remarks by the Editor" from James White, ed., *The Early Life and Later Experience and Labors of Elder Joseph Bates* (Battle Creek, MI: Seventh-day Adventist Pub. Assn., 1877). Pagination is from the original.

# EDITOR'S PREFACE.

THE body of this work is a reprint of the Auto-biography of Elder Joseph Bates, which received great public favor. A large edition of it has been sold, and the book has been out of print more than a year. The call for it continues. The author was one of those noble and godly men who though " dead yet speaketh."

The editor of this work was an intimate and close fellow-laborer with Elder Joseph Bates for more than a quarter of a century. And it is with great pleasure that we give his life sketches, with introduction and closing remarks, in this volume.

J. W.

BATTLE CREEK, MICH., AUGUST 16, 1877.

(vi)

# INTRODUCTION.

LIFE sketches of great and good men are given to the world for the benefit of generations that follow them. Human life is more or less an experiment to all who enter upon it. Hence the frequent remark that we need to live one life to learn how to live.

This maxim in all its unqualified strength of expression may be a correct statement of the cases of the self-confiding and incautious. But it need not be wholly true of those who have good and wise parents to honor, and who have proper respect for all prudent and good people who have made life a success.

To those who take along with them the lamp for their feet, found in the experiences of those who have fought the good fight, and have finished their course with joy, life is not altogether an experiment. The general outlines of life, to say the least, are patterned by these from those who have by the grace of God made themselves good, and noble, and truly great in choosing and defending the right.

Reflecting young men and young women may take on a stock of practical education before they leave parental care and instruction which will be invaluable to them in future life. This they may do to a considerable extent by careful observation. But in reading the lives of worthy people, they may in their minds and hearts live good lives in advance, and thus be fortified to reject the evil and to choose the good that lie all along the path of human life.

Second to our Lord Jesus Christ, Noah, Job, and Daniel are held up before us by the sacred writers as patterns worthy of imitation. The brief sketches of the faith, patience, firmness, and moral excellence of these and other holy men of God found in the pages of sacred history have been and are still of immense value to all those who would walk worthy of the Christian name. They were men subject to like passions as we are. And were some of them at certain unfortunate periods of life overcome of evil? Erring men of our time may bless that record also which states how they overcame evil, and fully redeemed past errors, so that becoming doubly victorious they shine brightest on the sacred page.

In his Epistle to the Hebrews, Paul gives a list of heroes of faith. In his eleventh chapter he mentions Abel, Enoch, Noah, Abraham, Isaac, Jacob, Joseph, Moses, and the prophets, who through faith subdued kingdoms, wrought righteousness, obtained promises, and stopped the mouths of lions. The apostle calls up this cloud of witnesses to God's faithfulness to his trusting servants as patterns for the Christian church, as may be seen by the use he makes of them in the first verse of the chapter which follows :—

"Wherefore, seeing we also are compassed about with so great a cloud of witnesses, let us lay aside every weight, and the sin which doth so easily beset us, and let us run with patience the race that is set before us." Heb. 12 : 1.

The life of Elder Joseph Bates was crowded with unselfish motives and noble actions. That which makes his early history intensely interesting to his personal friends is the fact that he became a devoted follower of Christ, and a thorough practical reformer, and ripened into glorious manhood a true Christian gentleman, while exposed to the evils of sea-faring life, from the cabin-boy of 1807, to the wealthy retiring master of 1828, a period of twenty-one years.

Beauty and fragrance are expected of the rose, planted in the dry and well-cultivated soil, and tenderly reared under the watchful eye of the lover of the beautiful. But we pass over the expected glory of the rose to admire the living green, the pure white, and the delicate tint of the water-lily whose root reaches way down into the cold filth of the bottom of the obscure lake. And we revere that Power which causes this queen of flowers, uncultivated and obscure, to appropriate to itself all valuable qualities from its chilling surroundings, and to reject the evil.

So, to apply the figure, we reasonably expect excellence of character in those who are guarded against corrupting influences, and whose surroundings are the most favorable to healthy mental and moral development. In our hearts, pressing upon our lips, are blessings for all such. But he who, in the absence of all apparent good, and in the perpetual presence of all that is uncultivated and vile, with no visible hand to guard and to guide, becomes pure and wise, and devotes his life to the service of God and the good of humanity, a Christian philanthropist, is a miracle of God's love and power, the wonder of the age.

It was during his sea-faring life, while separated from the saving influences of the parental, Christian home, and exposed to the temptations of sailor life, that the writer of the following pages became thoroughly impressed with moral and religious principles, and gathered strength to trample intemperance and all other forms of vice beneath his feet, and rise in the strength of right and of God to the position of a thorough reformer, a devoted Christian, and an efficient minister of the gospel.

J. W.

## REMARKS BY THE EDITOR.

CAPTAIN BATES retired from the seas in the month of June, 1828. He had acquired more than a competency. He immediately began to devote his time and means to moral reforms, and labored ardently and successfully in this way for about twelve years, when he became an Adventist. He soon entered the lecturing field, and labored as a speaker and writer, and employed his means and energies in the cause of Bible truth and reform during the remainder of his useful life until near his death, in 1872, a period of thirty-two years.

During this long period of his ministry, reaching from the noon of life to old age, he lost none of his ardor in the cause of moral reforms. In fact, his Second-Advent views, that the divine Son of God, and all the holy angels with him, would soon come to receive his people and take them to a pure Heaven, gave the inspired exhortations to purity of life, and the warnings to be ready for the coming of that day, a double force to his mind. While addressing the people upon the subject of readiness to meet the Lord at his coming, we have often heard him apply these texts with great force :—

"And take heed to yourselves, lest at any time your hearts be overcharged with surfeiting and drunkenness, and cares of this life, and so that day come upon you unawares." Luke 21 : 34.

"And what agreement hath the temple of God with idols? for ye are the temple of the living God; as God hath said, I will dwell in them, and walk in them, and I will be their God, and they shall be my people. Wherefore, come out from among them, and be ye separate, saith the Lord, and touch not the unclean thing, and I will receive you, and will be a Father unto you, and ye shall be my sons and daughters, saith the Lord Almighty. Having therefore these promises, dearly beloved, let us cleanse ourselves from all filthiness of the flesh and spirit, perfecting holiness in the fear of God." 2 Cor. 6 : 16–18; 7 : 1.

"Know ye not that ye are the temple of God, and that the Spirit of God dwelleth in you? If any man defile the temple of God, him shall God destroy; for the temple of God is holy, which temple ye are." 1 Cor. 3 : 16, 17.

When we expect a visit from friends we love and honor in our hearts, how natural to wash up, put things in good order, and dress up for the occasion. This simple fact in natural life may well illustrate the action of those Adventists who are really Adventists, in adopting the clean, pure rules of practical hygiene.

The principles of reform which had been written upon the mind and heart of Captain Bates while upon the seas, were still moving his soul to the very depths when among his friends at home. He still moved forward. His table reform commenced about this time.

We first met Elder Bates at his home at Fairhaven, Mass., in the year 1846. He had at that time discarded flesh-meats of all kinds, grease, butter, and all kinds of spices, from his own plate. When asked why he did not use them as articles of food, his usual reply was, "I have eaten my share of them." He did not mention his views of proper diet in public at that time, nor in private unless interrogated upon the subject. At his meals he took only plain bread and cold water. These, so very common, were readily obtained by those who entertained him, and in respect to diet he caused his friends but little trouble, excepting their anxieties that he would starve on bread and water.

When we first became acquainted with Elder Bates, in 1846, he was fifty-four years old. His countenance was fair, his eye was clear and mild, his figure was erect and of fine proportions, and he was the last man to be picked out of the crowd as one who had endured the hardships and exposure of sea life, and who had come in contact with the physical and moral filth of such a life for more than a score of years. He had been from the seas the period of eighteen years, and during that time his life of rigid temperance in eating, as well as in drinking, and his labors in the pure sphere of moral reform, had regenerated the entire man, body, soul, and spirit, until he seemed almost re-created for the special work to which God had called him. "Be ye clean that bear the vessels of the Lord."

Elder Bates was a true gentleman. We might suppose that a man of his natural firmness and independence, after twenty-one years of sea-faring life, and commander of rough sailors a large portion of that time, would be exacting and overbearing in his efforts to reform others. True, he would speak what he regarded truth with great freedom and boldness; but after he had set forth principles, and urged the importance of obedience, he was willing to leave his hearers to decide for themselves.

We need not say that when many of his fellow-laborers embraced the principles of health reform, and began to advocate them about the year 1860, he joined them with great gladness of heart. From this time he began to speak freely upon the subject both in public and private life. Up to this time he had refused all fruits and nuts because of the custom to eat them between meals. But when many of his brethren adopted two meals only a day, and furnished their tables with fruits and nuts, he would partake freely of them with his meals.

At a health reform convention held at Battle Creek, Mich., in the spring of 1871, the venerable Elder Bates, in his seventy-ninth year, made a speech of remarkable interest, into which he incorporated some items of his personal history and experience. It is of such living interest that the reader will pardon us for repeating it here.

"In early life, before finishing my second European voyage, I was impressed into the British naval service, and stationed on board a British war-ship, associated with about seven hundred men, on a daily stated allowance of hard bread, salt provisions, and one pint of inferior wine. Thus I was held for about two years and a half, until, soon after the declaration of war by the United States against England, the American citizens on board our ship petitioned, and became prisoners of war, and were placed on two-thirds of what had been allowed us before, and no wine. In this state I continued some two years and a half. The last eight months I was associated with about six thousand sailors and soldiers on that most dreary waste called Dartmoor, fifteen miles from Plymouth, in England. Five years' experience in these two schools of vice and debasement of moral character, seriously convinced me of the necessity of reform.

"What seemed most important of all at that time was the disuse of spirituous liquors. A few weeks after my return home from my imprisonment, in the summer of 1815, I was offered, and accepted, the office of second mate on board a new ship fitting for a European voyage. This was some twelve years before temperance societies were organized. I soon learned that it was indeed a warfare to attempt to stem so strong a current of vice single-handed. I was urged to take a social glass, again and again, for some time. After awhile I yielded, to use it moderately, and finally confined myself to one glass only in twenty-four hours. Wine, beer, and cider were not then considered spirituous liquors. These I used but seldom.

"In the fall of 1821, on my passage from South America to Alexandria, D. C., feeling more serious respecting the unnecessary habit of using one glass a day, I spoke out earnestly, saying, I will never drink another glass of spirituous liquors while I live. And I am not aware that I ever have. But this temperance reform was not yet accomplished. So, on my next voyage from Buenos Ayres, South America, round Cape Horn, in 1822, I fully resolved never to drink wine. By watchfulness and perseverance

I broke up my habit of using profane language, and before I left the Pacific Ocean, I had forever discarded the use of that filthy weed, tobacco. These victories strengthened and encouraged me in the work of reform.

"In the summer of 1824, on leaving the capes of Virginia for another voyage, I resolved from henceforth never to drink ale, porter, beer, cider, nor any liquor that would intoxicate. I now felt strengthened, and fully relieved from this burden to reform, which had been balancing in my mind for upward of ten years. I had been prospered in my business far beyond what I deserved, and was now setting out on another successful voyage, loading myself down with the cares and business of the world. Turning my attention more to reading the Bible than I had done, I was led to see what a feeble worm of the dust I was —an unpardoned sinner, under condemnation. I began and pleaded with God for pardoning mercy, for many days. I did then believe, and still believe, that he freely forgave me, for his dear Son's sake. My prospect then for this life, and the life which is to come, was most cheering. I then covenanted with the Lord that I would serve him evermore.

"Some thirty-three years ago, on becoming satisfied of the poisonous nature of both tea and coffee, I resolved never more to use them.

"In February, 1843, I resolved to eat no more meat. A few months after, I ceased using butter, grease, cheese, pies, and rich cakes. Since the introduction of the health reform several years ago by my brethren, I have been endeavoring to conform in my eating more strictly to the hygienic practice, and confine myself to two meals only in twenty-four hours. If the reader wishes to know what I have gained by my efforts from the first to reform, I answer :—

" 1. From the ruinous habits of a common sailor, by the help of the Lord, I walked out into the ranks of sober, industrious, discerning men, who were pleased to employ and promote me in my calling, so that in the space of nine years I was supercargo, and joint owner, in the vessel and cargo which I commanded, with unrestricted commission to go where I thought best, and continue my voyage as long as I should judge best for our interest.

"The morning after my arrival at the wharf in New York, among the laborers who came on board to discharge my vessel, was a Mr. Davis, one of my most intimate friends during my imprisonment. We had spent many hours together talking over our dismal position, and the dreadful state and ruinous habits of our fellow-prisoners, and there agreed that if ever we were liberated, we would labor to avoid the dreadful habits of intemperance, and seek for a standing among sober, reflecting men. Aside from his associates, we conversed freely, and he readily admitted our feelings and resolutions in the past, but with sadness of heart acknowledged his lack of moral courage to reform ; and now, in this uncertain way, he was seeking for daily labor when his poor state of health would admit of it.

" 2. When I reached this point of total abstinence, God in mercy arrested my attention, and on the free confession of my sins, for his dear Son's sake, granted me his rich grace and pardoning mercy.

" 3. Contrary to my former convictions, that

if I was ever permitted to live to my present age, I should be a suffering cripple from my early exposure in following the sea, thanks be to God and our dear Lord and Saviour, whose rich blessing ever follows every personal effort to reform, that I am entirely free from aches and pains, with the gladdening, cheering prospect that if I continue to reform, and forsake every wrong, I shall, with the redeemed followers of the Lamb, stand 'without fault before the throne of God.'"

No comment on the foregoing is needed. And it is hardly necessary to state that the speech, from one who had nearly reached his four-score years, and who could look back upon a long life of self-control, marked all the way with new victories and new joys, electrified the audience. He then stood as straight as a monument, and would tread the side-walks as lightly as a fox. He stated that his digestion was perfect, and that he never ate and slept better at any period in his life.

Elder Bates was in the hearts of his people. Those who knew him longest and best, prized him most. When his younger and most intimate fellow-laborers told him that his age should excuse him from the fatigue of itinerant life and public speaking, he laid his armor off as a captured officer would surrender his sword on the field of battle. The decision once made, he was as triumphant in hope and faith as before. Mrs. White wrote to him, recommending a nutritious diet, which called out the following characteristic statements from his pen thirty-three days before his death :—

"God bless you, Sister White, for your favor of yesterday, the 12th. You say I must have good, nutritious food. I learn from report that I am starving myself and am withholding from my daughter, who is with me, and alone a good part of the time in my absence; and that when I ask a blessing at my table, I ask the Lord to bless that which I may eat, and not that which is on the table. This is what I am not guilty of, nor ever was in all my family worship for some fifty years, but *once;* and I do greatly marvel how my industrious neighbors found out this one exception. But I will tell you the circumstance.

"Several years ago I was with the church in Vassar, Tuscola Co., Mich., and was invited to address them and their children in a barn on the Fourth of July, and also to dine with them. The tables were soon up and loaded with tempting eatables; and I was invited to ask the blessing. The swines' flesh upon the table, I knew was abominable and unclean from creation, Gen. 7 : 2, 8; and God had positively, by law, forbidden the eating or touching of it. See Lev. 11 : 7, 8 (law, verse 46); also Deut. 14 : 1-3, 8. I therefore very quietly distinguished, and asked a blessing on the clean, nutritious, wholesome, *lawful* food. Some whispered, and some smiled, and others looked, and so on.

"Starving, with more than enough to eat! Now allow me to state what, by the providence and blessing of God, we have in our house from which to choose a daily bill of fare.

"90 pounds of superfine white flour.
"100 pounds of graham flour.
"5 bushels of choice garden corn.
"Pop and sweet corn in abundance.

"Corn meal, rice, and oatmeal.
"Corn-starch, butter, sugar, salt.

### "VEGETABLES.

"Three varieties of potatoes.
"Sweet turnips, parsnips, squashes.
"Two varieties of onions.

### "PRESERVES.

"11 cans of sweet peaches.
"6 cans sweet grapes.
"Strawberries preserved and dried.
"Quince and grape jelly.
"Tomatoes by the jug.
"20 pounds of dried sweet peaches.
"Box of Isabella grapes, most consumed.
"Three varieties of apples and quinces.

"But the people say, and they think they know what they say, that he refuses to furnish his table with tea and coffee. That's true! They are poison. Some thirty-five years ago I was using both tea and coffee. After retiring from a tea-party at midnight, my bed companion said, 'What is the matter, can't you lie quiet and sleep?' 'Sleep! no,' said I. 'Why not?' was the next question. 'Oh! I wish Mrs. Bunker's tea had been in the East Indies. It's poison!' Here I forever bade adieu to tea and coffee. After a while my wife joined me, and we discarded them from our table and dwelling. That's the reason they are not on my table.

"They say, too, that this man does not allow any ardent spirits or strong drink in his house. That's true. Please hear my reason: Fifty years ago I was by myself on the boundless ocean. My thoughts troubled me. Said I to Him who always hears, I'll never drink another glass of grog or strong drink while I live. That's why I have no intoxicating drink on or about my premises.

"Well, there is another thing that he is fanatical about, and differs from more than half his countrymen. What is that? He will not have about him nor use any TOBACCO. Guilty! My reason: Forty-eight years ago I was away toward the setting sun; our gallant ship was plowing her way through the great Pacific. During the nightwatch we were called to take some refreshment. I then tossed my chew of tobacco into the ocean, never, no, never, to touch, taste, or handle any more. And allow me to say that when I had gained the victory over this deadening, besotting, benumbing vice, I went on deck the next morning a better man than ever I was in all my former life. Why? I was free. I could appreciate God's handiwork in sea and sky, even in the tumbling, rolling waves. I could breathe freely, inhaling the pure air of heaven, and shout. I was a free man.

"Therefore, if any demand is ever made on me for tobacco, tea, coffee, or strong drink of any kind that intoxicates, they must present me an order from the Court Above.

"Here comes half a barrel of graham crackers and a lot of farina, a natural breadstuff of the native South Americans. I think I am now well supplied with good, nutritious food. And if there is any lack I have some good, faithful brethren who seem to be waiting to serve me.

"I am your brother, now on retired pay in Monterey, Michigan.

"JOSEPH BATES.

"*Feb. 14, 1872.*"

Elder Joseph Bates died in the eightieth year of his age, at Battle Creek, Mich., March 19, 1872. The writer of his obituary says :—

" His last hours, though characterized by pain such as few men have been called upon to pass through, afforded a marked evidence of the superiority of a faith in Christ over the bodily suffering and the prospect of certain and rapidly approaching death. Having in early manhood chosen the service of God, and having for many years faithfully endeavored to live the life of the righteous, his last end was such as those alone can expect who have sedulously endeavored to preserve a conscience void of offense toward God and man.

" On Thursday, the 21st of March, his remains were taken to Monterey, Allegan Co., Mich., where they were interred on the following day in Poplar Hill Cemetery by the side of his wife."

The Michigan Conference of S. D. Adventists, at their session, September 5, 1872, passed this resolution :—

" That, as a tribute of respect, we recognize in the decease of our beloved brother, Elder Joseph Bates, the loss of a great and good man, eminent for piety and Christian virtue ; a pioneer in the third angel's message, always at his post of duty. We miss him in our assemblies, at our Conference, in our churches, at our fireside homes ; and while we deeply mourn our loss, we will remember his counsels, imitate his virtues, and endeavor to meet him in the kingdom of God."

# Appendix B

The "Editor's Preface" from C. C. Crisler, ed., *Life of Joseph Bates: An Autobiography*, abridged and edited (Washington, DC: Review and Herald, 1927). Pagination is from the original.

# Editor's Preface

DURING my boyhood days my beloved father presented me with a volume entitled, "Life of Joseph Bates." This was the third book I ever owned for myself. It had been written by Captain Joseph Bates originally as a series of articles for the young people's periodical known as *The Youth's Instructor,* during the years 1858 to 1863, and had been published in book form on the first "steam press of the Seventh-day Adventist Publishing Association," in November, 1868. The copy that came into my hands was of the second edition, prepared by Elder James White and published in the fall of 1877, and first read by me in 1886, when I was nine years old. I have since reread it again and again. The stories Captain Bates told of his early life have never lost their charm. All through the years his autobiography has remained one of my most treasured possessions.

Three years ago I began an inquiry among friends to learn how many had read the "Life of Joseph Bates," and to my surprise I found that only a few had had this privilege. Several had never heard of the book. Students in our schools have been unable to obtain it. For a third of a century it has been out of print. The volume is rarely found even in large libraries.

During the last year I have had occasion to make three long sea voyages, and have been carrying in my portfolio my copy of the autobiography of Captain Bates, in the hope of preparing it for republication in abridged form. These stories, which are chiefly of the sea, have thus been made ready anew while I have been journeying to and fro across the broad waters of the Pacific Ocean, and up and down the China and Inland Seas. The little volume has been brought into as brief a form as seems consistent with the preservation of the Captain's quaint and racy style.

Captain Bates closed his story with a brief account of the advent movement of William Miller's day, and of his uniting with others in an effort to find the light of Bible truth as related to the closing messages of the everlasting gospel now being proclaimed by the denomination known as Seventh-day Adventists. His story does not set forth in detail the important work he undertook and accomplished in preaching, in publishing, in founding churches, and in attending general meetings. Many of the incidents and providences connected with his later labors have been made familiar to us through the reminiscent and historical writings of Elder J. N. Loughborough, and have been repeated in varying forms in " Origin and Progress of Seventh-day Adventists," " Story of the Advent Message," " Advent Stories," and " Publishing Department Story." I have finally decided not to attempt to add supplemental chapters to the story as told by the Captain himself, but to let his autobiography close just as he left it.

At the time Captain Bates prepared his life-story for the press, late in the 60's, he had reached the venerable age of seventy-five; yet his heart was ever young, and he was " possessed of a strong and clear memory, an independent mind, a noble and courageous soul." " The life of Captain Joseph Bates was crowded with unselfish motives and noble actions," declares Elder James White in an introduction prepared for the 1877 edition of the autobiography. " That which makes his early history intensely interesting . . . is the fact that he became a devoted follower of Christ, a thorough, practical reformer, and ripened into glorious manhood.

" Captain Bates retired from the seas in the month of June, 1828. He had acquired more than a competency. In physical appearance, his countenance was fair, his eye clear and mild, his figure erect and of fine proportions. He devoted his time and means to moral reforms, and labored ardently and successfully in this way for about twelve years, when he became an Adventist. He soon entered the lecturing field, and labored as a speaker and writer, and employed his means and energies in the cause of Bible truth and reform during the remainder of his life, following his retirement from the sea.

"Elder Bates died in the eightieth year of his age, at Battle Creek, Michigan, U. S. A., March 19, 1872. On the 21st his remains were taken to Monterey, Allegan County, Michigan, where they were interred on the following day in Poplar Hill Cemetery by the side of his wife."

On the occasion of his death, some who had been his intimate associates paid a tribute of respect to their beloved friend, characterizing him in a published statement as "a great and good man, eminent for piety and Christian virtue; a pioneer in the third angel's message, always at his post of duty. . . . We miss him in our assemblies, in our churches, at our firesides; and while we deeply mourn his loss, we will remember his counsels, imitate his virtues, and endeavor to meet him in the kingdom of God."

C. C. CRISLER.

*Shanghai, China,*
*July 15, 1926.*

**Gary Land,** professor of history at Andrews University and chair of the department, earned a Ph.D. in history from the University of California at Santa Barbara. He has co-authored *Seeker after Light: A. F. Ballenger, Adventism and American Christianity* and edited such works as *Adventism in America* and *The World of Ellen G. White.*

**George R. Knight,** professor of church history at Andrews University, is an authority on Adventist history. The lengthy list of his published works includes *Millenial Fever and the End of the World: A Study of Millerite Adventism; A Brief History of Seventh-day Adventists;* and *A Search for Identity: The Development of Seventh-day Adventist Beliefs.*